NEW EDITION

first certificate

Gold

teacher's book

Sally Burgess

with Richard Acklam

Longman

Pearson Education Limited
Edinburgh Gate
Harlow
Essex CM20 2JE
England
and Associated Companies throughout the World.

www.longman-elt.com

© Longman Group Limited 1996
© Pearson Education Limited 2000

The right of Sally Burgess and Richard Acklam to be identified as
authors of this Work has been asserted by them in accordance
with the Copyright, Designs and Patents Act 1988

First published 1996. This new edition published 2000.
Third impression 2000
ISBN 0 582 42968 4

Set in Frutiger 9/11.5pt

Printed in Spain by Graficas Estella

Authors' Acknowledgements
We would especially like to thank the following people:
Sue and Emma for their support and encouragement, Jess for
being such a tolerant author's partner. And Gordon, Amy and
Martin for providing a roof over my head during my various trips
to London in the early stages of the project. All the Longman team.
In particular, Judith King, Frances Woodward and Emer Wall for
their contributions to the original edition and Heather Jones
(Senior Publisher), and Ann Hislop (Senior Development Editor)
for their contributions to the Revised Edition. Matthew Barnard,
Charlie Crawford and Kristina Teasdale for their comments
and advice at an early stage of the project.

Contents

Introduction

Profile of an FCE Student

The students with whom you will be using *First Certificate Gold* can broadly be described as late intermediate students. This means that they will have studied English for between 500 and 600 hours. They may have taken other English examinations such as the PET (Preliminary English Test), though this is not a requirement for FCE entry or preparation.

A typical FCE student will have studied many of the main structures of English and have met many basic vocabulary items as well as more specialised vocabulary in certain areas. The courses they have followed will also have introduced a number of the communicative functions of English. These courses will also have given your students opportunities to read and listen for general understanding and for detailed information. Your students will also have had practice writing descriptive, narrative and possibly discursive compositions, as well as a number of other text types such as formal and informal letters, memos and reports. Throughout the time that they have been studying English they will probably also have had plenty of speaking practice.

It is important to remember, nevertheless, that students at this level do make errors with much of the language they have met in the past and also periodically experience difficulty with some aspects of skills work. This is to be expected and will not prevent them from preparing for FCE successfully.

Preparing for FCE

Basically, preparing for FCE involves consolidating, refining and extending what your students already know and providing them with the specific techniques the examination requires.

Grammar and vocabulary

It will be necessary to revise and practise many of the grammatical structures students have met at lower levels (verb tenses, reported speech, relative clauses, etc.) and to introduce some more complex structures (expressing hypothetical meanings, mixed conditionals, causative *have*, etc.). Students' use of even basic structures (third person Present Simple singular 's', direct questions, etc.) may not be entirely error-free and it is important to 'iron out' errors with these basic structures before they tackle the examination as

it is just these errors that are often heavily penalised.

Vocabulary will also require a lot of work. Basic lexical sets will need to be revised and extended. Students will need to learn more about word formation and to extend their knowledge of phrasal verbs. A limited knowledge of vocabulary is something that can seriously affect your students' chances of exam success.

The skills

In terms of reading and listening skills, they will need to be able to listen to or read a text and find the main ideas, distinguishing these from secondary ideas. They should be able to listen or read for gist as well as extract specific information or detail. In the case of reading, they will also need to learn to identify structure within the text, to work out what different pronouns, etc. are referring to, to work out the meaning of unknown words and to infer meaning from context.

In terms of writing, your students will need to learn to produce texts of between 120 and 180 words. To write successfully at FCE level they will need to learn to generate ideas, organise these ideas, express them accurately and check their work thoroughly. Most FCE writing tasks demand that students address the requirements of specific audiences and demonstrate knowledge of the layout and style of a range of text types, including letters, reports and articles, so they will need to become familiar with these.

Your students will need to get as much speaking practice as possible. By the time they take the FCE examination, their spoken English should be reasonably fluent and accurate. Their pronunciation should be clear and intelligible and they should be able to use a range of structures and vocabulary in speech to express their ideas. In addition to these abilities, they should be able to interact in a comfortable and natural manner with the other candidate and/or the examiner.

Features of the *First Certificate Gold* course

The *First Certificate Gold* course is made up of the *First Certificate Gold Coursebook* and cassettes, the *First Certificate Gold Exam Maximiser* and cassettes, the *Teacher's Book* and the *First Certificate Gold Practice Exams* and cassettes.

First Certificate Gold Coursebook

General features

The *First Certificate Gold Coursebook* offers progressive preparation for FCE through fifteen graded units. There are *Review* pages, each of which includes at least one exam-style exercise, to revise the language taught. These *Review* pages occur at the end of all units except 5, 10 and 15. These units are followed by *Progress Checks* designed to test your students' knowledge of the language presented in the previous five units. The *Progress Checks* include Paper 3 (Use of English) exam-format tasks covering all five parts of Paper 3.

In addition to the units themselves, at the back of the *First Certificate Gold Coursebook* you will find a *Phrasal verb reference*, a *Writing reference*, a *Grammar reference*, *Language index* and *Communication activities*. The *Phrasal verb reference* contains an alphabetical listing of all the phrasal verbs presented in the *Coursebook* and provides definitions as well as examples of the verbs used in context. The *Writing Reference* provides model answers for all the genres tested in Paper 2 (Writing). These are annotated with 'dos and don'ts'. In addition, the *Writing Reference* includes useful expressions for each genre. The *Grammar reference* is a mini-grammar covering and extending all the grammar points presented in the units.

Each unit in the *First Certificate Gold Coursebook* provides an integrated package containing the presentation and practice of grammar and vocabulary as well as reading, listening, speaking and writing development activities all linked to a theme. A feature of each unit is an *Exam focus* section which presents and practises the techniques required for a specific task in one of the five papers in the FCE examination. Phrasal verbs are also regularly practised and presented throughout the *First Certificate Gold Coursebook* and more basic errors typical of FCE are dealt with through *Watch Out!* boxes. The communicative functions crucial to the exam are revised and practised throughout and many units also contain communication activities involving an information gap of some kind. Finally, individual sounds and other features of pronunciation including stress and intonation are covered in pronunciation sections.

Grammar

Various different approaches are used for the presentation and practice of grammar points. Structures are either taken from the authentic texts used in the unit, presented through error analysis or through matching rules to examples. Each grammar presentation is followed by a number of controlled practice activities, both spoken and written, and freer practice activities in which students have a further opportunity to put the structures to use in either speech or writing. Each grammar section is cross-referenced with the *Grammar reference*. The *Teacher's Book* suggests alternative procedures for dealing with the grammar sections depending on level and class-size. Grammar sections are also cross-referenced with the *First Certificate Gold Exam Maximiser* so that students can do further practice in class or at home.

Vocabulary

Vocabulary presentation always builds on what students already know, for example through getting them to list words they know in a particular lexical set before they learn new words to add to the set. A wide variety of presentation and practice techniques is used. Dictionary use and ways of recording and learning new vocabulary are emphasised. The practice activities provide students with techniques for organising vocabulary in various ways as well as giving them the opportunity to use what they have learnt in speech or writing. Word formation is another area that *First Certificate Gold* pays particular attention to. Students' awareness of word formation rules is raised by getting them to work out the meaning of affixes, identify parts of speech and form words through combining affixes and stems. There are also regular phrasal verb sections (see page 6). The *First Certificate Gold Coursebook* is cross-referenced to further word formation and vocabulary exercises in the *First Certificate Gold Exam Maximiser*.

Reading

Authentic texts from a range of sources (newspapers, magazines, reference books, etc.) are used to develop reading skills. Many texts are accompanied by photographs or illustrations which can be used as a means of generating interest in the text and getting students to predict what the text will be about. Students read first for gist, answering a specific question or questions the first time they read, for example, how far predictions they have made on the basis of the illustration or title are accurate. They then go on to read for more detailed information or to distinguish main from subsidiary ideas, recognise text structure, etc. There is also regular practice with working out the meaning of unknown words. Activities practising these sub-skills reflect the task types used in the actual exam. Earlier units provide a lead-in to these tasks by offering shorter simpler texts and easier versions of the tasks for students to tackle first.

Listening

Again, a range of sources is used for listening texts and the recordings offer students practice with a variety of accents. Pre-listening tasks help students to predict what they will hear. In earlier units key vocabulary is presented before students listen. Activities provide practice in listening for specific information, for gist and inferring through tasks which reflect the Paper 4 listening tasks. There is a gradual build-up in terms of difficulty of text and task as the course progresses.

Songs are another feature of the listening component of the course. The songs are related to the theme of each unit and provide a motivating use of authentic material.

Writing

Writing activities in each unit provide practice in descriptive, narrative and discursive writing within the parameters of the text types students are expected to produce in the exam itself (letters, reports, articles and compositions). Pre-writing activities get students to brainstorm ideas in pairs or groups. They are also given practice in planning their work. Earlier units often provide a plan while later units expect students to produce their own plans. They are encouraged to produce more than one draft after discussing their work with another student. Penultimate drafts are also frequently discussed with others, who help with editing and error correction (spelling, grammar and vocabulary, style and layout). Students are told to keep a record of errors that occur in their written work and to be particularly alert to these errors. Many writing activities build on sample answers to typical FCE writing tasks which means that students have an opportunity to see the way other students write and to improve the sample answers.

Speaking

The grammar, vocabulary, reading, listening and writing activities above will involve students in speaking practice through pair and group work. In addition, specific speaking activities in each unit give students an opportunity to discuss issues in open-class or small groups and to take part in roleplays. As well as these speaking activities many of the units in the *First Certificate Gold Coursebook* contain a communication activity in which students work in pairs. These are information gap activities in which each student looks at different information. All these speaking activities help to develop and refine students' spoken English while providing them with solid preparation for Paper 5.

Exam focus

Each unit contains at least one *Exam focus* section which provides information about an exam task and a procedure to adopt for that task. By working through these sections students become increasingly familiar with the exam itself and develop the appropriate strategies for dealing with each of the task types so that they approach the final examination with confidence.

Phrasal verbs

Graded presentation and practice of phrasal verbs is another important element of the *First Certificate Gold Coursebook*. Phrasal verb presentation is always integrated with the other work in the unit. A variety of approaches to presentation is used. Sometimes the focus is on the overall meaning of the particle while on other occasions students learn a stem plus a number of particles. Extensive practice is provided with cross-referencing to the *First Certificate Gold Exam Maximiser*. Students can use the *Phrasal verb reference* at the back of the *Coursebook* to test themselves.

Watch Out! *boxes*

The *Watch Out!* sections are designed to pick up on errors that are common to FCE students from a range of language backgrounds. They are typically the kinds of language points that have often been taught at lower levels but with which many students continue to have difficulty.

With stronger classes, or with points that you feel will not present great difficulties for the majority of your students, the most appropriate procedure is to use them diagnostically, that is to get students to work individually before checking their answers with the whole class. Then elicit or provide an explanation.

With weaker groups, or if you feel the point is a problem common to many of your students, it may be preferable to elicit or provide students with an explanation first.

Grammar reference

Students are referred to the *Grammar reference* throughout the *First Certificate Gold Coursebook*, but they will also use the *Grammar reference* to revise grammar points, especially in the lead-up to the exam itself.

Writing reference

Like the *Grammar reference* this section can be referred to as students meet and practise each of the key text types, but they will also turn to the *Writing reference* while revising in the weeks immediately prior to doing the exam itself.

First Certificate Gold Exam Maximiser

The other major component of the *First Certificate Gold* course is the *First Certificate Gold Exam Maximiser*. Working through the exercises in the *Exam Maximiser* will help students revise and consolidate language and skills presented and practised in the *First Certificate Gold Coursebook* and provide them with crucial further exam-specific preparation. The *Exam Maximiser* comes in two versions, one with and one without an answer key and tapescript.

General features

Each of the fifteen units corresponds thematically to the *First Certificate Gold Coursebook* and contains exercises specifically designed to recycle grammar and vocabulary presented in the *Coursebook*. Like the *Coursebook*, the *Exam Maximiser* is graded and provides a gradual progression from easier exercises and shorter texts to exercises and texts at the level of difficulty of the FCE exam itself.

A feature of the *Exam Maximiser* is a more explicit focus on exam strategies. Each unit contains a number of tasks like those in the exam itself. Students are provided with information about specific items in each paper and with strategies to ensure they answer these items successfully. Activities in the *Exam Maximiser* then ensure that students put these strategies into practice. *Hot tips!* throughout the *Exam Maximiser* are designed to give students pointers on how to get extra marks or to avoid losing marks in specific papers. *Learner training* sections extend the development of exam strategies and provide ideas for keeping in contact with English outside the classroom. In the final units of the *Exam Maximiser* students practise timing their answers and transferring them to sample answer sheets. There is also a complete *Practice Exam* at the back of the *Exam Maximiser* which can be done in the lead-up to the exam itself, before students go on to tackle the *First Certificate Gold Practice Exams*.

The *Exam Maximiser* makes extensive use of annotated sample answers and is accompanied by cassettes with simulated Paper 5 tasks. Students have the opportunity to evaluate these sample answers and simulate tasks themselves.

Using the Exam Maximiser

The *Exam Maximiser* can be used in class in tandem with the *First Certificate Gold Coursebook* as a means of providing immediate follow-up work on specific grammar or vocabulary and key exam practice. Alternatively students can do the appropriate exercises as homework.

Another way of organising your FCE programme is to first work through the *First Certificate Gold Coursebook* and to then use the *Exam Maximiser* for intensive exam preparation in the term leading up to the exam itself.

The *First Certificate Gold Exam Maximiser* can also be used by students preparing for the exam independently.

First Certificate Gold Teacher's Book

The third element in the *First Certificate Gold Course* is the *Teacher's Book*. The *Teacher's Book* provides suggestions as to how to use the material in the *First Certificate Gold Coursebook* to best advantage, answers to all exercises and an integrated tapescript. Alternative procedures are almost

always offered so that you can adapt the material in accordance with the individual characteristics of your class. Extra activities are suggested to provide your students with more fluency activities including debates and projects.

At the back of the *Teacher's Book* you will find a bank of fifteen tests, including twelve Unit tests to be used after your students have completed the *Review* pages and three Progress tests to be used once they have completed the *Progress checks* at the end of Units 5, 10 and 15. The Unit tests are multiple choice tests which are easy to administer and correct. They should take no more than 30 minutes for students to complete. An answer key is provided so that, if preferred, students can correct their own work. The Progress tests make use of the tasks in Paper 3 (Use of English) in the FCE examination. These tests should take no more than one hour for students to complete. Answer keys to these tests are also provided. If class time is short, students can be asked to do the tests outside class.

First Certificate Gold Practice Exams

The final element in the *First Certificate Gold* package is the *First Certificate Gold Practice Exams*. There are five exams including all five papers at the level of the examination itself. These tests are exactly like the examination and will make sure your students know exactly what to expect.

Teaching methodology

Marking written work

Throughout the *First Certificate Gold* course students are encouraged to develop the ability to edit and evaluate their own and other students' work. Nevertheless, final versions of written work will usually be marked by the teacher.

Teach your students the correction code which follows. Encourage them to use it when correcting one anothers' work and use it yourself.

vf	= verb form	
	e.g. *My father always play tennis on Saturdays.*	
vt	= verb tense	
	e.g. *Last year I have visited Italy.*	
ww	= wrong word	
	e.g. *We arrived to the airport half an hour late.*	
wo	= word order	
	e.g. *I go usually to the beach in the summer.*	
g	= grammar	
	e.g. *Why you not tell me you were Spanish?*	
sp	= spelling	
	e.g. *I'm really looking forward to my hollidays.*	

p	= punctuation
	e.g. *Do you come here often.*
?	= meaning or handwriting unclear
	e.g. *I was very happy to see my brother next weekend.*
/	= missing word
	e.g. *I went to / United States.*

Write in the correct form wherever you feel the error is one involving language beyond the scope of an FCE student. Add a short comment on layout and task achievement as appropriate.

Give back work marked up with the code and tell students that you will collect their work again after they have tried to correct their errors. Initially this error-correction phase should be done in class so that you can supervise students and provide help where necessary. Make sure that they keep a record of their errors and make a note yourself of any errors that are common to many of your students.

During the early stages of the course it is probably unnecessary to grade students' written work. As the course progresses you should begin to grade. Provide global grades e.g. Unsatisfactory, Satisfactory, Good or Excellent, but base your assessment on the following: use of vocabulary; use of grammar; spelling and punctuation; task achievement. Continue to use the correction code and to comment on students' work briefly throughout the course.

Dealing with speaking tasks

Avoid 'assessing' students when they are doing fluency activities in the *Coursebook*. Unobtrusively monitor speaking activities, noting errors to go through with the whole class after the activity. During these feedback sessions, do not say who made the errors.

During controlled practice immediately correct basic errors and encourage students to correct themselves and one another. If these errors occur while students are engaged in fluency activities, mention them in the feedback session at the end.

Towards the end of the course you may choose to do practice Paper 5 tests with your students. Evaluate these for grammar and vocabulary, discourse management, pronunciation and interactive communication.

Exploiting background reading texts

By covering the background reading texts you give your students another option in Paper 2. Even if your students do not intend to do this question in the exam, the background reading texts provide:

- an invaluable source of extended reading practice and vocabulary input.

- variety in terms of sources of language input and practice.

- an excellent starting point for integrated skills work.

- a stimulus for roleplay and simulation.

Set regular reading tasks involving the set texts. Ask students prediction questions in class and get them to read a chapter for homework as well as answering gist comprehension questions (e.g. *Which of the following events does not happen in this chapter?*). Follow-up activities (e.g. reading for detailed information) can be done in class.

If you have access to the film versions, these can be used for listening practice. Roleplays and simulations can also be designed (e.g. students roleplay the production team for a film version and decide where to film, who to cast in each role, etc.).

Writing work can be extended to take the form of project work with students finding additional information about the authors or the books and preparing poster presentations.

Students who take this option can choose between two general questions applicable to any of the set texts.

Recycling and revision

First Certificate Gold provides many opportunities to revise and recycle language presented. Each unit of the *Coursebook* concludes with a *Review* page or a *Progress check*; the *Exam Maximiser* offers a range of activities to recycle language from the *Coursebook* as well as a complete course-linked practice exam; the *Teacher's Book* includes revision tests for all fifteen units. The *First Certificate Gold Practice Exams* are a final element so that you can check your students' mastery of exam techniques and language.

Sample answer sheets

There are sample answer sheets exactly like those used in the exam at the back of the Teacher's Book. Students need practice in filling in these sheets. Use them with the practice exam at the end of the *First Certificate Gold Exam Maximiser*.

UNIT

1 A sense of adventure

Speaking p.6

1 Students discuss the questions in pairs. *(The man is motorsledging)*

ALTERNATIVE PROCEDURE: conduct a teacher-fronted class discussion on the questions.

2 Students complete the questionnaire individually and then compare answers in pairs. When they have read the descriptions, ask if they agree with them. What changes would they make?

ALTERNATIVE PROCEDURE: after answering the questionnaire, students try to guess how you scored and compare their answers with yours or they try to guess how other students scored. Who do they think is the biggest thrill-seeker in the class? Do they agree with the descriptions?

Vocabulary: feelings p.7

1 Students work individually before comparing their answers with the whole class.

ANSWERS

1 a) *excited*: all the other words describe feelings of fear. You can be excited without being afraid.
   b) *lucky*: all the other words refer to reactions to particular situations or circumstances.
   c) *confused*: all the other words describe feelings of unhappiness. You can be confused without being unhappy.
   d) *upset*: all the other words describe feelings of surprise. You can be upset without being surprised.
   e) *nervous*: all the other words describe feelings of anger. You can be nervous without being angry.

2 a) 'frightened ex'cited 'terrified scared
   b) 'happy 'lucky thrilled glad
   c) de'pressed 'miserable sad con'fused
   d) a'stonished up'set a'mazed sur'prised
   e) 'angry cross 'furious 'nervous

Watch Out: *nervous*

1 It's very *irritating*.
2 I get very *nervous* just before an exam.

Reason: *nervous* means 'frightened or worried'. Someone whistling would be unlikely to make you feel like this; *irritating* means 'making you angry or excited in an unpleasant way'. This is a much more likely reaction to someone else's behaviour, especially noises like whistling.

2 Work with the whole class.

ANSWERS

1 frightening   2 frightened

Reason: *-ing* adjectives describe the experience or action; *-ed* adjectives describe the person's feeling about the experience.

Adjectives from Exercise 1 with *-ed* and *-ing* forms: excited, terrified, thrilled, depressed, confused, astonished, amazed, surprised.

Highlight spelling changes: infinitives ending in *-y* have *-ied* in the *-ed* form e.g. *terrify – terrified*; infinitives ending in *-t* double the consonant in the *-ing* form e.g. *upsetting*; infinitives ending in a consonant + *e* drop the final *-e* in the *-ing* form e.g. *excite – exciting*

3 Students work individually before comparing their answers with a partner and then with the rest of the class.

ANSWERS

1 sad/depressing 2 astonished/amazed/surprised
3 angry/cross/furious 4 thrilled 5 exciting

4 Students work in pairs discussing the questions.

ALTERNATIVE PROCEDURE: elicit answers from individuals open-class.

POSSIBLE ANSWERS

1 thrilled/glad/astonished/amazed/surprised
2 frightened/terrified/scared
3 angry/cross/furious
4 frightened/terrified/scared

5 Students work in pairs describing situations.

ALTERNATIVE PROCEDURE: students write one or two sentences about a situation in the past without actually using the adjective. They then read their sentences and the class try to guess the adjective.

6 Ask the class about other ways they know to record vocabulary in addition to the ones suggested. Ask what they have done in the past. Discuss the advantages and disadvantages of the different methods. How would they advise someone learning their language to record vocabulary?

Remember to get students to regularly monitor and evaluate their vocabulary recording techniques. Are they recording vocabulary systematically? Are they satisfied with the techniques they are using? Do they test themselves from time to time?

FURTHER PRACTICE: **First Certificate Gold Exam Maximiser Unit 1, p.12 Vocabulary Exercises 1 and 2.**

Reading p.8

1 Students work in pairs. One student describes an illustration without indicating which one s/he is describing. The other student tries to guess which one it is. The second student then describes an illustration while the first student listens and guesses.

ALTERNATIVE PROCEDURE: instead of describing the illustrations with a partner, students listen while you describe one or two of them and work out which one(s) you are describing. Then individual students describe the remaining illustrations while the rest of the class listen.

2 Give the students five minutes to read the text and match the pictures to the paragraphs. Then allow another three or four minutes for students to discuss their answers.

ANSWERS

Para. 1: D	*Para. 4*: A
Para. 2: E	*Para. 5*: C
Para. 3: B	

3 **1** Go through the first example with the class. Refer students to what comes before and after the phrase *In their quest for* in the text to show that *quest* cannot mean 'fear'. Ask them to work individually before checking their answers with a partner and then with the whole class.

ANSWERS

1a); 2a); 3b); 4b); 5a); 6b); 7a)

2 Students choose two words and work out the meaning from the context individually. Encourage students to think of an *English* explanation for the words they have chosen, but accept L1 equivalents in monolingual classes. Help any students who are having difficulty. Students then compare notes with a partner. Did they choose the same 'unknown' words to guess from context? Can they help their partner with any other unknown words?

Grammar: questions pp.9–10

1 Students work individually or in pairs (put weak and stronger students together so they can help each other). Go through the answers with the whole class, asking individuals to tell you which section of the information in the box corresponds to each mistake.

ALTERNATIVE PROCEDURE: use this as a diagnostic test. Students work individually *without* referring to the information in the box. Go round making a note of individual difficulties. After they have done the exercise, students read the information in the box and modify their answers where necessary. Go through the answers with the whole class, making sure they understand the explanations in the box.

Direct the class to the *Grammar reference* on pages 162–177 of the *Coursebook*. Tell them that they should revise grammar points covered in class regularly by reading through the appropriate section.

ANSWERS

1 Why **do** people take such dangerous risks?
2 Can you tell me how you **felt** afterwards?
3 **Was** he waiting for you to jump?
4 Let's go home, **shall we**?
5 When **did you go** bungee-jumping?
6 **Do** you agree?
7 **How long** have you been doing this sport?
8 **What** are you afraid **of**?
9 Who **asked** the instructor?
10 Do you know if **he is** coming?
11 He used to hate motorbikes, **didn't** he?

2 **1** Pause the cassette after each question and check the answer. Play the cassette again, pausing after each question so that students can repeat.

ANSWERS

a) not very sure *(You've got two brothers, haven't you?)*

b) fairly sure *(You've got two brothers, haven't you?)*

2 Follow the same procedures as in Exercise 1, pausing the cassette to check the answers and to get students to repeat.

TAPESCRIPT

a) You haven't told him, have you?

b) She's going to tell him, isn't she?

c) They won't see him until the summer, will they?

d) You don't eat meat, do you?

e) He didn't use to like her, did he?

ANSWERS

a) fairly sure b) not very sure c) fairly sure
d) not very sure e) not very sure

3 Put headings such as *Age*, *Family*, *Education*, *Hobbies* on the board and elicit various possible questions which students might then use to ask one another. Students work in groups of two or three or get up and mingle, asking everyone in the class at least two questions.

3 Elicit or give meanings for *flapping* and *sawdust*. Divide the class into groups of four. Give each group a three-minute limit to prepare two questions to ask you. Go round answering each group's questions while the other groups listen. Only answer questions which are grammatically correct. Remember to only answer with *Yes/No*. When all the questions have been answered, give the groups another three minutes to prepare two more questions. After you have been round three more times, tell each group to work out their version of what happened to tell the other groups.

ANSWERS

1 Cindy and Sebastian are goldfish. A cat came in through the window and tried to get them out of their goldfish bowl. As she was doing this the bowl fell to the floor and smashed. This is why there was broken glass, water and two dead fish on the floor. The crash frightened the cat and she ran away.

2 The dead man was the smallest circus dwarf in the world. The second man was the second smallest circus dwarf in the world and was very jealous of the first man. The smallest circus dwarf was also blind and because of this had a very strict routine. He kept a piece of wood which was exactly the same height as him by his bed. Every morning as soon as he got up he would measure himself to make sure he hadn't grown during the night. One night the second smallest dwarf crept into the smallest dwarf's caravan, cut the stick in half and ran away. When the smallest dwarf woke up, he measured himself as

usual, but found that he appeared to have got twice as tall overnight. In a fit of despair he got his gun and shot himself. The second smallest dwarf came along later to check what had happened, saw his rival was dead and smiled as he was now the smallest dwarf in the world.

4 **1** Students work in pairs before checking their answers with the whole class.

ALTERNATIVE PROCEDURE: elicit possible questions from the students open-class.

POSSIBLE ANSWERS

a) How long have you been living in England/working as an actress?

b) What's your favourite food?

c) What are you afraid of?

d) Who do you most admire?/Who's your favourite female vocalist?

e) What's your worst habit?

f) What do you hate doing?

g) How often do you buy a new car/change boyfriends/ visit your parents/say something interesting/go to the theatre?

h) You're twenty-one, aren't you?

i) Have you ever smoked?

j) How would you describe your relationship with X?

k) Which of your features would you most like to change?

l) What is your best characteristic?

m) Who's your best friend?

---

2 Use this as an opportunity to pair students who haven't had an opportunity to talk to each other before.

ALTERNATIVE PROCEDURE: students ask you questions.

5 **1** When students have written their questions, ask them which famous people they have chosen. Have any pairs chosen the same famous people?

2 Students act out their interviews. When in the role of journalist, they should take notes of the famous person's answers. They then report back on the interviews to the rest of the class.

ALTERNATIVE PROCEDURE: students take it in turns to perform their interviews in front of the rest of the class.

FURTHER PRACTICE: *First Certificate Gold Exam Maximiser*
Unit 1, pp.12–13. The game *Animal, vegetable, mineral?*
described in the text *Travel Games* on p.8 can also be played
in class to practise question forms.

Exam focus: Paper 1 Reading: Part 4 (multiple matching) pp.10–11

Before students read the text get them to look at the titles
and the covers of the Lonely Planet guides. Ask them to note
down:

- three things people on holiday often mention in postcards
  home to friends

- three things guidebooks should tell travellers about their
  country or region

- three things they would like to know about each of the
  places on the covers of these guidebooks.

List students' ideas on the board.

Tell them to read the text once quickly to find out how many
of their ideas were mentioned.

Focus attention on the *About the exam* section and read it
through with the class. Now look at the *Procedure* with the
class. Point out that the general advice on looking at the title
and trying to predict as well as the first point in the specific
Part 4 procedure is what they have just done. Focus attention
on points 2 and 3 in the Part 4 procedure and tell students to
do the task. Set a time limit of fifteen minutes.

ANSWERS

1 D; 2 C; 3 D; 4 B; 5 A; 6 C; 7 D; 8 A; 9 B (in any
order); 10 D; 11 C; 12 D; 13 C; 14 A; 15 C.

EXTRA ACTIVITIES

1 Students work in groups to produce illustrated brochure-
type descriptions of local tourist attractions.

2 Groups of students focus on different holiday destinations
and find out as much as they can about them from
libraries or by writing off for information to embassies or
tourist authorities. They later present the information to
the rest of the class.

FURTHER PRACTICE: *First Certificate Gold Exam Maximiser*
Unit 1, pp.8–9.

Writing: informal letters p.12

1 This exercise is designed to get students used to the
idea of checking their own and other students' work. It can
operate as a diagnostic test of students' knowledge of a
variety of language points. The letter is intended to simulate
the kind of letter an FCE level student would produce. The
suggested corrections would produce a letter that would
receive an *Excellent* grade in the exam. It is therefore
unnecessary to focus on or correct language other than that
indicated.

CORRECTED VERSION

Dear Chris,

*Thanks for your last letter. I am really sorry I didn't write
back earlier, but I have only just got back from holiday. I
went with three friends to a little place called Mojacar
which is <u>near Almeria</u>, but it wasn't exactly <u>what</u> we
expected!*

*We booked some rooms in <u>a hotel</u> in the village, but
when we arrived <u>at the hotel</u>, we were very
<u>disappointed</u>. It was very old, rather dirty and we
<u>couldn't see</u> the sea. So, we <u>decided to change</u>.*

*The next hotel was <u>perfect</u>. It was very clean and it had
the <u>biggest</u> <u>swimming</u> pool <u>I have ever seen</u>. But <u>there
was</u> one problem – it was <u>too expensive</u>! We <u>stayed</u> one
night, but then <u>it was time</u> to change again!*

*<u>In the end</u> we found <u>a</u> beautiful apartment with a
balcony and it was cheap. <u>Unfortunately</u>, we only had
four days of our holiday left!*

*Anyway, I must go and unpack my suitcase! I will write
again soon.*

Love,

Natalia

2 Focus attention on the letter in Exercise 1 and elicit
answers to the questions from the whole class.

ANSWERS

1 In the top right hand corner.

2 No.

3 You sign your name at the bottom.

4 Below your address.

5 *Dear* + the addressee's first name.

6 *All the best, Best wishes, Love, Lots of love* + your
first name

7 No.

3 Do this first writing exercise in class. Students brainstorm ideas in pairs, but write the letter individually. Go round and help where necessary. When they have finished writing their letters, ask them to work with their partners to check grammar and vocabulary.

ALTERNATIVE PROCEDURE: if students find the idea of another student seeing their writing threatening, give out blank pieces of paper for them to use for their final draft. Tell them *not* to put their names on their letters. After they have finished, collect the letters and redistribute them so that nobody gets their own letter back.

Explain that they can improve their ability to correct their own work if they learn to correct each other's mistakes. Teach students the correction code on pages 7–8 of the Introduction. Tell them to use the code as they mark the letters and go round helping. Collect the marked letters and put them in a folder. Pass the folder round so that each student can take her/his letter out. Students correct as many of the indicated mistakes in their letters as they can. Finally collect the letters again to mark yourself using the code. If students have not been able to correct errors indicated by their classmates, give hints e.g. *-ing* or *-ed* form? *at the school* or *at school*? If a student has made errors (e.g. of style) which at this level s/he would not be able to correct her/himself, write in the correct form.

When you return the marked written work, allow five minutes for individual error correction. At the end of that time, ask them to swap letters with a partner, who will try to correct any errors they have not been able to deal with. When students have their work back, go round pointing out and helping them to correct any errors they have missed. Go over any common errors with the whole class without saying who actually made them.

4 Tell the class that it is very important to keep a record of mistakes so that they learn to check their work more effectively – something they will, of course, have to do in the exam itself. Explain to students that you will collect their notebooks on a regular basis to check that they are keeping their record up to date. Keep a record of common errors that your students make and go over these areas in class from time to time.

Tell students that there is a *Writing reference* on pp.178–186 of the *Coursebook*. Explain that they can use the *Writing reference* to check layout and useful expressions when they are doing writing exercises.

*FURTHER PRACTICE: **First Certificate Gold Exam Maximiser** Unit 1, p.11.*

Vocabulary: transport p.13

1 Elicit other means of transport from the class.

POSSIBLE ANSWERS
by sea: yacht, raft, rowing boat, hovercraft, ferry, swimming, windsurfing.
by air: plane, balloon, helicopter, zeppelin, hang-glider, magic carpet.
by land: hitchhiking, walking, skateboarding, roller-skating, on a donkey/horse/bicycle/motorcycle, by tram/rickshaw/cable car.

2 Elicit the items from the students open-class.

ANSWERS
(underlined words can go in more than one category)
ships: Customs, a lifeboat, a cabin, a deck, a liner, a cruise, a passenger, a port, a ferry, a life-belt, first-class, a steward, a yacht.
trains: a guard, Customs, a platform, a compartment, a fare, a ticket, a passenger, a single, an inspector, first-class, a track, a steward.
planes: to check in, Customs, a fare, a ticket, a seatbelt, a passenger, to take off, a departure lounge, a flight, first-class.
cars: a dual carriageway, the fast lane, roadworks, a lay-by, a seatbelt, a passenger, a parking meter, a driving test.
buses: a fare, a ticket, a passenger, an inspector, a stop.

3 Put the table on the board and elicit the answers open-class.

ANSWERS

	car	bicycle	train	motor-bike	plane	bus
get into/out of	✓	✗	✗	✗	✗	✗
get on/off	✗	✓	✓	✓	✓	✓
drive	✓	✗	✓	✗	✗	✓
ride	✗	✓	✗	✓	✗	✗
catch/miss	✗	✗	✓	✗	✓	✓

Watch Out! *journey/trip/travel*

1 I've got to go on a business *trip*... (a *trip* is a short journey for pleasure or for a particular purpose)
2 The *journey* to New York ... (a *journey* is a trip from one place to another over quite a long distance)
3 *Travel* makes you ... (*travel* means the general concept of moving around to different places)

Speaking p.13

Get students to ask you the questions so that you can demonstrate that they should answer each question with a couple of sentences, not just with a few words. Explain that this is very important in Paper 5. While students are doing the activity in pairs go round and listen to their answers noting errors to correct with the whole class. Pay particular attention to question forms.

ALTERNATIVE PROCEDURE: this can be done as a game. The rest of the class 'interrogates' individual students. The student who keeps talking and takes the longest to answer all the questions is the winner.

Explain to the students that this task is very similar to Paper 5, Part 2 (individual long turn) except that in the exam they would only hear the questions. Ask them to work in pairs, taking it in turns to ask and answer. Follow the pair work up with a teacher-led discussion of the photos.

FURTHER PRACTICE: First Certificate Gold Exam Maximiser **Unit 1, pp.7–8.**

Listening: disaster at sea p.14

1 1 Elicit as much information as possible from the class and write up key points on the board for students to refer to while they listen.

2 Check that students know the meaning of each of the words. They are key words in the listening extract and understanding the cassette is dependent on students knowing these words. Discuss with the whole class why the words might be important.

2 Play the first part of the story through once. Allow time for students to discuss with a partner if their ideas for Exercise 1 were correct and then go through the answers with the whole class.

TAPESCRIPT

The sea was calm and the sky shining with stars, when Frederick Fleet, the look-out at the top of the ship, saw the towering grey mountain of ice. 'Iceberg right ahead,' he shouted down his telephone to the bridge. And so began two hours and forty minutes of disbelief, fear and finally horror for the 2,300 passengers of the 'unsinkable' *Titanic*. For that was all the time that it took for the biggest and supposedly safest liner in the world to sink beneath the icy waters of the North Atlantic.

It was 11.40 p.m. on April 14, 1912 when the warning call came. Immediately the huge ship swung away – but not soon enough. On the bridge, the officers were congratulating themselves on a near miss, but below the water line, the Atlantic Ocean was pouring in.

The myth of the *Titanic*'s unsinkability was only one of an incredible combination of human errors, without which neither the liner nor the 1,513 lives need have been lost.

Why was the *Titanic* travelling so fast – twenty-two knots – when a mass of icebergs had been reported in the area?

Why was the *Titanic*'s radio out of contact with other shipping?

Why also did the *Titanic* have only sixteen lifeboats – with just 1,250 seats for the 2,300 people on board?

ANSWERS

The *look-out* saw the *iceberg* that the *Titanic* hit. The officers were standing on the *bridge* congratulating themselves on a near miss, but the ship had actually hit the iceberg. This was what caused the *Titanic* to *sink*. The water in the North Atlantic is described as *icy*. There were not enough *lifeboats* for all the passengers.

3 Play the cassette again while students answer. Allow them to compare answers with a partner before playing the cassette again, pausing after each relevant section to check the answers.

ANSWERS

a) *2,300*: the number of passengers on board the *Titanic*.
b) *11.40 p.m.*: the time when the warning was given.
c) *1,513*: the number of people who were killed.

d) *22 knots*: the speed at which the *Titanic* was
   travelling.

e) *16*: the number of lifeboats.

4 If students have difficulty predicting, ask the following
questions:
- *How do you think the passengers felt?*
- *What do you think the crew and captain did?*
- *How many people do you think were saved?*

Play the cassette through once. Compare students'
predictions with what is said on the cassette.

TAPESCRIPT

Aboard the *Titanic*, <u>the passengers were at first puzzled
rather than frightened</u> by the way the ship was leaning
and although the *Titanic* struck the iceberg at 11.40
p.m., it was not until five minutes after midnight that
the order was given, 'Uncover the lifeboats!' At this
point the passengers began to realise that they were in
danger.

In one of the last overcrowded lifeboats to leave the
Titanic stood Mrs Emily Richards, then twenty-four, and
<u>going off to join her husband in the USA. She had her
ten-month-old baby, George, in her arms.</u> She said later,
'We pulled away from the liner. The sea was full of
wreckage and bodies. Some people had jumped
overboard and were screaming for help. The sea was
very icy. <u>We wanted to pick them up, but our boat was
overloaded already.</u>'

As the lifeboats drifted away, <u>at 2.20 a.m. the *Titanic*
began to slip beneath the surface. The band was still
playing.</u>

One of the strangest aspects of this disaster was that it
had been foreseen in extraordinary detail in a <u>novel
published fourteen years earlier. The book, written by
Morgan Robertson,</u> told the story of the biggest and
most luxurious liner ever built ... of how it set out from
Southampton to New York on its maiden voyage ... of
how it hit an iceberg in the North Atlantic ... of how its
hull was torn open beneath the water line ... and of
how it sank with a terrible loss of life because it failed to
carry enough lifeboats. The name of the ship was the
Titan.

---

5 Check that the students understand the True/False
statements. Play the cassette again while students answer
the questions. Allow them to compare their answers before
playing the cassette a third time. Once again allow them to
compare answers before playing the cassette through a final
time and checking the answers. Pause the cassette after the
relevant sections.

ANSWERS

(see underlined sentences in tapescript)

1 True 2 False: she was going *to* the USA. 3 False: she
had *one* child with her. 4 True 5 False: it only *began* to
disappear below the surface at this time. 6 True
7 False

---

6 This can be done in groups with a secretary to report
back to the rest of the class or as a whole-class discussion.

EXTRA ACTIVITY: Show the film *Titanic* to your class. There is
an earlier version of the Titanic story called *A Night to
Remember*. This could also be shown and the class asked
to compare the two versions.

Vocabulary: word formation p.14

1 Focus students' attention on the sentence from the
Titanic listening and elicit or teach that *dis-* is a prefix used to
form the opposite of *belief*. Give students time to look at the
prefixes and then elicit answers open-class.

ANSWERS

2 *dis-/im-/il-/un-/ir-/in-* all form opposites. Point out that
im- il- ir- are all versions of *in-*, with *il-* added to stems
beginning in *l-*, *ir-* to stems beginning in *r-*, and *im-* to
stems beginning in *p-* or *m-*.

3 *over-*: too much

4 *under-*: too little

5 *post-*: after

6 *ex-*: former

7 *sub-*: under

---

2 Students work with a partner before checking their
answers open-class.

ANSWERS

1 *-ly, -wards*: adverb

2 *-ment, -ness, -ion* and *-ism*: noun (abstract)

3 *-ee, -er, -or*: noun (people or instruments)

4 *-ous, -y, -ful, -ish, -less*: adjectives

---

3 Students work individually or in pairs.

ALTERNATIVE PROCEDURE: divide the class into two or more
teams. The team that creates the most words wins. If the
game ends in a draw, ask one team to make sensible and
meaningful sentences to show the difference in meaning
between two of the words e.g. *helpless* and *unhelpful*.

Set a time limit of three minutes for this. Then give the other team(s) an opportunity to do the same. The first team to win three tie-breakers like this wins the game.

POSSIBLE ANSWERS

(Students at FCE level are unlikely to know the words in brackets.)

excitement, excitable, disappoint, disappointment, appointment, honesty, honestly, dishonest, dishonesty, dishonestly, patiently, impatient, impatiently, successful, unsuccessful, successfully, unsuccessfully, directly, direction, directness, indirect, indirectly, indirectness, kindness, unkind, unkindness, kindly, unkindly, profitable, unprofitable, profitably, unprofitably, helpful, helpless, unhelpful, helpfully, unhelpfully, helplessly, friendly, friendliness, unfriendly, (friendless), unfriendliness, friendship, lucky, luckily, unlucky, unluckily, (luckless), dislike, likely, likeable, likeness, unlikely, (unlikeable).

Tell students to record important forms of new items of vocabulary in their vocabulary notebooks.

4 Students work individually writing sentences before comparing answers with a partner and open-class.

FURTHER PRACTICE: **First Certificate Gold Exam Maximiser Unit 1, pp.9–10.**

Unit 1 Review

ANSWERS

1 1 d) *(passenger and clerk in British Rail ticket office)*

2 f) *(people in a car or on a coach stuck in heavy traffic)*

3 a) *(ticket inspector and passenger on train or bus)*

4 b) *(announcement over the tannoy and a passenger with a ticket for the flight mentioned talking to another passenger in an airport)*

5 c) *(someone who has returned from a cruise or voyage describing it to a friend)*

6 e) *(passenger with a problem and driver who doesn't want to stop yet, travelling by car on a motorway)*

2 1 examiner 2 unfriendly 3 underestimated
4 overcrowded/crowded 5 conductor 6 useless
7 Luckily 8 disbelief 9 backwards 10 disappointed

3 A frightened, scared, terrified B astonished, amazed, surprised C miserable, depressed, sad D angry, furious E surprised, thrilled, astonished

4
181 Dover House Rd.,
Putney,
London
SW5 5AE
19/5/96

Dear Natalia,

Thanks very much for your letter. Your holiday sounds like it was very interesting!

I have been very busy at work recently, but Sam and I are going on holiday to Greece next week for ten days. We are really looking forward to it. I promise I'll send you a postcard!

Hope to see you soon.

Best wishes,

Chris

5 1 What do you like doing in your free time? *(I like + -ing ...)*

2 What is the most interesting place you have ever been to? *(The most interesting place I have ever been to is ...)*

3 What kind of holidays do you like best? *(I like ... holidays best because ...)*

4 How long have you been studying English for? *(I have been studying English for/since ...)*

5 What do you find the most difficult thing about learning English? *(The thing I find most difficult is ...)*

6 Do you think you will pass the First Certificate exam? *(Yes, I think so./Yes, I will.)*

Now your students are ready to do the test for Unit 1 on page 121.

UNIT
2 Work and play

Speaking p.16

Elicit the words for the jobs shown in the photographs.

> **ANSWERS**
>
> A miner B dentist C nurse D dustman
> E football player F pop star G policeman H teacher

Students work individually first and then compare their views with a partner.

ALTERNATIVE PROCEDURE: after students have decided individually who should be paid the most and the least, write the jobs up on the board and find out how many students put each one in first position, second position, etc.

Vocabulary: jobs p.16

1 Students work in groups of four and think of a description for each job. Explain that they can use English–English dictionaries for any words they do not know, but *only* for these words. Set a time limit of five to ten minutes at the end of which they report back to the rest of the class. Write the most acceptable definitions up on the board.

ALTERNATIVE PROCEDURES:

1 For weaker groups write descriptions up on the board in jumbled order. Include two or three descriptions of jobs which do not correspond to any of the items e.g. *someone who makes and repairs wooden objects (a carpenter), someone who stands at the entrance to a building and checks people who enter (security guard)*. Students work individually matching the descriptions to the words.

2 Write the names of the jobs on pieces of paper, fold them and put them in a jar or hat. Divide the class into two teams. Each team picks out twelve items and works together to arrive at complete descriptions. They take it in turns to read their descriptions aloud. If the description is acceptable, the team gets a point. The other team can challenge if they feel the description is incomplete or inaccurate. If you allow the challenge, that team wins a point.

> **POSSIBLE ANSWERS**
>
> *A debt collector* collects debts from people and companies that owe others money.

An undertaker arranges funerals.

A referee makes sure that players obey the rules and decides what to do if the rules are broken in games like football and rugby.

A tax inspector checks that people and companies have paid the right amount of tax.

A bouncer works on the door of clubs and discotheques and keeps troublemakers out.

A plumber fits and repairs water pipes.

A traffic warden checks that cars and other vehicles are not parked in the wrong place and issues fines if they are.

A conductor
a) collects fares from passengers on buses and trains.
b) directs the playing of a group of musicians while standing in front of them.

A bookmaker takes money that people bet on races or competitions and pays the winners.

A social worker tries to improve bad social conditions and helps people in need.

A surgeon is a doctor who performs medical operations.

A dustman empties rubbish bins left in the street.

An artist paints, draws or produces pieces of art.

A chef is the chief cook in a restaurant.

A miner works underground digging out mineral substances.

A private investigator collects evidence and information about people and crimes and is paid by an individual or private company.

A librarian works in a library and decides what books to buy and how to classify them, as well as helping people find the books they want to borrow or use.

A caretaker is paid to look after a large public building such as a school and is responsible for small repairs and cleaning.

A stockbroker buys and sells stocks and shares in companies.

An editor
a) checks and corrects books, newspaper/magazine articles or films before they are published or shown.
b) is in charge of a newspaper or magazine.

A vet treats sick and injured animals.

A *wrestler* fights by holding on to an opponent and trying to throw her/him to the ground.

A *lifeguard* helps swimmers if they are in danger at a beach or pool.

2   Say which of the jobs you would be interested/not interested in doing and why so that students understand that they should answer the questions in two or three sentences, not just in a few words. Emphasise again that this is very important in Paper 5 of the exam. Students work in groups taking it in turns to respond to the questions.

ALTERNATIVE PROCEDURE: lead the discussion yourself asking individuals to respond to the questions. Write up the jobs on the board and keep a 'score' of how many people are interested/not interested in each of the jobs.

3   Make it clear that students can only ask *Yes/No* questions. Choose a job yourself and tell the students to prepare two questions to ask you. Go round monitoring question formation. Note any problems and direct these students to page 9 in Unit 1 and to page 172 (13.1) of the *Grammar reference*. Get the class to ask you their questions. Write all acceptable questions up on the board and answer them. The class should continue asking questions until they have worked out what your new 'job' is. Students then work in pairs asking and answering questions.

ALTERNATIVE PROCEDURE: individual students are 'interrogated' by the rest of the class. If the class cannot guess the job after ten questions, the student 'wins'.

EXTRA ACTIVITIES

1 Check that students know the English for the jobs they do themselves or those that members of their families do. Students write definitions of these jobs.

2 Students choose one of the jobs in Exercise 1 and interview someone who does the job about its advantages and disadvantages. They report their findings to the rest of the class.

3 Students look at newspaper advertisements from English language and local newspapers for some of the jobs in Exercise 1 to see how much people doing these jobs actually earn in their country and the UK.

FURTHER PRACTICE: First Certificate Gold Exam Maximiser Unit 2, p.17.

Listening: unpopular jobs p.17

1   Ask students which of the jobs in Exercise 1 they think might be unpopular jobs. Emphasise that the first time they listen they only need to work out which job is being talked about and write it down. Play the cassette once straight through. Ask which of the 'hated jobs' the class mentioned were on the cassette.

TAPESCRIPT

1 **(Sue Roberts, private investigator)**

I used to be a policewoman so this was an obvious line of work to get into. It can be quite a dangerous job and you can meet some really nasty types. I suppose it's not really very surprising, but some people don't like it much if they find out you've been spying on them ... they can get pretty unpleasant. The other thing which isn't much fun is the nights of sitting in cars watching people or waiting to see what they will do. On the other hand, quite often I'm asked to try and find missing people, especially children. That's great ... it's really satisfying to be able to bring a family together again.

When people ask me why I do the job, it's quite hard to pick on one thing, but to be honest, <u>what I really like best about it is the pay cheque at the end of the month!</u>

2 **(Mike Cooper, debt collector)**

For several years I worked as an accountant for a large firm, but then I was made redundant. So I decided to start my own company and now I'm really quite proud of my job and what I've managed to build up. We collect anything from £100 to thousands for clients. I think it's very unfair that this kind of work has such a bad reputation. In fact, we all have to be licensed and follow strict guidelines.

The worst part about the job? Well, I've had several abusive phone calls in the office, and <u>one individual said he would break my legs if I kept on asking him for money</u>. But that's rare – most people know that I'm just a go-between.

What do I like most about it? ... lunch hours probably ... no, seriously, I think it's the fact that there's lots of variety. I'm certainly always busy.

3 **(Jill Woods, tax inspector)**

It can be hard because we often see people get very emotional. They can get angry and frustrated and I did once have someone who broke down and cried. Usually though, it's not personal, it's to do with the whole system. Of course I do feel sympathy for people, but in the end, my job is to just make sure that they end up paying the correct amount of tax.

Outside work I try to avoid telling people directly what I do because what usually happens is that they start telling you all their financial problems and I get quite enough of that already.

I suppose every job has its ups and downs, but I think possibly the worst moment in my career was early on, soon after I'd started in the office – I managed to mix up some demands for a number of quite large payments. One way or another they got sent to the wrong people and needless to say they were very upset. I felt like a real idiot. It took ages to sort out.

4 **(Harry Bains, nightclub bouncer)**

I'd done various jobs, but these often involved working on my own. What I wanted was work where I could meet people, as that's what I really enjoy. I'm well over six feet tall and I was in the army for a while. As well as that I've always been keen on boxing and the martial arts – so that all helped me get into this line of work.

We're very strict about who we let in. Obviously that reduces the chance of trouble inside the club. Occasionally there are fights, but I hardly ever get physical except in self-defence. I will first of all call the police.

Without a doubt, it's the people that I like most about the job. I love seeing a lot of faces, both different and familiar. I work pretty hard, usually six evenings a week, for quite long hours, but I still have time for friends and family.

ANSWERS
1 private investigator 2 debt collector 3 tax inspector
4 nightclub bouncer

2 Focus attention on the instructions. Make it clear that the students do not need to use one of the sentences. Ask the class to read the sentences through silently. Check they understand *threatened*, *salary* and *embarrassing*. Play the cassette, pausing at the end of each extract. Ask which sentence they have matched with the extract, but don't indicate if they are right or wrong. Play the cassette again, straight through this time. Check the answers by playing the cassette and pausing on the key phrases.

ANSWERS
(see underlined sentences in tapescript)
A 2; B 1; D 4; E 3
Sentence C is the distractor. Speaker 3 doesn't mention having cried at work. She says *other people have cried in front of her.*

3 Phrasal verbs are presented and revised throughout *First Certificate Gold* in a variety of ways. In this case the consistent general meaning of the particle *on* is highlighted as it is helpful for students to be aware of meaning relations such as these.

Ask students if they know any phrasal verbs. Ask if they know how phrasal verbs are usually formed. Point out that phrasal verbs can be dealt with just like other vocabulary and that students should record and learn them in the same way that they record and learn other items. Focus attention on the meanings and the sentences and elicit the answer from the class.

ANSWER
c) to continue

Tell students that they will be doing regular work on phrasal verbs and that there is an alphabetical list with definitions and example sentences of all the phrasal verbs in the Coursebook on pp.196–198.

4 Begin by asking two students if they would be interested in doing any of the 'hated' jobs on the cassette. Encourage them to answer in more than a few words, saying why they would or would not be interested. This should elicit some of the vocabulary for the second question. Put up a list of possible qualities and abilities on the board e.g. *patience, physical strength, courage, intelligence, mathematical ability, curiosity, a desire to help people, ability to get on with people, a bright personality, ambition, attractive appearance, knowledge of foreign languages, driver's licence,* etc.

Ask students to work in groups saying which of these qualities/abilities apply to the jobs and adding any that have not been included.

Grammar: present tenses pp.17–18

1 Students work individually and then compare answers with a partner before checking the *Grammar reference* on page 175 to see if they were right.

ANSWERS
a) 5; b) 2; c) 1; d) 4; e) 3

2 Give students time to prepare answers before asking them to work with a partner.

ALTERNATIVE PROCEDURE: elicit a sentence for each of the situations from each of the students in class.

3 Follow the same procedure as in Exercise 1.

ANSWERS

a) 5; b) 1; c) 2; d) 3; e) 6; f) 4

4 **1** Students write answers individually in their notebooks. Go round helping and pointing out any errors.

ANSWERS

a) will paint/have b) won't start/arrives c) finds/will leave d) will move/find e) comes/will tell

2 Students write five sentences and then read them aloud to a partner.

3 Start this off by describing your own routine. Exaggerate a bit for humorous effect e.g. say you get up at midday and spend two hours in the bath, have an enormous breakfast, etc. Tell students that they should take notes while the other members of their group describe their routines. Get each group to report back to the whole class. This should elicit plenty of third person 's' practice. Monitor this carefully.

5 Before they start to fill in the gaps, tell students to read the dialogue all the way through and answer the following question:

• Which of these things are not mentioned?
a) Rupert's work b) Rupert's girlfriend c) Rupert's family
(answer: b) Students read the dialogue again filling in the gaps individually before comparing answers with a partner. Check the answers through with the whole class, asking them to match the answers to the rules in Exercises 1 and 3.

ANSWERS

1 work 2 are you doing 3 am having 4 do you think
5 like 6 get up 7 plan 8 is getting 9 teach 10 finish
11 go 12 are you going back 13 leaves 14 see
15 stops 16 is playing 17 think 18 is trying 19 are you doing

*FURTHER PRACTICE: **First Certificate Gold Exam Maximiser** Unit 2, p.19.*

Vocabulary: employment p.19

1 Encourage students to check words they are not familiar with in English–English dictionaries. Tell them to make a note of the definition, the examples and the phonemic transcription. Ask them how they are going to record and learn the new words and expressions.

2 Once students have worked out the meanings of all the items, ask them to work in groups of three or four to discuss the questions.

ALTERNATIVE PROCEDURE: set Exercise 1 for homework, again encouraging students to use English – English dictionaries and to record vocabulary in their notebooks. At the beginning of the next class ask two students how they recorded the new words. The questions can be discussed in groups or with the whole class.

*FURTHER PRACTICE: **First Certificate Gold Exam Maximiser** Unit 2, p.17.*

Watch Out!

1 He did a scientific *experiment* in the laboratory. (*a scientific test*)

2 He has a lot of *experience* as a salesman.(*uncountable: knowledge or skill that comes from doing something for a long time*)

3 He had some terrible *experiences* while he was travelling in the USA. (*countable: something that happens to you and has an effect on your mind or feelings*)

Exam Focus: Paper 3 Use of English: Part 5 (word formation) p.19

Read the instructions and exam advice aloud to the whole class. Write an example on the board e.g.
I'm afraid there is no .... of arriving on time. POSSIBLE.
Ask what part of speech is missing (*noun*). Tell students to read the text through and answer the following two questions:

• Why did Stephen Bidwell sack his son? *(Because he was lazy.)*

• How many jobs has Stuart had in the last ten years? *(One.)*

Now tell them to decide which part of speech is missing from each gap.

ANSWERS

1 dishonesty (*noun*) 2 complaint (*noun*) 3 employee (*noun*) 4 numerous (*adjective*) 5 manager (*noun*)
6 useless (*adjective*) 7 qualifications (*noun*) 8 resignation (*noun*) 9 refusal (*noun*) 10 unfairly (*adverb*)

Tell students to study *Writing Reference* pp.178–186

*FURTHER PRACTICE: **First Certificate Gold Exam Maximiser** Unit 2, p.16.*

Listening: song p.20

1 Discuss the questions open-class (*rat race*: the endless competition to succeed, especially in business).

2 Students discuss the question in pairs and then open-class. Play the song once straight through and then discuss the question with the whole class.

> **TAPESCRIPT**
> **9 to 5**
> Tumble out of bed,
> And I stumble to the kitchen,
> Pour myself a cup of ambition,
> And yawn and stretch,
> And try to come to life,
> Jump in the shower,
> And the blood starts pumping,
> Out on the streets,
> The traffic starts jumping,
> With folks like me,
> On the job from 9 to 5.
>
> *Chorus*
> Working 9 to 5,
> What a way to make a living,
> Barely getting by,
> It's all taking and no giving,
> They just use your mind,
> And they never give you credit,
> It's enough to drive you crazy,
> If you let it.
>
> 9 to 5 for service and devotion,
> You would think that I,
> Would deserve a better promotion,
> Want to move ahead,
> But the boss won't seem to let me,
> I swear sometimes,
> That man is out to get me.

3 Students work in pairs putting the lines of the song in the correct order. Play the song through once for them to check their answers and then again if necessary.

Exam focus: Paper 2 Writing: Part 1 (transactional letter) pp.20–21

1 Focus attention on the exam information and read it aloud to the class. Emphasise that this question is compulsory.

Put these True/False statements on the board and ask students to answer them as they look at the task.

- You have to do two things in your letter. (*True: say why you are suitable and ask for information.*)
- This task is called a 'guided letter writing' task because you are told what questions to ask. (*True: the questions are indicated in the notes.*)
- You only have to read the notes to answer the question well. (*False: you also have to read the advertisement so as to be able to say why you are suitable.*)
- You can write this letter in the same way as you would write a letter to a friend. (*False: you have to decide on an appropriate style. In this case the letter would be formal.*)

2 Look at the table with the class. Briefly explain or elicit explanations of each of the descriptors e.g. *answers the question directly and completely* would mean saying why you are suitable, asking for the information in the notes and not talking about other irrelevant things; *communicates the message effectively* would mean that even if you made some mistakes, it would still be easy for someone to understand what you meant.

Ask students to read the letters individually and complete the table. Students then compare answers in pairs or in an open-class discussion. Elicit or give reasons for the answers.

ANSWERS

	Letter A	Letter B
• answers the question directly and completely (*The writer of Letter B has not asked for any information other than when the job starts.*)	✓	✗
• communicates the message effectively (*Both letters communicate their message effectively.*)	✓	✓
• begins and ends the letter appropriately (*Letter B does not end appropriately. 'Lots of love' would only be appropriate at the end of an informal letter to a close friend or relative.*)	✓	✗
• organises it well with clear paragraphs (*Letter A is not organised into paragraphs at all.*)	✗	✓

	Letter A	Letter B
• has a good range of grammatical structures and vocabulary *(Letter A shows a good range of structures and vocabulary e.g. 'I am writing with reference to ...', 'I am afraid that I will only be available for interview in the evening.' Letter B is rather limited.)*	✓	✗
• uses the grammatical structures and vocabulary accurately *(Generally the writer of Letter A uses vocabulary and structures accurately. An exception to this is 'communication' for 'communicate'. There are some basic errors in Letter B e.g. 'I ... can be start ...', 'I need knowing ...', 'I had interested ...'.)*	✓	✗
• has correct punctuation and spelling *(There are some errors of punctuation and spelling in Letter A e.g. 'english', 'britain', the comma after 'start'; spelling mistakes include 'advertisment', 'intrested', 'begining' 'countrys' and 'cultur'.)*	✗	✓
• includes a range of linking expressions e.g. *although, furthermore (The writer of Letter A has not used any linking expressions.)*	✗	✓
• uses language of an appropriate style *(Both letters use an appropriate style, except for the ending 'Lots of love' in Letter B.)*	✓	✓

3 The task can be done in class or for homework. Remind students to check carefully for any of the errors you marked in their last compositions. They should use the table in Exercise 2 as a checklist for their own work.

FURTHER PRACTICE: **First Certificate Gold Exam Maximiser Unit 2, p.20.**

Reading pp.22–23

Look at the photographs with the class and ask what they think each of the people is doing and whether they would ever think of doing something like that.

1 Tell the class about something dangerous you have done before getting students to relate dangerous/exciting experiences in pairs.

ALTERNATIVE PROCEDURE: put a list of dangerous/exciting activities on the board e.g. parachute jumping, downhill skiing, bungee-jumping, riding a horse bareback, swimming in a very rough sea, white-water rafting. Ask the class to add to the list any other dangerous or exciting things they have done. Give the English words for any activities they have done if necessary.

2 Preteach the following words: *launch*, *sub-aqua*, *sky diving*, *fencing*, *wrestling*, *trampolining*, *bounce*. Draw attention to the fact that sentences have been removed from the text, but explain that students should still be able to answer the questions. Set a time limit of five minutes. Explain that this should encourage them to skim the text rather than reading sentence by sentence.

ANSWERS
1 She is a stuntperson.
2 She didn't think she could work as a dancer for long and her father suggested working as a stuntperson.
3 No.
4 This is a matter of opinion, but considering the risk of injury most people would not consider her to be well paid.

3 Focus attention on the step-by-step procedure for this task.

- *(Step 1)*: elicit a summary of the text (the dangers and joys of working as a stuntperson).

- *(Step 2)*: look at each of the sentences with the class, eliciting or suggesting a general subject for each one as follows: **A** says that something earlier in the text is not true; **B** things that can and cannot be used for stuntpeople to fall on; **C** being on fire; **D** groups and categories; **E** types of fall; **F** what she likes about the job; **G** how long it took her to decide.

- *(Step 3)*: work together to decide which sentence is missing in gap 1 (sentence **E**). Point out or elicit the fact that *this* refers back to *the really dangerous bits of acting work in films or on TV*.

• (Step 4): students work individually. Go round helping any students who are having trouble. Elicit answers from the whole group without saying whether they are wrong or right before going through the answers with the whole class.

ANSWERS
1 E; 2 G; 3 B; 4 F; 5 C; 6 A; 7 D

4 Students discuss their answers in pairs or open-class.

ANSWERS
A *that's* = stuntpeople must *be completely mad*
B *that* = a pile of cardboard boxes
D *They* = six of the categories
E *This* = the really dangerous bits of acting work
G *it* = doing stunt work

5 Check that students understand the words for the various sports and activities. Ask them to discuss the questions in groups of three or four, appointing a secretary to report back in an open-class discussion.

ALTERNATIVE PROCEDURE: get the students to ask you the questions before conducting an open-class discussion.

FURTHER PRACTICE: **First Certificate Gold Exam Maximiser Unit 2, p.15.**

Vocabulary: sports p.23

1 Before students look at the task, ask what sports they play and elicit as much vocabulary as possible. Then tell them to match the words in the box to a sport, before comparing answers with a partner. As you check the answers open-class, elicit or explain the meaning of each of the items.

ANSWERS
1 **tennis:** a racket, a net, an umpire, a court, a linesman, a club (as in an association), to serve, a set.
2 **golf:** a glove, a hole, a green, a club (association and stick), a round.
3 **football:** a goal, a pitch, a club (association), a referee.
4 **volleyball:** a net, a court, a referee, a club (association), to serve.
5 **boxing:** a glove, a ring, a referee, a round.

EXTRA ACTIVITY: get students to bring in photos of the sports mentioned from newspapers or magazines and ask the class to label them using some of the vocabulary presented.

2 Check that students understand the meanings of each of the sports in Exercise 1. Tell them to choose two pairs of sports they know how to play individually. Put them in pairs so that each pair will discuss four sports.

POSSIBLE ANSWERS:
1 *volleyball/basketball*: volleyball involves punching or propelling a ball over a high net. The ball must not touch the ground. In basketball each team tries to throw the ball through the other team's basket. The ball can be bounced. Both sports are scored in points and are played with the same type of ball. Height is an advantage in both games.
2 *tennis/table-tennis*: tennis is played with a racket and table-tennis is played with a bat. A tennis ball is larger and heavier. Table-tennis is generally played indoors on a special table whereas tennis can be played on a court either indoors or in the open air. They are similar in that they both involve hitting a ball over a net and in that they are scored in points rather than goals.
3 *boxing/wrestling*: in boxing you fight with tightly closed hands and wear gloves. The object of the sport is to score points or win outright by knocking your opponent out. In wrestling you do not hit your opponent but try and hold him/her down for a designated period of time. Both are types of fighting and can involve physical injury.
4 *football/American football*: in football you can kick the ball or bounce it off your head but you may not run with the ball or throw it. Both are permitted in American football in which players can carry the ball over the line to score points. In American football players wear helmets and heavily padded clothing. The ball is a different shape in the two games. In both games you can tackle an opponent.
5 *surfing/windsurfing*: surfing involves using the power of waves to propel you through the water, while windsurfing involves using the power of the wind. Both sports use boards of a similar shape, though surfboards are often shorter than windsurfing boards, which have a small sail attached to them. It is possible to surf without a board.

3 While the students are discussing the questions, go round helping with any extra vocabulary.

Writing: sequencers p.24

1 Get students to describe what they think is happening in the pictures. Ask students if they have ever seen sumo wrestling or know anything about it. Allow three to five minutes for the reading task.

ANSWERS

1 C; 2 B; 3 E; 4 D; 5 A

2 **1** Do this with the whole class.

ANSWERS

On entering ... / ... first ... / Having done that, ... /
Next ... / Then ... / After that, ... / Finally, ...

2 Students describe a typical morning to a partner.

ALTERNATIVE PROCEDURE: students write paragraphs about a
daily routine. Then you read them aloud to other students
who try to guess whose routine it is.

3 Ask a strong student to describe a sport to you. Ask
lots of questions to elicit a clear explanation e.g. *Do you hit
the ball with your hand? How many people are in each
team? Can you play this inside or do you have to be outside?
What do you do then?*

While students work in groups, go round prompting them to
ask questions and to give explanations that include as much
of the language practised in Exercise 2 as possible.

ALTERNATIVE PROCEDURE: students describe how to cook a
favourite meal, what they do when they have guests for
dinner, how to knit an item of clothing, how to play
Scrabble, Trivial Pursuit, etc.

4 Set the writing activity for homework.

Unit 2 Review

1 **POSSIBLE ANSWERS**

2 *kindness*: dentist, social worker 3 *patience*: nurse,
teacher 4 *reliability*: conductor, caretaker
5 *creativity*: artist, chef 6 *attention to detail*: editor,
private investigator

2 **ANSWERS**

1 An *employer* employs other people; an *employee*
works for an employer.

2 You *win* a game, competition or race; you *earn* a
salary or wages.

3 Office workers and professional people earn
salaries; other workers earn *wages*. *Salaries* are
often paid monthly whereas *wages* are usually
paid weekly.

4 To be *unemployed* is to be without a job, in
which case you may receive money from the
government to live on; to be *on a pension* is to
receive money from the government or a private
company because you are elderly and have
stopped working.

5 You can be *sacked* because your employer is
dissatisfied with your work; you are *made
redundant* when your employers no longer need
anyone to do your job.

6 A *perk* can be money, goods or any other
advantage e.g. the use of a company car, you get
from your work; a *bonus* is extra money you are
paid because you have been working very well or
at certain times of the year such as Christmas.

7 You *retire* at the end of your working life; you
resign from a particular job and usually go on to
work somewhere else.

3 resig'nation/re'sign; em'ployment/em'ploy;
ad'vertisement/'advertise; appli'cation/a'pply;
re'placement/re'place; infor'mation/in'form;
speciali'sation/'specialise; pro'tection/pro'tect;
concen'tration/'concentrate

4 1 is slowly getting 2 only occasionally go
3 don't believe 4 am staying 5 see 6 am
probably playing

5 1 B; 2 A; 3 C; 4 B; 5 B; 6 C; 7 D; 8 A; 9 B; 10 C;
11 B; 12 A; 13 A; 14 B; 15 A

**Now your students are ready to do the test for Unit 2
on page 122.**

UNIT

3 Nearest and dearest

Advance preparation

Ask students to choose some family photographs to bring to class for Exercise 3 on page 30 in this unit.

Speaking p.26

Ask students to describe the photo in as much detail as possible in pairs or open-class.

1 Explain to the class that rhyme will help them complete the poem. Tell them to read the poem through once before they start to fill in the gaps. Do the first two gaps with the whole class, highlighting the fact that *pain* and *again* rhyme. Students then complete the poem individually before comparing answers in pairs.

Play the cassette, pausing after each couplet to elicit the missing words from the class.

> **ANSWERS**
> 1 pain 2 again 3 same 4 blame 5 win 6 twin 7 out
> 8 shout 9 trick 10 sick 11 sin 12 twin

EXTRA ACTIVITY: simple poems of this type offer an excellent opportunity for rhythm and sentence stress practice. Get the class to chant the poem with you after they have heard it a second time. Exaggerate the stress and intonation. They then mark the stressed syllables in each line. Get students to chant the poem again with their books closed.

2 Students discuss the questions in pairs or open-class.

ALTERNATIVE PROCEDURE: put jumbled up advantages and disadvantages of being an only child, having brothers and sisters, or being a twin on the board e.g. *being over-protected, other children to play with, lots of attention from parents, borrowing toys and clothes, help with homework, sharing parents' affection, friends of different ages, no chance to be alone, too much time alone, learning to be independent, learning to cooperate with others, etc.*

Students then put them in the two groups of advantages and disadvantages.

EXTRA ACTIVITY: divide the class into three or four groups made up of the following:

- people who are eldest children
- people who are youngest children
- people who are middle children
- people who are only children.

Ask each group to make a list of advantages and disadvantages of being in that position in the family. Regroup students so that each group is made up of at least one person from each position in the family and get students to compare lists.

Reading pp.26–27

Focus attention on the photograph. Ask students to describe the Chaplin sisters physically and ask them how they imagine their characters and lifestyle to be.

1 Check that students understand the meaning of *reunited, lifetime apart, trapped* and *bringing up*. Set a three-minute time limit for students to answer the gist question.

> **ANSWER**
> b) is the most suitable title

2 Tell students to read through the True/False statements before reading the article a second time.

> **ANSWERS**
> 1 True (*para. 1: This is everyday East London, where everyone knows Greta and Freda Chaplin, the identical twins.*)
> 2 True (*para. 2: Listening to them talk is like hearing one person with a slight echo a split second later.*)
> 3 True (*para. 2: They have two black coats, but one came with green buttons and one black. They swapped the buttons around so that each twin had two green and two black buttons on each coat.*)
> 4 False (*para. 3: Some people are frightened of their strange telepathic bond, others laugh at them.*)
> 5 False (*para. 3: They rely a great deal on the protection and friendship of Jack Davenport who has been like a father to them.*)

6 False (*para. 4: From babies their mother treated them as one and encouraged their dependence on each other; para. 7: The mother of Freda and Greta Chaplin tried to bring them up as a single child and didn't give them the chance ever to be separated.*)

7 True (*para. 5: As Jack Davenport remarks, 'They do have different personalities although they won't admit it. Greta is the softer, more sensible one. Freda is the one who tends to dominate her sister and lose her temper more quickly.*)

8 True (*para. 6: 'These two are an extreme case, but I'm quite sure there is often telepathy between twins. If you shared the womb and your life together, there is bound to be.*')

9 True (*para. 7: 'My concern is to help parents with the emotional stress of having two babies or more at the same time.*')

3 Explain that students are not expected to understand every word in a text, they can learn to work out the meanings of words from the context and that exercises like this are intended to help them.

Students work individually, comparing notes with a partner before discussing the answers open-class.

ANSWERS

1 at the same time = *in unison*
2 to hold tightly = *grasp*
3 a very short time = *a split second*
4 to exchange = *swap*
5 part of your body above your hips = *waist*
6 a flat surface in a shop where you go to be served = *counter*
7 to keep together = *stick to each other*
8 to agree that something is true = *admit*
9 to become angry suddenly = *lose (her) temper*
10 part of a woman's body where a baby develops before it is born = *womb*
11 certain, sure = *bound*
12 anxiety, pressure = *stress*

4 **1** Explain that there are often questions of this type (involving inference) in the exam. Allow time for students to read the text again before discussing the answer open-class.

ANSWER

The writer feels sorry for the twins because they are so dependent on each other, because people are not always sympathetic towards them, because they have not been able to develop separate identities and because they have never had the 'love, friendship and understanding' they need.

2 Discuss the other questions with the whole class. As always, try to get students to speak for as long as possible.

Vocabulary: phrasal verbs (family) p.27

1 Students think of English definitions or equivalents. In monolingual classes students can provide translations. Play the cassette twice to give students a chance to note meanings. With weaker classes the sentences can be dictated.

TAPESCRIPT

1 I *grew up* in a small town in the north of England. I left there when I was seventeen.

2 It was really my mother who *brought* me *up*. My father was often away on business trips.

3 Could you *look after* Jimmy for a couple of hours while I go out shopping?

4 I don't *get on very well with* my younger sister. We're always arguing.

5 He always *looked up to* his father. He wanted to be like him and he wanted his father to be proud of him.

6 I think she particularly *takes after* her mother. They are both very open, generous people.

7 What are the children *getting up to* now? It's very quiet ... too quiet!

8 His mother never *tells* him *off*. That's why he's so naughty all the time.

POSSIBLE ANSWERS

1 to grow up = *to develop from being a child into an adult*

2 to bring (someone) up = *to educate and care for a child until s/he is grown-up*

3 to look after = *to take care of*

4 to get on (with) = *to form or have a friendly relationship with*

5 to look up to = *to respect and admire*

6 to take after = *to look or behave like (an older relative)*

7 to get up to = *to do something bad (especially of children)*

8 to tell someone off (often done by a teacher, parent or boss) = *to speak angrily to*

2 Give students a few minutes to prepare before telling a partner.

ALTERNATIVE PROCEDURE: this can be done as a competition. Individual students talk in front of the rest of the group and describe their family situation. Students are given points for every phrasal verb they use correctly. Bonus points can be given for phrasal verbs from Units 1 and 2. The student who uses the most phrasal verbs and keeps talking for the longest time is the winner.

Exam focus: Paper 3 Use of English: Part 4 (error correction) p.28

Read the information about the exam and the advice on how to deal with this question aloud to the class. Ask the students to read the text through once quickly to answer the question: *Who is the speaker describing?* (*his brother and sisters*) Ask them to read the text again and find the four lines which are correct.

> **ANSWERS**
> Lines 1, 7, 8 and 9 are correct

Focus their attention on the kind of extra words to look for and get them to check the eleven incorrect lines for these items individually.

> **ANSWERS**
> *line 2:* delete *are*
> *line 3:* delete *the*
> *line 4:* delete *on*
> *line 5:* delete *a*
> *line 6:* delete *to*
> *line 10:* delete *to*
> *line 11:* delete *am*
> *line 12:* delete *she*
> *line 13:* delete *all*
> *line 14:* delete *more*
> *line 15:* delete *a*

Grammar: making comparisons pp.28–29

1 Tell students to underline all the phrases in the error correction text in which there is a comparison. Explain that the line numbers in brackets in the grammar rules for comparison indicate the lines of the text where an example of each rule occurs. Students then work individually to

complete the rules before checking their answers with a partner. Refer them to page 164 of the *Grammar reference* to check and correct their answers if necessary. Go through the answers with the whole class.

> **ANSWERS**
> a) adding *-er* and *-est* b) double the consonant first
> c) drop the *-e* d) good/better/best, bad/worse/worst;
> far/farther/farthest e) using *more* or *most* + adjective
> f) dropping the *-y* and adding *-ier* g) the same; not the
> same. h) a small i) a big j) *more* and *most*

2 Do this exercise with the whole class. Give students a few moments to look at the first picture before going through the answers as a class.

> **ANSWERS**
> Sentences 2, 6, 7, 9 and 11 are true.

3 Students work individually writing in the missing words before checking their answers with a partner and with the whole class.

> **ANSWERS**
> 1 No one I know works as hard **as** my father.
> 2 She is **the** most intelligent person I've ever met.
> 3 They have **a** lot more money than we do.
> 4 I am **not** nearly as old as Simon.
> 5 She plays tennis better **than** I can.
> 6 Last time the ticket was a little **less** expensive.

4 Explain to the class that some of them are going to take the role of salespeople and others the role of customers or clients. Make it clear that the two salespeople are trying to get C to buy what they are selling. Tell them that this is an opportunity for them to use some of the language of comparison they have just practised. Students listen to the example on the cassette and decide which sales pitch they prefer. Give Students A and B two minutes to plan how they are going to sell their items to Student C.

> **TAPESCRIPT**
> **A:** I think it would be much better for you to go on holiday to England than to the United States. To start with, it's a lot nearer and so it will be much cheaper to get there. That means you will have far more money to spend when you get there.
>
> **B:** That may be true, but think about when you get

there. There is so much more to do in the United States, there are so many different things to see and places to go. Imagine ... you could go to New York, San Francisco, the Grand Canyon, Disneyworld ...

A: Exactly, Disneyworld! Think of all the history there is in England, all the amazing castles to visit ...

B: Okay, but what about the weather? The weather isn't nearly as good in England as in the United States – everybody knows that.

When Students A and B have finished selling their product, get them to change roles so that Student C takes on the role of a salesperson and Student A becomes the customer. Then students change roles again so that Student B becomes the customer. Get students to choose a different product to sell each time they are in the role of the salesperson.

ALTERNATIVE PROCEDURE: Students A and B try to sell their items to the whole class, who then vote on which item to buy. Another pair of students tries to sell another pair of items, the class votes and so on until all the items have been presented.

5 Check that students know what a *world record* is and that they understand the abbreviations *cm* (centimetres) and *m* (metres).

Get students to describe each of the illustrations in groups of three or four before comparing answers with the whole class.

ANSWERS

1 55.8 cm = *the bubble gum blowing record. The largest bubble ever blown is one measuring 55.8 cm in diameter by Susan Montgomery of Fresno, California, USA on 30 June 1985.*
2 35 m 55 cm = *the greatest measured distance for the flight of a champagne cork.*
3 92 hours = *the longest period of non-stop play of computer games by Terry Smith of Hull to raise money for the Council of Disabled People.*
4 1,009,152,000 = *the greatest number of continuous hiccups. Charlie Osborne of Iowa, USA hiccoughed from 1922 to 1994 without stopping.*
5 8.61 seconds = *this is the fastest recorded time for consuming 115 m of spaghetti plus sauce.*

FURTHER PRACTICE: **First Certificate Gold Exam Maximiser Unit 3, p.24–25.**

Pronunciation: /ʌ/ p.30

1 If students do not know phonemics explain that /ʌ/ is the phoneme that represents the sound in *son*. Refer them to the pronunciation page in their dictionaries.

Tell students to say the words in the exercise quietly and to list the words with the sound /ʌ/. Read the words aloud to students so that they can check their answers.

ANSWERS

mother, uncle, cousin, company, money, love, drunk, trouble, enough, young, blood, won, Monday, cup, shut, butter, much, London

2 Play the cassette. Students note down the words in the box which they hear.

TAPESCRIPT

1 Shut the door, will you love?
2 Your uncle's got a bad cough.
3 Apparently they're having some trouble at the bank.
4 Give this cap to your mother.
5 There's blood on my ankle.
6 Your cousin came home. He won the match.
7 I drank too much on Monday.

ANSWERS

1 shut/love 2 uncle/cough 3 trouble/bank
4 mother 5 blood 6 cousin/home/won
7 drank/much/Monday

Teach the phonemic symbols for the vowel sounds that occur in the other words on the cassette: nephew /e/; bank, drank, cap, ankle /æ/; cough /ɒ/; home /əʊ/.

Ask them how many ways /ʌ/ can be spelt (o, u, ou, oo).

Tell students to remember to note the pronunciation of new words as they learn them.

Students work individually reading aloud quietly. When they have had a chance to rehearse, get a couple of students to read to the whole class. If they mispronounce a word with the sound /ʌ/, encourage self-correction by pretending you did not hear. Say: 'I'm sorry. I didn't quite catch that.' or 'Sorry, did you say "uncle" or "ankle"?', etc.

Vocabulary: describing people (1) p.30

1 Explain or elicit the fact that *related by blood* means related by birth. Students answer questions 1 and 2 referring to the words in the box. Tell them to use a dictionary to help them where necessary.

ANSWERS

1 *Relations that can be male or female*: twin, cousin.
2 *Relations that cannot be related to you by blood*: stepmother, sister-in-law.

Revise other family relationships by teaching or eliciting the following words: *stepfather/stepsister/stepbrother; father-in-law/mother-in-law/brother-in-law; great-grandmother/great-grandparents; half-brother,* etc.

EXTRA ACTIVITIES: give students slips of paper with instructions such as these written on them (the instructions can be changed according to what you know about your students):

Find the person with the most cousins.
Find someone who has at least one niece or nephew.
Find someone whose great-grandfather is still alive.
Find the person who has the most uncles and aunts.
Find someone who has a sister-in-law, brother-in-law, mother-in-law or father-in-law.
Find someone who has four grandparents.

Students get up and mingle, asking everyone in the room *Have you got ...?* or *How many ... have you got?* until they have found people who fit the descriptions.

2 1 Students work individually matching words to definitions before checking their work in pairs or open-class.

ANSWERS

a) 14; b) 2; c) 5; d) 9; e) 7; f) 11; g) 6; h) 4; i) 1; j) 8;
k) 10; l) 13; m) 12; n) 3

2 Demonstrate this to the class by telling them about friends and relatives of yours without telling them who they are. See if they can guess what your relationship is to the person you describe. Students work in pairs describing their friends and relatives.

ALTERNATIVE PROCEDURE: put sentences describing people on the board. Students match them to the words and then write other sentences of their own. e.g.

He wants to be president of the company by the time he's thirty. (ambitious)

They never let their children eat sweets or watch television during the week. (strict)
He buys everybody really expensive presents for their birthday. (generous)
She's really talented and clever, but if you compliment her on her work, she always says it was nothing. (modest)
He noticed my umbrella was torn and broken so he bought me a new one. (thoughtful)
Last time we went out, they gave the babysitter a terrible time. They threw talcum powder all over the stairs and stuck all the baby's disposable nappies together. (naughty)
She's always willing to listen to new ideas and opinions even if she thinks you're wrong. (open-minded)
She's not at all beautiful in the classical sense, but people always want to be with her. (attractive)
She can walk into a roomful of strangers and seem completely relaxed. (self-confident)
You know somehow that he'll be your friend for life no matter what happens. (loyal)
If she says she'll be there at 8 o'clock, you can guarantee she will be. (reliable)
He never takes a day off and only stops for lunch for half an hour. (hard-working)
Now she's decided, she won't change her mind. (stubborn)
She's so easily offended. She feels really hurt by anything anyone says about her. (sensitive)

3 Students work in groups of three or four and think of opposites for the adjectives.

ALTERNATIVE PROCEDURE: elicit opposites from the students open-class.

POSSIBLE ANSWERS

a) lazy b) mean c) flexible d) insecure
e) unreliable f) disloyal g) easy-going
h) narrow-minded i) thoughtless j) well-behaved
k) unattractive l) insensitive m) arrogant n) unambitious

3 Pass round some of your family photos and explain who each person is. Ask students to work in pairs and describe members of their families. Go round monitoring use of the language of describing people and comparison. Note any errors to go over with the class at the end of the activity.

Watch Out! *sensible/sensitive*

1 sensitive *(easily upset)*
2 sensible *(showing good sense)*

ALTERNATIVE PROCEDURE: students prepare short talks about their families and posters of their family trees to present to the rest of the class.

FURTHER PRACTICE: First Certificate Gold Exam Maximiser **Unit 3, p.21 and pp.26–27 (Writing: transactional letter).**

Listening: Man's best friend p.31

1 Play the cassette once while students work individually and decide which picture is not mentioned. Check the answer with the class. (Picture C is not mentioned).

TAPESCRIPT

P = Presenter J = Jane

P: In *All in the family* this morning we'll be looking at the only member of the family we can actually choose – the family pet! With me in the studio to talk about choosing and looking after a pet is vet, Jane Herriot. So Jane, what advice would you give a family thinking of getting a dog or cat?

J: Well, the first thing I'd tell them is to think twice! <u>Dogs and cats can live up to twenty years or more</u> and they don't stay cute and tiny for very long. Looking after an animal is a big commitment so if you're thinking of getting a pet make sure that everyone in the family is willing to accept this responsibility.

P: Okay, so first let's look at dogs. What kinds of things should you be prepared for when you get a puppy?

J: Assuming you and your family opt for a puppy as opposed to an adult dog… and that's an important decision in itself …

P: Yes, I'd like to come back to that in a moment.

J: You need to make sure that your home is 'Puppy-proof'.

P: 'Puppy-proof'? What do you mean, Jane?

J: Well, puppies are very good at escaping so you need to make sure that they can't get out and onto the road where they inevitably will be in danger. <u>Even if you've blocked all exits you need to keep an eye on your puppy at all times. Leaving him unsupervised for even a few minutes can lead to a mishap or a serious accident.</u> The second thing to remember is that puppies chew, and chew and chew and chew. <u>They can't tell the difference between a stick that they find in the park that can be chewed and the leg of the antique coffee table. You must teach them.</u>

P: How should we go about training a puppy?

J: Puppies need consistency, so make sure everyone in the family <u>agrees</u> on what the rules are and train your puppy to follow those rules. <u>It's no good if one person tells the puppy off for jumping up on the sofa and someone else encourages him to get up and sit on their lap. Small, cuddly puppies that were once 'lap dogs' may still climb onto your lap when they are fully grown and this can be a rather uncomfortable experience with the bigger breeds.</u> Secondly, it's important to remember that puppies make many mistakes because they don't retain information and this can be frustrating. <u>No matter how infuriating he is, you should never hit your puppy, even when he's naughty.</u> Remember! No puppy is perfect – and neither are we for that matter.

P: No, no, far from it, I'm afraid. What about exercise? Is it all right to keep a puppy in a flat as long as he's taken out regularly?

J: Well, personally I'm not in favour of keeping puppies and dogs in small apartments or flats. In fact, some blocks of flats establish restrictions on size and weight to stop people keeping big dogs in too small a space. <u>Puppies and dogs have a lot of energy and they need plenty of daily exercise and space for lots of play, so it's best not to think about having one unless you've got room. As I said before they do have some annoying habits like digging and they do this especially when they're bored, so never leave a puppy outdoors unattended – he'll almost certainly be lonely and may do something diabolical like eating the washing! One way to avoid this is to fill his time with more acceptable activities, particularly playing, walking and running.</u> If you don't have a fenced garden or live in an apartment, you'll have to walk him several times a day.

P: What costs should dog owners expect?

J: Well, basically dogs get more expensive the longer they live…

---

2 Focus attention on the *Yes/No* statements and get students to read them through. They can try to answer from memory before a second listening. Play the tape again while students listen and answer. Check the answers open class, playing relevant sections of the tape again if necessary.

ANSWERS
1 Yes 2 No 3 Yes 4 Yes 5 No 6 No 7 Yes

3 Students work in groups of four discussing the questions and then reporting back to the rest of the class.

ALTERNATIVE PROCEDURE: Conduct a whole class discussion.

Writing: drafting and redrafting p.31

1 Focus attention on the posters and slogans. Elicit or explain that there are many animal rights and animal protection organisations in the UK and elsewhere in Europe. Highlight the fact that this task is similar to Paper 5, Part 3 (Collaborative Task) and that they should discuss all the possible combinations before they decide which combination of photo and slogan they think would be most effective. Get each pair to tell the rest of the class why they chose their combination.

Tell students to look at *Writing Reference* pp.178–186.

2 Allow plenty of time for this. Emphasise the importance of drafting and redrafting as a way of improving writing. Set time limits for each phase as follows

- *5–10 minutes*: students work in pairs and brainstorm ideas together.

- *10–15 minutes*: students write the first draft in pairs.

- *5 minutes*: students exchange the first draft with another pair of students.

- *5–10 minutes*: students rewrite the first draft in pairs in response to the other students' comments.

- *5 minutes*: students go through the final version checking carefully for mistakes. Collect the stories at the end for correction. Use the correction code as for earlier writing tasks.

Reading pp.32–33

1 Focus attention on the photographs and ask students to think about the question. Tell students to read the section entitled **Open House** and answer the gist question. Explain that there is an exercise later to help them with unknown vocabulary, which is why some words in the text are underlined.

> **ANSWER**
>
> The families are going to record themselves for a TV documentary.

2 Point out that this activity is very similar to Part 2 of Paper 5 and that students should aim to talk for as long as possible. Students work in pairs describing the photographs.

ALTERNATIVE PROCEDURE: stronger students can talk about the photographs in front of the whole class.

3 Set a five-minute time limit for this initial reading of the text. Ask students if their opinions about the families have changed.

> **ANSWERS**
>
> - Daniela and Claudia Chiappi mention a row, but in general both the Chiappi and the Gibson brothers and sisters get on well.
> - Luciano Chiappi owns a garage and Diane Chiappi is a teacher. Jack Gibson is a geography teacher and Pauline Gibson works as a doctor's receptionist.
> - Neither the Chiappis nor the Gibsons seem strict. It was the children who arranged to be on the programme in both cases. Both lots of children tease their parents.
> - In both cases the families seem close. The Chiappis are described as 'fiery but fiercely loyal'. The Gibsons have a lot of fun together including water fights.

4 Set a time limit of ten to fifteen minutes for this. Tell the class to read the questions before re-reading the text. Students work individually and compare their answers in pairs, before checking with the whole class.

> **ANSWERS**
>
> 1 the Chiappis (*'There was one point when I wished the camera had been turned off,'* admits Daniela./ *'Sometimes it all became annoying when you didn't want to be filmed,'* says Enza.)
> 2 the Chiappis (*'Everything we've shot is true to life, except Luciano and I fall out much more than you see on the film.'*)
> 3 Luciano Chiappi. (*'His jokes are really bad and he tells them a hundred times. Ever since we've been filming he has said, "You must talk to my agent first." and he still thinks it's funny!'*)
> 4 the Gibson family (*The fun-loving family obviously had a fantastic time with their camcorder.*)
> 5 the Chiappis (*Loud laughter and even louder arguments can be heard from the Chiappi's house.*)
> 6 Suzanna Gibson (*Suzanna retaliated by lying in wait at 7.30 a.m. for her mum to come out of the shower.*)
> 7 the Gibsons (*'They're worse than teenagers, they take absolutely ages to get ready,'* he complains.)
> 8 Luciano Chiappi (*'The irritating part is they didn't ask me, they have no respect. It's always the same,'* he moans.)

5 Students work individually before checking answers with the whole class.

> **ANSWERS**
> *row* = noun; *yell* = verb; *grumpy* = adjective (in a bad mood); *fall out* = verb; *moan* = verb, *downfall* = noun; *grin* = noun; *keep up* = verb; *drench* = verb (make thoroughly wet). The two words with inappropriate meanings are *grumpy* and *drench*.

6 Students work in groups of three or four and discuss the questions.

ALTERNATIVE PROCEDURE: lead a discussion of the questions with the whole class.

Vocabulary: describing people (2) p.34

1 Focus students' attention on the photo of the Chiappi family on page 32 and play the cassette. Ask if any of the students noticed any differences. Play the cassette again, pausing after the underlined words in the tapescript to elicit the eight differences between the cassette and the photo.

> **TAPESCRIPT**
>
> **E = Enza B = boyfriend**
>
> **E:** So this is the whole family again, when we were doing that thing I told you about for the TV.
>
> **B:** Yeah? That must have been really weird.
>
> **E:** Well, it was okay, quite a laugh really, I've still got it on video somewhere, I'll show you later.
>
> **B:** So, anyway that's your Dad with the blue jeans.
>
> **E:** Yeah, that's right, sitting in the armchair. Doesn't he look funny with a beard and a moustache? He's only had the beard for a while. I think he's just trying it out.
>
> **B:** He's going a bit bald, too.
>
> **E:** Well, he never had much hair!
>
> **B:** And I guess that's your mum in front of the sofa.
>
> **E:** Yeah, she doesn't normally look like that 'cos she wears glasses usually. I think she took them off there for the photo, and that silk scarf she's got on, I gave her for her birthday the week before.
>
> **B:** Yeah, it's nice. And who are the two on the sofa?
>
> **E:** Oh, them ... they're my sisters, Daniela and Claudia. Daniela's just turned sixteen and Claudia's nearly

fourteen. I told you about them. They're alright, I suppose, but they can get on my nerves.

> **B:** Like all girls!
>
> **E:** Hey, watch it you!
>
> **B:** So is it Claudia with the plain green top and the trainers?
>
> **E:** Yep, and Daniela with that crazy look on her face.
>
> **B:** Yes, they both look as if they're having fun! So, you're the only one with short hair?
>
> **E:** Yeah. I used to have shoulder-length hair, pretty much like my sisters, but I got it cut like this a little while ago and in fact this photo was taken soon after.
>
> **B:** And you're doing the filming ... Mrs Stephen Spielberg no less! I like that polo-neck you've got on in the picture.
>
> **E:** Haven't you seen it before? It was the one ...

> **ANSWERS**
> *(see underlined sentences in tapescript)*
> 1 not wearing jeans 2 sitting in the armchair 3 with a beard and moustache 4 in front of the sofa 5 she wears glasses usually 6 plain green top 7 the only one with short hair 8 polo-neck you've got on

2 Focus attention on the table and check that students understand all the items. If possible, illustrate the meaning of any unknown items with realia or magazine pictures. Tell students to circle the items they hear mentioned on the cassette.

> **ANSWERS**
> a beard/a moustache, is going a bit bald, glasses, silk scarf, has just turned sixteen, short hair, shoulder-length hair

3 Students work in pairs and classify the items, using a dictionary where necessary.

> **ANSWERS**
> **Age:** getting on, teens
> **Hair:** a fringe, a ponytail, wears it in a bun, wavy
> **Build:** plump, frail
> **Face:** (thin/thick) eyebrows, high cheek-bones
> **Body marks:** a tattoo, freckles, wrinkles
> **Accessories:** contact lenses
> **Attitude:** pleased with herself, fed-up

Remind them to add to these lists themselves when they meet new vocabulary for describing people.

4 Set the writing task for homework. Tell students to write a paragraph about each member of the family.

EXTRA ACTIVITY: at home students write descriptions of photographs of their families. They bring the photographs and the descriptions to the next class. Number the descriptions and display them on the walls of the classroom with the photographs (numbered a,b,c, etc.) in jumbled order. Students read the descriptions and match them to the photographs.

If students do not have family photographs, give them magazine or newspaper pictures of families to describe.

5 This information gap activity must be done in pairs. If you have an odd number of students, form one group of three in which two students work together describing one photograph to another student working on her/his own. Monitor the pairs noting any errors in language for describing people. Go through the errors later with the whole class without saying who made each error.

ANSWERS

In Picture B:
1. The daughter's hair is wavy.
2. The elder son has not got any freckles.
3. The elder son is wearing an earring.
4. The grandfather has got a scar on his face.
5. He has got a little hair on his head.
6. The grandmother is wearing a gold chain.
7. The mother is the same height as the father.
8. The mother looks as if she is happy.
9. The father has not got any eyebrows.
10. The youngest son is fat.

*FURTHER PRACTICE: **First Certificate Gold Exam Maximiser** Unit 3, p.21 and pp.26–27 (Writing: transactional letter).*

Unit 3 Review

ANSWERS

1 1 looking after 2 was brought 3 has grown 4 get on well with 5 told us off 6 takes after 7 looked up to 8 getting up to

3 a) stubborn b) ambitious c) open-minded d) reliable e) loyal f) lazy

4 1 much 2 sunglasses 3 ponytail 4 moustache 5 well-built 6 as 7 wavy 8 in 9 wearing 10 looked

Now your students are ready to do the test for Unit 3 on page 123.

UNIT
4 Seeing is believing

Speaking p.36

Students discuss the questions in groups or open-class. List students answers to questions 3 and 4 on the board. Tell the students that the other versions were painted by Jess Artem (the middle picture) and Marcel Duchamp (the top right picture).

Reading pp.36–37

1 Set a three to four minute time limit for the skim reading task before going through the answers to the questions open-class.

> **ANSWERS**
> 1 Yes. In August 1911. 2 It's not possible to say for certain.

2 Explain to students that they should first decide what the main idea of each paragraph is and that this will help them to choose between the two headings.

> **ANSWERS**
> 1 A mysterious theft
> 2 A dishonest craftsman
> 3 An international conspiracy
> 4 A successful conspiracy – a fake *Mona Lisa*?
> 5 Would *Mona Lisa* pass a scientific test?

Speaking p.37

1 Students discuss the questions in pairs and then open-class. Ask how important it is for clothes e.g. trainers, jeans or jewellery e.g. watches, to be authentic.

2 Divide the class into two groups. Each group appoints a spokesperson to argue their case. Tell one group that they should prepare to argue that the *Mona Lisa* in the Louvre is the original and the other group that they should argue that the painting was not painted by da Vinci. The groups work with the spokespeople to prepare a three to five minute presentation to the enquiry. If possible, another class at this or a more advanced level could be asked to listen to the presentations and reach a decision on whether or not the painting is the original. If this is not possible, the teacher should decide.

FURTHER PRACTICE: **First Certificate Gold Exam Maximiser Unit 4, pp.28–29.**

Vocabulary: science and technology p.38

1 Ask students what kinds of dictionaries they normally use. Ask questions about the way they use their dictionaries, e.g.
Do they only use them to look up unknown words when they are reading?
What kinds of information do they record?
Do they only write down the meaning or do they also record other information such as pronunciation, grammatical information and examples?
Do they use dictionaries when they are writing?
If students do not normally bring English–English dictionaries to class, tell them some of the advantages of using an English–English dictionary e.g. *they generally provide more information about pronunciation and grammar and provide more examples than bilingual dictionaries; they have grammar pages; they have labelled illustrations to teach lexical sets and exercises.*

2 Students work individually, reading the definitions. Then ask the class what kinds of information they noticed. Put a complete list of dictionary uses on the board. Mention the *Longman Active Study Dictionary* as a suitable English–English dictionary for this level.

3 Students work individually filling in the gaps.

> **ANSWERS**
> 1 realistic 2 revolutionize 3 laboratory
> 4 chemicals/produce 5 theoretically 6 developments
> 7 invention 8 production

4 Emphasise *in natural speech*. Students should not count orthographic syllables. Students do this first without looking at the dictionary entries. They then use the entries to check their answers.

ANSWERS

1 rea'listic – four syllables
2 revo'lutionize – five syllables
3 la'boratory – four syllables
4 'chemicals – three syllables
  pro'duce – two syllables
5 theo'retically – four syllables
6 de'velopments – four syllables
7 in'vention – three syllables
8 pro'duction – three syllables

FURTHER PRACTICE: **First Certificate Gold Exam Maximiser**
Unit 4, p.33 (Vocabulary and grammar: open cloze).

Grammar: *like* p.39

1 Discuss the questions open-class.

ANSWERS

1 The girl was not impressed.
2 *Like* means 'similar to'.

2 Students work individually, comparing answers with a partner and then the whole class. They can then check their answers by referring to page 177 of the *Grammar reference*.

ALTERNATIVE PROCEDURE: this can be set for homework or self-access work.

ANSWERS

The following sentences should be corrected as shown:
2 My brother is the same age **as** me.
4 He **looks** like a banker *or* He **is** like a banker.
5 What **do** you like doing at the weekends?
9 Would you like me **to make** some tea?

Watch Out! *like to do/like doing*

Gavin enjoys getting up, Pete chooses to get up. *Like + -ing* means 'to enjoy', *like* + infinitive means 'you think it is a good idea and you do it if possible'.

3 1 Students work individually writing their questions.

POSSIBLE ANSWERS

a) What do you like doing at the weekends?
b) What time do you like to get up in the morning?
c) What's your girlfriend/cousin/teacher, etc. like?
d) What's the weather going to be like tomorrow/this weekend/on Wednesday, etc.?
e) What's the town/city where you live/you are from like?
f) What does your brother/friend/cousin, etc. look like?

2 Students work in pairs asking each other their questions.

ALTERNATIVE PROCEDURE: students ask you their questions.

4 Students discuss the photograph in pairs or open-class before checking to see if their ideas were correct.

FURTHER PRACTICE: **First Certificate Gold Exam Maximiser**
Unit 4, p.30.

Exam focus: Paper 4 Listening: Part 3 (multiple matching) p.40

Read the exam information aloud to the class. Point out that one of the prompts is not needed. If you think your students need extra help, get them to work in pairs trying to predict what each of the speakers will say. Give them this example for item A 'Maybe someone went for dinner at a friend's house and the food was awful'. Play the tape once straight through while students answer, working individually. After a short pause play the tape again. Check the answers open-class. Play the relevant parts of the tape again if necessary.

TAPESCRIPT

1 I suppose it was a bit stupid really, but I was desperate to get this job, so at the interview when they asked me about my computer experience, I told them I had used all the different software packages that had been mentioned in the advertisement. They were really pleased and a few days later I got a letter offering me the job. Well, this morning, my second day there, <u>my boss asked me to integrate some statistics in a report using this software that I had said I knew all about. I sat there for ages, I had no idea what to do.</u> In the end, I went and told him. He was very nice about it, but I was so embarrassed!

2 I never tell lies normally. I pride myself on that, but there was one occasion when this aunt came to stay with me and she had just bought this amazing pink suit with a bright orange hat to match and worst of all, the hat had this artificial fruit on it. I think it is probably the most hideous set of clothes I have ever seen. <u>Anyway, unfortunately, just before we went out one evening, she put this on and asked me what I thought of it. I couldn't bring myself to tell her the truth.</u> I told her I thought it was wonderful.

---

3 The other day I was just coming out of school and I saw Karen, this good friend of mine, kissing the new boy who has only been in the school a few weeks. All the girls like him 'cos apparently they all say he's really good-looking. Anyway, she saw me and came over and told me that I mustn't say anything to Pete about it. She's been going out with Pete for ages and Pete's my best friend. <u>I said I wouldn't say anything, but that evening I was round at Pete's house. I felt really awkward and Pete asked me if everything was alright. I said, 'Yeah, yeah, everything's fine.'</u>

4 I had quite a funny experience just the other day in a small newsagent's near my house. Well, when I say 'funny' it wasn't really funny at all! There were these two youngsters, probably about ten and eleven years old, and <u>while the woman behind the counter's back was turned I saw them taking handfuls of sweets off the shelves and stuffing them into their pockets. I was just about to say something when a couple more customers came in and in the end I didn't say anything. I wish I had now.</u>

5 I suppose it was a bit naughty of me but I really wanted to see the Wimbledon tennis finals on TV this afternoon, so I called in this morning to work and put on an 'ill' voice and told them I had been very sick in the night, had got no sleep and still had a terrible headache. Anyway, they were completely taken in and were very sympathetic and told me to take it easy. The tennis was great, but I did feel a bit bad about not going in to work. <u>Still, lots of other people take time off work when they aren't really ill, so why shouldn't I?</u>

ANSWERS
(see underlined sentences in tapescript)
1 F; 2 A; 3 E; 4 D; 5 B

FURTHER PRACTICE: ***First Certificate Gold Exam Maximiser* Unit 4, p.31 (Listening).**

Speaking p.40

1 Students work in groups of three to four to discuss the questions.

ALTERNATIVE PROCEDURE: lead an open-class discussion.

2 Begin by telling the class a fabricated and a true story yourself. Make sure that the fabrication sounds as though it could be real, so don't include bizarre or exaggerated detail e.g.

I was waiting for my friends outside the cinema on Saturday evening when a girl came up to me and said, 'Hi! How are you? I haven't seen you for such a long time. Have you been away somewhere?' I was pretty sure that I had never seen her before in my life, but since I am a bit forgetful and since she was so certain she knew me, I pretended to know her too. 'No. I've been here, working away as usual. What have you been up to?', I asked. 'Oh, studying for my exams. How's that friend of yours? Oh ... what's his name? I've forgotten,' she said. Well, that really put me in a difficult situation, but I just picked a name and pretended I knew who she was talking about. 'Oh, you mean Nick. He's fine, too. He's just passed his driving test, actually,' I said. She looked very surprised. 'But he told me he was working as a driving instructor,' she said. Just at that moment one of my friends arrived. 'Tim, this is ... I'm terribly sorry. I've forgotten your name,' I said. 'Oh, Nicola. My name's Nicola Andrews,' said the girl. 'And how do you know (insert your name)?' asked Tim. The girl went bright red. 'Oh I'm so sorry,' she said. 'I've got you mixed up with someone else. You look so like her. It's incredible. Oh, this is so embarrassing. I'm so sorry,' she said and rushed off down the street.

See if students can work out which story was true before telling similar stories in groups.

ALTERNATIVE PROCEDURE: get more confident students to tell their stories to the whole class.

Vocabulary: phrasal verbs (*take*) pp.40–41

1 Accept one word (e.g. *deceived*) or equivalents in the students' own language.

2 Students work individually before checking their answers in pairs and with the whole class.

ANSWERS
1 e); 2 g); 3 a); 4 c); 5 b); 6 d); 7f)

3 Students write suitable responses individually.

> **POSSIBLE ANSWERS**
>
> 1 Why don't you *take up* jogging?
> 2 She has *taken over* a lot of the work I was finding it hard to finish.
> 3 You probably need to *take* a few days *off*.
> 4 I've *taken up* tennis actually.
> 5 Yes, *they've taken on* a lot of new staff.
> 6 No, I was completely *taken in*.
> 7 The teacher caught him *taking off* the headmaster again.

FURTHER PRACTICE: **First Certificate Gold Exam Maximiser Unit 4, p.31 (Phrasal verbs).**

Watch Out! *actually*

Actually is used correctly in Sentence 1; in Sentence 2 the speaker should have said *at the moment/now*.

Grammar: narrative tenses pp.41–43

1 Focus attention on the photo. Ask if anyone knows who the person in the photo is. Tell the class to look at the two questions. Read the text aloud to the class while they follow in their books. Elicit answers to the two questions open-class.

> **ANSWERS**
>
> 1 People thought the United States was being invaded by Martians. 2 A radio station was broadcasting a radio play.

2 Students work individually noting each example of the tenses under the headings.

> **ANSWERS:**
>
> **Past Simple:** interrupted, beamed out, caused, was;
>
> **Past Continuous:** were moving
>
> **Past Perfect:** had landed

3 Students work individually. Check the answers open-class

> **ANSWERS**
>
> 1 Past Perfect 2 Past Simple 3 Past Continuous

Refer students to the corresponding section of the *Grammar reference* on page 176.

4 Students work individually before comparing their answers with a partner and then open-class.

> **ANSWERS**
>
> 1 A play was being broadcast. 2 The programme on the other station was not very interesting. 3 There was music between the announcements and sometimes silence. The announcer sounded frightened. 4 People panicked and left their homes in an effort to escape. 5 It made him famous.

5 Students work individually. Check the answers open-class

> **ANSWERS**
>
> 1 said 2 had begun 3 heard 4 contained 5 followed 6 was going on 7 came 8 was changing/had changed 9 had taken over 10 were moving 11 were racing 12 pretended 13 were 14 was trying 15 fled 16 had told

6 Students discuss the questions in groups of three or four with one student reporting back their views to the rest of the class.

ALTERNATIVE PROCEDURE: conduct an open-class discussion. Students write a summary of the discussion in class or for homework.

EXTRA ACTIVITY: students conduct a survey asking as many people outside the class as possible questions 1–4. They should write up their findings and report them to the rest of the class.

7 **1** Divide the class into two groups, A and B. Members of each group work individually and fill in the gaps before comparing answers. This exercise provides further practice of narrative tenses

> **ANSWERS**
>
> **Joke A:** 1 came 2 was doing 3 went 4 put 5 were staring 6 had finished 7 asked 8 had never been 9 told 10 was hopping 11 was feeling 12 called
>
> **Joke B:** 1 was sitting 2 had reserved 3 have 4 was 5 seemed 6 went 7 remarked 8 to enjoy 9 liked 10 replied 11 read

2 Give students time to learn their jokes before pairing students from Group A and students from Group B to tell their jokes.

ALTERNATIVE PROCEDURE: ask stronger students from each group to tell their jokes to the whole class.

EXTRA ACTIVITY: students collect jokes to tell in the next class. They can either translate from their language or find jokes in books of English jokes.

FURTHER PRACTICE: ***First Certificate Gold Exam Maximiser*** **Unit 4, p.32 (Writing, exercises 1 and 2).**

Listening: extracts p.43

1 Explain that the extracts are taken out of context and that it is like overhearing part of a conversation. Tell them they will hear each extract twice. Focus attention on the prompts.

Tell the class to note any clues the first time they listen. Play the first extract once and elicit any clues the class picked up e.g. *class, teaching.* Play it again and ask which prompt the class would match it to. Play the cassette straight through to the end. Check the answers with the whole class.

TAPESCRIPT

1   T1 = teacher 1   T2 = teacher 2

T1: Did you hear what happened in Mike's class this afternoon?

T2: No ... what?

T1: Well, apparently he was <u>teaching his fourth year group ...</u>

T2: <u>Oh, what, that noisy 4F lot?</u>

T1: That's right. They were doing some experiment, mixing some chemicals or something when there was this explosion ...

T2: Explosion, really, was it serious, I mean was there a fire?

T1: Oh no, nothing like that, but ... look, I must rush, I've got to be at a rehearsal for the school play in five minutes.

2   C = customer   R = receptionist

C: Look, I'm sorry to bother you, but we actually booked a room with a view of the beach and sea and we are in fact looking back inland onto the main road in front of the hotel.

R: Could you just tell me your surname, please sir?

C: Of course. It's O'Leary, O'-L-E-A-R-Y.

R: Oh yes, here we are, staying until the 14th.

C: That's right.

R: But on the booking form it doesn't say anything about a sea view.

C: Well, I'm sorry, but I definitely told my travel agent.

R: <u>Well, look, let me just see what else is available. I'm sure we can arrange something ...</u>

3   T = Tim   S = Simon   A = Andrew

S: No, go on, tell us it.

T: Okay, but you've been warned ...

A: Oh no, they're always so awful.

S: Oh shut up, go on, Tim.

T: Well, there's this young schoolboy who goes up to his Maths teacher at the beginning of a lesson to ask him a question.
'Yes, what is it?' asks the teacher.
'Excuse me, sir,' says the boy, 'but do you think it is right to punish people for things they haven't done?'
'Of course not!' replied the teacher. 'That's perfectly obvious.'
<u>'Oh good,' said the boy, 'because I haven't done my homework.'</u>

A: You see, I told you it was going to be awful ...

4   P = policeman   W = woman

P: Stand well back, please, come on now, all move back.

W: What is it officer? What's going on?

P: Just routine precautions, madam, nothing to worry about, but it would help if everyone could just move back.

W: <u>But my car's through there.</u> Can't I quickly go and get it? I won't be a second.

P: No, I'm very sorry, madam, but no one's being allowed through just for the moment.

5   M = man   W = woman

M: So, are you trying to tell me that you actually believe in UFOs?

W: Well, I suppose it does depend exactly what you mean by UFOs. I mean, I don't have an image of little green men with antennae, but it is true that there have been a large number of sightings of things looking like alien spaceships in different parts of the world.

M: <u>Now come on.</u> You know as well as I do that in all of these cases, in the end, there is always a rational, scientific explanation.

W: <u>Well, it's all very well for you to say that, but what about the case where ...</u>

ANSWERS

A 3; B 5; C 1; D 4; E 2

2 Focus attention on the questions. Allow a minute or so for students to read them through before playing the cassette a third time.

ANSWERS

(see underlined sentences in tapescript)

1 B; 2 B; 3 B; 4 A; 5 B

Writing: narrative p.44

Read the exam information aloud to the class.

1 Students work individually putting the parts of the story in order before comparing notes with a partner and the rest of the class.

ANSWERS

1 F; 2 C; 3 E; 4 D; 5 G; 6 B; 7 A

Watch Out! *after/afterwards/after that*

1 *afterwards* and *after that*, both of which can begin independent clauses

2 *After,* which is an adverbial conjunction and can begin a dependent clause.

2 Do this exercise with the whole class.

ANSWERS

suddenly: all of a sudden, out of the blue, without warning, from out of nowhere.

enormous: gigantic, huge, vast, massive.

strange: weird, odd, peculiar.

after that: following this, afterwards, some time later, after a while.

3 Allow plenty of time for this. Students work together planning and drafting their stories. The final version can be written at home. When correcting this exercise, pay particular attention to the use of narrative tenses and linkers. Use the correction code outlined on pages 7–8 of the *Introduction*.

FURTHER PRACTICE: First Certificate Gold Exam Maximiser Unit 4, pp.32–33.

Unit 4 Review

ANSWERS

1 1 scientist 2 revolutionary 3 chemistry 4 inventor
5 product 6 realistic 7 ambitious 8 theoretically
9 disappointment 10 discovery

2 1 How much time have you taken off this year?
2 I think things are really going to take off soon.
3 We just can't take on any more staff at the moment.
4 Playing football on Saturdays takes up too much time.
5 Why has Bill taken up tennis again after so many years?
6 I gave him the money before I realised I had been taken in.
7 It is amazing how well he can take off his history teacher.
8 Could you take over from me while I'm at lunch?

3 1 was doing/heard 2 didn't see/had told
3 was painting/was cleaning 4 realised/had left
5 had/ate/went 6 was standing/walked

Now your students are ready to do the test for Unit 4 on page 124.

UNIT
5 All you need is love

Advance preparation

Page 51 of the *Coursebook* deals with background reading texts. If you plan to work on these texts, tell students to read one of the set books in preparation for the lesson.

Speaking p.46

1 The photos show the following musicians: A Janet Jackson, B Madonna, C Sting, D Elvis Presley, E The Beatles, F Elton John, G Oasis, H The Back Street Boys.

This can be done as a whole class activity or in pairs.

2 Ask students to work in groups appointing a secretary to report back on the answers to the questions to the whole class.

ALTERNATIVE PROCEDURE: ask students to note answers to the questions individually and then conduct a whole-class discussion. Encourage students to talk freely and extensively about their musical interests.

EXTRA ACTIVITY: students bring music cassettes or videos of their favourite artists to the next class and play extracts that illustrate the points they made in the questions for discussion.

Listening: song pp.46–47

1 Students listen to the song and think about the questions. Check the answers open-class. Do they like the song? Have they heard it before? Do they know any other songs by the same singer?

ANSWERS

1 Elton John 2 Writing a song for someone he loves.

2 Focus attention on the words in the box. Play the first verse again and point out that *funny* and *money* and *inside* and *hide* rhyme and that this will sometimes help them choose the missing words. Students read through the other verses before listening to the song straight through and filling in the gaps.

ALTERNATIVE PROCEDURE: write the song out again, photocopy it and cut it into strips with one line of the song on each strip. Tell students to work in pairs. Give each pair an envelope containing the strips of paper. Students listen to the song first and put the strips in order and then once again fill in the gaps.

ANSWERS

1 funny 2 hide 3 live 4 sculptor 5 show 6 gift
7 simple 8 world 9 roof 10 cross 11 kind 12 blue
13 sweetest

3 Students work in pairs or open-class.

ANSWERS

 1 Love for the person he's writing the song for.
 2 His feelings.
 3 I
 4 Because he can't imagine being a 'sculptor'.
 5 medicines
 6 Because the person he is writing the song for might be embarrassed to have a song dedicated to her/him.
 7 Because he had trouble writing some parts of the song.
 8 shining
 9 forgetting
10 The person's eyes.

Vocabulary: phrasal verbs (*down*) p.47

1 Students work in pairs or open-class.

ANSWERS

1 c); 2 b); 3 d); 4 a)

2 Students work in pairs or groups and compare answers open-class.

POSSIBLE ANSWERS

a) Someone writing a love letter or love song.
A boss to a secretary.

b) A passenger talking to the driver of a taxi or bus.
A close friend talking to someone who eats too much chocolate.

c) The police trying to get into a house where they know a criminal is hiding.
Two neighbours discussing damage to trees.

d) Someone informing other people at a meeting about a phone conversation s/he has just had with John.
A description of a teacher or lecturer in a class where everybody has been laughing at something that happened.

3 Go through the answers open-class.

ANSWERS

1 c); 2 d); 3 a); 4 b)

Reading p.48

Read the introduction aloud to the class and then focus attention on the film stills. Tell them to work in pairs saying who they think is shown in each still and what they think is happening.

1 Students read the extract individually and check their answers open-class.

ANSWERS

The photos from top down show 1 Heathcliffe and Cathy, 2 Cathy and Edgar Linton, 3 Heathcliffe.

2 Students work in pairs to answer the four questions

ANSWERS

1 Cathy tells Nelly that Edgar has proposed to her and that she has accepted. 2 Nelly is irritated by Cathy's behaviour and refuses to promise to keep the secret. 3 Her love for Heathcliff is deeper because she feels as if he's a part of her. 4 If she marries Edgar, she will never be completely happy and Heathcliff will never forgive her. If she marries Heathcliff they will be poor and her brother will probably make their lives unbearable.

Students work in groups discussing question 2. Suggest that students read the book to find out who Cathy marries and what the consequences are.

3 Students in pairs. If students have difficulty thinking of character adjectives, put the following adjectives on the board and ask them to use their dictionaries to decide who they best apply to.

materialistic (Cathy) understanding (Nelly) spoilt (Cathy) loyal (Nelly) indecisive (Cathy) snobbish (Cathy) fussy (Cathy) moody (Cathy) passionate (Cathy) patient (Nelly) sensible (Nelly) obstinate (Cathy) pessimistic (Cathy) wise (Nelly) irresponsible (Cathy) realistic (Nelly) logical (Nelly) immature (Cathy)

Grammar: reported speech p.49

1 Refer students back to the reading *Wuthering Heights* and tell them to find direct speech equivalents of the sentences in reported speech.

ANSWERS

1	*line 7*	'I'm very unhappy!'
2	*lines 13–14*	'Today Edgar Linton has asked me to marry him ...'
3	*line 20*	'Why do you love him?'
4	*line 22*	'... you must tell me why.'
5	*line 28*	'And because he loves me.'
6	*line 68*	'We can never be separated.'
7	*lines 75–76*	'Will you keep this one?', she asked. 'I'll not promise.'

2 Give students time to compare reported and direct speech versions, then elicit the differences. Put the differences up on the board, classifying them under these headings:

Verb tense   Word order   Other changes

ANSWERS

1 Present Simple becomes Past Simple.
2 *today* becomes *that day*; Present Perfect becomes Past Perfect.
3 Present Simple becomes Past Simple; reported *wh-* questions are formed with statement word order.
4 *must* + present infinitive becomes *had to* + present infinitive.
5 Present Simple becomes Past Simple.

6　*can* becomes *could*.

7　*will* becomes *would*; *this* becomes *that*; reported *Yes/No* questions are formed with *if* + statement word order.

Ask students to check the *Grammar reference* on pages 173–174 for any other changes you have not covered.

3　**1** Play the cassette through once while students answer the question.

TAPESCRIPT

M = Mike　T = Tom

M:　Hi, Tom. How are you?

T:　Actually, I'm really fed up. It's Sarah.

M:　Sarah, who's Sarah?

T:　Oh nobody really, just the most stunningly attractive girl in my year at school.

M:　Oh, is that all? So, what's the problem?

T:　Well, the thing is, I just don't know how to make her notice me or ...

M:　Wait a minute, I've got a brilliant idea. Why don't you try talking to her?

T:　But I wouldn't know what to say, I ...

M:　Look, she's in your Maths class, isn't she? You're good at Maths ... you could offer to help her with her Maths homework. How about that?

T:　Not bad. Just one problem.

M:　What?

T:　She's better than me at Maths.

M:　Okay then, well, there's that party at Steve's on Saturday night, you could invite her.

T:　Just another small problem ... Steve's her boyfriend.

ANSWER

He likes a girl in his class, but he doesn't know how to get her to notice him.

2 Play the cassette again pausing after each line in the tapescript so that students can write their reported speech version.

3 Encourage students to check each other's work for mistakes of grammar in using reported speech. Play the cassette again eliciting a reported speech version for each line from the class. When you get an acceptable version, write it up on the board

POSSIBLE ANSWER

Mike saw Tom and asked him how he was. Tom said he was really fed up because of Sarah. Mike asked who Sarah was and Tom explained that she was the most attractive girl in his year at school. Mike didn't think this was terribly important and asked what the problem was. Tom said that he didn't know how to make her notice him. Mike said that Tom should try talking to her, but Tom said that he wouldn't know what to say. Tom remembered that Mike was good at Maths and told him to offer to help her with her Maths homework. Tom said that the problem with that idea was that Sarah was better at Maths than him. Tom then said that Mike should invite her to a party at Steve's house the following Saturday night, but Mike said that would be a problem too as Sarah was Steve's girlfriend.

Watch Out! *to suggest*

He suggested them to go. is grammatically incorrect.

Reporting verbs

4　Do this with the whole class. Check that students understand the verbs in the box. Write the verb patterns up on the board and elicit the answers.

ALTERNATIVE PROCEDURE: students work in pairs looking up verbs they are unsure of in a dictionary before checking their answers with the whole class.

ANSWERS

a)　**verb** + **object** + **infinitive**: advise, encourage, invite, remind, warn.

b)　**verb** + **(that)**: admit, agree, decide, deny, explain, insist, promise, recommend, suggest.

c)　**verb** + **object** + **(that)**: advise (meaning 'inform'), promise, remind, warn.

d)　**verb** + **gerund**: deny, recommend, suggest.

e)　**verb** + **object** + **preposition** + **gerund**: accuse, blame, congratulate.

f)　**verb** + **infinitive**: agree, decide, offer, promise, refuse, threaten.

g)　**verb** + **preposition** + **gerund**: apologise, insist.

5　Students work individually before checking their answers with a partner and then with the whole class.

ANSWERS:

1　She apologised for being late.

2　He warned me not to touch the chair.

3　She promised that she would do/to do her

homework after the film.

4 He suggested going/that we should go/that we went to the beach for a swim.

5 She refused to go to the party.

6 He accused me of stealing the money.

7 She reminded me to get Paula a birthday present.

8 He offered to take me to the airport.

9 She admitted lying/that she had lied about her age.

10 She threatened to tell the teacher if I didn't put it back.

6 Divide the class into groups of four. Give them five minutes to brainstorm ideas and fifteen to twenty minutes to write their stories. If an overhead projector is available, get students to write their stories on transparencies so that the rest of the class can read them. If this is not possible, a spokesperson from each group can be asked to read the story aloud.

ALTERNATIVE PROCEDURE: after brainstorming ideas in class, students write their stories for homework. The finished stories can then be put up around the classroom for everyone to read.

FURTHER PRACTICE: **First Certificate Gold Exam Maximiser Unit 5, pp.35–37.**

Speaking p.50

1 Tell the class about one of your favourite books first as an example. Write up the following words on the board: science fiction, horror, detective stories, romance, adventure stories. Ask the class if they can give you examples (including books in their own language) of any of these. Students then work in groups telling each other about their favourite books and saying why they liked them.

ALTERNATIVE PROCEDURE: conduct this as a teacher-fronted activity, getting more confident students to talk about their favourite books.

2 If possible, bring copies of the readers to class.

ANSWERS
1 E; 2 D; 3 A; 4 B; 5 C

3 Students discuss the questions in pairs.

ANSWERS
1 A; 2 B; 3 E; 4 C; 5 D

4 Students work individually putting the books in order before comparing answers in groups.

Writing: background reading texts p.51

1 Go over the exam information with the whole class.

• (Steps 1 and 2): give students enough time (probably about a week) to read the book once all the way through for homework. Give them a date by which they should be prepared to come to class and tell another student about the book they have read.

ALTERNATIVE PROCEDURE: groups of students who have chosen the same books prepare short talks explaining the basic story to present to the whole class. They should not mention the title of the book in their talks. They appoint a representative to give the talk while the rest of the class listen and try and guess which book they are referring to on the basis of the cover designs.

• (Step 3): tell the students that they should read their books again, underlining the key vocabulary and checking meaning in their dictionaries. Explain that they should come to class in a week's time with a list of words to explain to other students. In a subsequent class group students according to the books they read so that they can compare their lists. How many people looked up the same words?

• (Step 4): give two examples of what kinds of things students might write under each heading e.g.
Characters: Leo: young boy, shy, not from a rich family.
Relationships: Marian and Leo: Leo loves Marian, Marian uses Leo as a messenger, etc.

Ask students what other headings they would add to the list and why e.g. **Time:** early twentieth century.

In a subsequent class get students to compare their notebook entries with a partner who has read the same book. Students then change partners to work with someone who has read another book and talk about their books.

• (Step 5): give students examples of questions they might be asked e.g.
Suggest an alternative cover design for the book you have chosen and explain why you think it is appropriate.

Tell a friend who is thinking of reading the book you chose enough about it for her/him to decide whether to read it or not.

Ask students to suggest more questions. Do the questions focus on characters, relationships, places or events?

2 Initially, work with the whole class. Ask students to underline key words and phrases in the two questions.
(1: *most important event, account, for a student who has not yet read the book* 2: *most interesting person, report for your school magazine, why this person is interesting, contributes to the story as a whole*)

Get students to work with a partner who has read the same book. They choose a title and brainstorm ideas, making use of the notes they made in Exercise 1. They then group the points into paragraphs. The actual writing should be done individually in class or at home. Students then exchange compositions with their partners who check their work, paying particular attention to errors with reported speech. Once students have had a chance to correct any errors their partners pointed out, collect the compositions and mark them using the correction code on pages 7–8 of the *Introduction*. Return the compositions and get students to try and correct any of the errors you have corrected in class, before collecting them once more to give them a final grade.

FURTHER PRACTICE: ***First Certificate Gold Exam Maximiser* Unit 5, p.39 (Writing).**

Vocabulary: ways of talking p.51

1 **1** Write the table up on the board and complete it with the whole class.

ALTERNATIVE PROCEDURE: students work individually before comparing their answers in pairs and then with the whole class.

ANSWERS

	say	tell	speak
a lie	✗	✓	✗
'Yes'	✓	✗	✗
English	✗	✗	✓
a story	✗	✓	✗
something	✓	✗	✗
loudly	✗	✗	✓
me his name	✗	✓	✗

2 In monolingual classes this can be done with the whole class. In multilingual classes ask students to translate the verbs and compare notes with speakers of the same language if possible. Discuss the differences with the whole class.

2 **1** Tell students to read the text silently before discussing the source with the whole class.

ANSWER
The text comes from a letter to a friend (c).

2 Students work individually before comparing answers with a partner and then with the whole class.

ANSWERS
1 C; 2 B; 3 A; 4 C; 5 A; 6 C; 7 B

Use of English p.52

1 Students work in pairs. One student describes the photo in as much detail as possible, while the other listens without looking and tries to imagine what the photo is like.

ALTERNATIVE PROCEDURE: this can be done as a teacher-fronted activity with strong students being asked to describe the photo while the rest of the class listen and try to imagine it.

2 Focus attention on the headline and ask students what they think the article is going to be about. They read the article once through to see if their predictions were correct before working individually to fill in the gaps. Check the answers through with the whole class.

ANSWERS
1 still 2 on 3 be 4 has 5 was 6 who 7 being 8 when 9 their 10 had 11 to 12 that 13 to 14 will

Exam focus: Paper 5 Speaking: Part 2 (individual long turn) p.53

ADVANCE PREPARATION: Prepare sufficient strips of paper with instructions for interlocutors and examiners (see below).

Before looking at the exam information, ask students to tell you all they know about Paper 5. Write up what they say on the board and get them to compare this with the information in the *Coursebook*. Discuss what aspects of the paper they think will be the most difficult/the easiest/the most interesting, etc.

1 Students then work through the exercise deciding which are compare and contrast (C&C) and which are description (D). Check the answers open class.

ANSWERS
1 D 2 C & C 3 D 4 C & C 5 C & C 6 C & C

2 Focus attention on the photographs and ask students to say which candidate (Silvina or Carola) describes which pair of photographs. Play the tape and ask students to tick the sentences the candidates use. Check the answers open class.

ANSWERS

Sentences 2, 4, 5 and 6

Draw students' attention to the language of comparison and contrast. Ask them to underline 'In the first photograph … whereas the second photograph …' in sentence 2; '…but…' in sentence 4; 'They're both…' in sentence 5; and '…, on the other hand,…' in sentence 6.

Play the tape again and get students to note down other phrases that compare and contrast the two photographs. Write the sentences up on the board and get students to tell you to underline instances of the language of comparison and contrast. Tell students to use this language when doing the Part 2 tasks that follow.

ANSWERS

(see underlining in tapescript) .'…but although the women are also all roughly the same age, they're all dressed differently.'; … one important difference between the two photographs is that in one it's clear why the group of people are friends, while in the other it's not so obvious'… that's really where the similarity ends… I'm sure both couples

I = Interlocutor C = Carola S = Silvina

I: Carola, photographs 1 and 2 show groups of friends. Silvina, you can look at them too. We'll look at your photographs in a minute. Carola, I'd like you to compare and contrast these photographs, saying why you think the people in them are friends. Remember, you have only about a minute for this so don't worry if I interrupt you.

C: Well, in the first photograph I can see a group of women, whereas in the second photograph it's a group of men. The women seem to be having a meal together, perhaps to celebrate a birthday, so they're inside a restaurant, but in the second photograph the men are outside. Umm I think it's a pub. The young men in the second photograph are all wearing the same kind of clothes, so I suppose this is one reason that they are friends? They like the same clothes and probably music, but although the women are also all roughly the same age, they're all dressed differently. I don't exactly know why they are friends. Perhaps they studied together at school or university or they could even be members of a club of some kind. Anyway, one important difference between the two photographs is that in one it's clear

why the group of people are friends, while in the other it's not so obvious.

I: Thank you. Silvina, which group of people do you think is having more fun?

S: I think the women look like they're having more fun than the young men. The young men look a bit self-conscious? As if they expected the photo to be taken but the women look very relaxed as if they are really enjoying being together.

I: Thank you. Now Silvina, photographs 3 and 4 show couples getting married. Carola you can look at them too. Silvina, I'd like you to compare and contrast these photographs, and say how you think the couples are feeling. Remember, you have only about a minute for this so don't worry if I interrupt you.

S: Right. They're both photographs of weddings, as you said, but that's really where the similarity ends. In the first one, it's a very formal church wedding. Perhaps, the couple are famous? Or were famous because it seems to have been taken quite a long time ago? The second photograph is more recent but again not the kind of thing you see today so much. They're hippies and they're getting married outside in a field or garden somewhere. The guests are all dressed very casually and so are the couple. In the church wedding, on the other hand, the bride is wearing white and the groom is dressed in a very formal suit. I think the first couple are probably feeling rather nervous. There are a lot of people in the church watching them and they might be a little worried about making a mistake when they say their vows. The hippy couple seem very happy and relaxed and they've probably written the service themselves. I'm sure both couples …

I: Thank you. Carola, which of the two weddings looks more familiar to you?

C: Oh definitely the first one. Most people in my country like to get married in a church and to have a white wedding like that. I'd hate to get married like the second couple. I think your wedding should be …

I: Thank you. That's great. Thank you.

3 Ask the interlocutors and examiners to come to the front of the room so that you can give them their instructions: Give each 'interlocutor' a slip of paper with the following instructions:

Decide which candidate you would like to start. This is what you must say to her/him. Do NOT show her/him this piece of paper.

(Name of first candidate), photographs 1 and 2 show groups of friends. (Name of other candidate) you can look at them too. We'll look at your photographs in a minute. (Name of first candidate) I'd like you to compare and contrast these photographs, saying why you think the people in them are friends. Remember, you have only about a minute for this so don't worry if I interrupt you.

*Time the first candidate and say '**thank you**' after they have been speaking for a minute.*

Then say to the second candidate:

(Name of candidate) which group of people do you think is having more fun?

*Say '**thank you**' when the second candidate has been speaking for twenty seconds.*

Then say:

Now (Name of second candidate), photographs 3 and 4 show couples getting married. (Name of other candidate) you can look at them too. (Name of second candidate) I'd like you to compare and contrast these photographs, saying how you think the couples are feeling. Remember, you have only about a minute for this so don't worry if I interrupt you.

*Time the second candidate and say '**thank you**' after they have been speaking for a minute.*

Then say to the first candidate:

(Name of candidate) which of the two weddings looks more familiar to you?

*Say '**thank you**' when the second candidate has been speaking for twenty seconds*

You should give each candidate a mark out of five for how well they communicated and how well they performed the task.

Give the 'assessor' the following checklist:

Explain that they should give each candidate a mark out of five in each category:

	Candidate A	Candidate B
Grammar and vocabulary		
Discourse Management*		
Pronunciation		

* Did the candidate compare and contrast the photographs clearly? Did s/he comment on the photographs in the way the interlocutor told her/him to?

Explain that the assessors can take notes of any good use of vocabulary (especially use of the language of comparison and contrast), any errors or anything that particularly impressed them about the 'candidates'' performance.

Tell the two 'examiners' that they can compare marks before explaining their assessment to the two candidates.

4 Follow the same procedure with the new examiners.

Give each new interlocutor a slip of paper with the following instructions

Decide which candidate you would like to start. This is what you must say to her/him. Do NOT show her/him this piece of paper.

(Name of first candidate), these photographs show landscapes. (Name of other candidate) you can look at them too. We'll look at your photographs in a minute. (Name of first candidate) I'd like you to compare and contrast these photographs, saying which landscape seems more attractive to you. Remember, you have only about a minute for this so don't worry if I interrupt you.

*Time the first candidate and say '**thank you**' after they have been speaking for a minute.*

Then say to the second candidate:

(Name of candidate) which of these two places would you prefer to live in?

*Say '**thank you**' when the second candidate has been speaking for twenty seconds.*

Then say:

Now (Name of second candidate), these photographs show people at concerts. (Name of other candidate) you can look at them too. (Name of second candidate) I'd like you to compare and contrast these photographs, saying why you think people enjoy going to concerts like these. Remember, you have only about a minute for this so don't worry if I interrupt you.

*Time the second candidate and say '**thank you**' after they have been speaking for a minute.*

Then say to the first candidate:

(Name of candidate) which of the two concerts would you rather go to?

*Say '**thank you**' when the second candidate has been speaking for twenty seconds*

You should give each candidate a mark out of five for how well they communicated and how well they performed the task.

Give the 'assessor' the following checklist:

Explain that they should give each candidate a mark out of five in each category:

	Candidate A	Candidate B
Grammar and vocabulary		
Discourse Management*		
Pronunciation		

* Did the candidate compare and contrast the photographs clearly? Did s/he comment on the photographs in the way the interlocutor told them to ?

Explain that the assessors can take notes of any good use of vocabulary (especially use of the language of comparison and contrast), any errors or anything that particularly impressed them about the 'candidates'' performance.

Go round monitoring performance yourself and making notes of any errors and also of good use of vocabulary and grammar. When all the groups have finished conduct a debriefing with the class, noting the errors and good language you heard on the board.

Vocabulary: love and marriage p.54

1 Students discuss these items in pairs before checking their answers in dictionaries.

> **ANSWERS**
>
> 1 *to go out with someone/to live with someone*: 'to go out with' is a near synonym of the American English 'to date'. It implies that the two people do not live together, but that they are having some kind of romantic relationship.
>
> 2 *to be infatuated/to fall in love*: infatuation is more superficial and usually based on initial impressions. It may also not last as long as 'being in love'.
>
> 3 *to get engaged/to get married*: people get engaged when they have decided to get married. The person you are engaged to is called your fiancé(e). The man usually gives the woman *an engagement ring*, usually with a precious stone such as a diamond. During their engagement they plan the wedding. If they change their minds about getting married, they *break off the engagement*. Nowadays people often get married without getting engaged. You 'get married' when you go through either a religious or civil marriage ceremony.
>
> 4 *to get pregnant/to have a baby*: a woman is pregnant for nine months and then she has a baby. We often say 'she's having a baby' to mean 'she's pregnant'.
>
> 5 *to have an anniversary/to have a birthday:* an 'anniversary' marks the day on which a significant event, other than your birth, occurred. It is often the day you met or married someone you love.
>
> 6 *to have rows/to have discussions*: 'a discussion' is an exchange of views which does not involve anger. 'A row' always involves anger and often shouting.
>
> 7 *to chat/to flirt*: if you 'chat' to someone you talk to her/him in a friendly, informal way; 'to flirt' means to talk to someone you find attractive in order to attract her/his attention.

> 8 *to get a divorce/to split up*: both involve separation from a partner; you 'split up' from your girlfriend/boyfriend or someone you live with; you 'get a divorce' from your wife or husband.

2 Students work in pairs discussing the questions and referring to dictionaries for words they do not understand.

> **ANSWERS**
>
> *a wedding*: a marriage ceremony with a party or meal afterwards.
>
> *a registry office*: couples who decide not to get married in a church can marry in a registry office. It is the place you go to register births, deaths and marriages and where records of these events are kept.
>
> *a church*: the majority of Christian weddings still take place in churches, even though the couple may not otherwise be religious.
>
> *the aisle*: the passage between the rows of seats (pews) in a church. At the beginning of the marriage ceremony the bride, arm-in-arm with her father or another male relative or friend, walks down the aisle to the altar.
>
> *a vicar*: in the Church of England, priests are often referred to and addressed as 'vicar'. The vicar performs the Church of England marriage ceremony.
>
> *the bride*: the woman who is to be married is the bride. Traditionally she dresses in white and arrives at the church after the other members of the wedding party.
>
> *the bridegroom*: the man who is about to be married. He waits at the altar for the bride.
>
> *the best man*: a close friend or sometimes a brother of the groom. He is responsible for the ring and also makes an amusing speech at the reception afterwards.
>
> *the bridesmaids*: they are usually the close friends or sisters of the bride or groom. They wear identical dresses and also carry bouquets of flowers.
>
> *the ring*: usually a plain gold band. Nowadays couples often exchange rings, though once it was only the bride who was given a ring.
>
> *the reception*: the party after the marriage ceremony which often takes place at a hotel or the bride's home. A meal is served and speeches are made about the bride and the groom. They cut a wedding cake during the reception and make wishes for a happy marriage.
>
> *the organist*: the person who plays the traditional church organ either solo or to accompany the choir and congregation in the singing of hymns.
>
> *the choir*: usually a group of young boys and men who lead the singing in church.
>
> *a bouquet*: a bunch of flowers that the bride carries.

a veil: a fine cloth, often very fine netting, used as a headdress and to partially cover the bride's face at the beginning of the marriage ceremony.

a honeymoon: the holiday that the bride and groom go on after the wedding.

Give students practice with this vocabulary by asking questions and getting them to call out the answers, e.g.

What do you call the bunch of flowers the bride carries? (a bouquet)

What does the best man have to remember to bring to the church? (the ring)

What do you call the party after the wedding ceremony? (the reception)

Where can you get married if you don't want to get married in a church? (a registry office)

FURTHER PRACTICE: **First Certificate Gold Exam Maximiser Unit 5, p.38.**

Listening: Do you take this man? p.54

1 Focus attention on the title and ask students if they know where it comes from (the marriage ceremony). Elicit or explain that it continues '… to be your lawfully wedded husband, to love, honour and cherish him in sickness and in health as long as you both shall live?' Look at the titles with the class and ask them to speculate about what each extract might be about. Point out that there is one extra title they don't need to use. Play the tape once. Allow time for students to compare answers in pairs and then check them open-class.

TAPESCRIPT

1: We all met at a disco two years ago. I'd gone along with Sue, my twin sister, and Toby was there with Sam, his twin brother. We've always done everything together: holidays, shopping, sports, picnics, so it seemed only natural to have a joint wedding. Our local vicar knew all four of us very well and knew that we were genuinely committed to each other, but he still needed some convincing, but when I pointed out that it would be much more economical for our families he agreed to perform the ceremony. Sue and I had one bridesmaid each and Toby and Sam had their older brother as best man. They've always been able to tell us apart but just in case, we wore different dresses. Actually, we sometimes have trouble with them but I'm pretty sure I married the right twin.

2: We went to this incredible wedding when we were in the States. Tina's cousin lives down near the Ozark

Mountains and he had just bought a houseboat which he had moored on one of the lakes there. Anyway, he and his fiancée decided to have their wedding on board and a local minister performed the ceremony. I couldn't believe it! The bride and groom wore white leather swimming costumes, the bridesmaids pink ones and the best man and the other groomsmen black swimming trunks … with bow ties, of course. The most amazing thing of all was that the minister wore a swimming costume too under his robe and led the recessional down a slide into the water. It certainly was spectacular … but hardly appropriate for such an important event.

3: I just couldn't go through with it. I'd been having doubts for months before but my friends kept telling me it was just pre-wedding nerves. Of course, I should have said something much sooner, but at least there was still time to cancel the honeymoon, the flowers and the reception. The bridesmaids were all quite glad to have their dresses. They don't know each other very well and they can wear them to parties without running the risk of finding someone else wearing the same dress! Unfortunately, he was terribly hurt. We haven't seen or spoken to each other since. I heard the other day that he's engaged to a girl we both went to school with. I wonder now if I made the right decision.

4: I married a couple recently who had, unknown to me, decided to include their dogs in the ceremony. They had special outfits made for each dog: shawls and bonnets for the two females and, for the male of the threesome, a top hat and tie. The plan was for the trio to walk proudly down the aisle at the end of the ceremony, accompanied by the bride's younger brother. Unfortunately, when the dogs came out of the holding area they were so delighted to see all their favourite friends gathered in one place that they went mad, running all over the church wagging their tails frantically and saying 'hello' to all the people they knew in the congregation. I thought the bride's brother would end up in hospital with a dislocated shoulder.

5: We decided to get married on the exact spot where we first met. It doesn't look very romantic … it's the corner of the High Street and another road … but for us it's the centre of the universe. Fortunately, it's just along the street from a church and the vicar was willing to marry us outside. The date was a year to the day after we first met. It was absolutely freezing and very windy so my veil had to be very firmly pinned down and we all wore thermal underwear under our wedding clothes. The only other problem was that the vicar really had to shout above the noise of the traffic. It attracted quite a lot of attention from passers-by and some of them joined us at a local café for cups of steaming hot chocolate. It was perfect!

ANSWERS

Extract 1: D; Extract 2: A; Extract 3: B;
Extract 4: F; Extract 5: C; E is the title that is not used

2 Focus attention on the statements. Point out once more that there is an extra statement they do not need to use. Play the tape again. Students answer individually before comparing their answers with a partner and then open-class. If necessary, play the relevant sections of the tape again.

ANSWERS

1 – B; 2 – C; 3 – E; 4 – A; 5 – F; Statement D is not used. (See underlining in tapescript)

EXTRA ACTIVITY: if you have access to the video of *Four Weddings and a Funeral*, you could show the class the four wedding segments, particularly the last. The tape could be played with the sound turned down and paused. Students can be asked to identify the people in the wedding ceremony and to try to work out what is happening.

Speaking p.54

Students work in pairs, with one student taking the role of interlocutor as in the exam and asking the other student(s) the questions. Tell the student(s) to answer the questions as fully as they can before changing roles.

ALTERNATIVE PROCEDURE: put the following headings on the board:

Before the wedding   Participants   Special clothes
During the wedding   After the wedding   Special food

Describe the last wedding you went to using the headings as an example for the class before asking for volunteers to do the same thing.

EXTRA ACTIVITY: students bring in photos or videos of family weddings they have attended and give a short talk on them. They can also be asked to prepare a list of items that are typical of weddings in their countries and explain them to you and the class in English.

Units 1–5 Progress check

ANSWERS

1 1 B; 2 C; 3 A; 4 D; 5 B; 6 D; 7 D; 8 C; 9 D; 10 B;
11 A; 12 D; 13 B; 14 C; 15 C

2 1 How old is Teresa?
2 What's she like?
3 Has she got a boyfriend?
4 What does she do?
5 What does she like doing/does she do in her free time?

3 1 Because/As/Since 2 gloves 3 them 4 they 5 club 6 like 7 as 8 such 9 net 10 very 11 out 12 umpire 13 has 14 goal 15 with

4 1 1 h); 2 c); 3 k); 4 j); 5 f); 6 e); 7 g); 8 i); 9 b); 10 l); 11 d); 12 a)
2 a disorganised b rewrite c subtitles d overeat e uncomfortable f illegal g irresponsible h underline i ex-wife j immature

5 1 I am *the best player* in our class.
2 My older brother *works as a social worker* in one of the big hospitals.
3 My friends *had left when I arrived* at the meeting point.
4 She admitted *that she had stolen* the money.
5 Jacky doesn't play *the piano as well as* Susan.
6 Badminton *is like tennis* in some ways.
7 She *invited us to stay* for dinner.
8 The Nigerian ran *2·5 seconds faster than* the Moroccan.
9 He asked me *to tell him* the time.
10 Are you *accusing me of* lying?

6 *line 1* – delete *out*
line 2 – delete *the*
line 3 – delete *it*
line 4 – delete *have*
line 7 – delete *did*
line 8 – delete *a*
line 9 – delete *it*
line 12 – delete *to*
line 13 – delete *it*
line 14 – delete *did*
line 15 – delete *in*

7 1 satisfaction 2 creative 3 attention 4 Familiarity 5 advertisement 6 Unconsciously 7 originality 8 characteristic 9 memorability 10 product

8 1 up 2 broke 3 off 4 Slow 5 off 6 die 7 up 8 down 9 over 10 on 11 kept/went 12 was brought

Now your students are ready to do the Progress test for Units 1–5 on pages 125–127.

UNIT
6 It's all in the mind

Reading pp.58–59

1 Students discuss their answers in groups of three or four or open-class. Write the list up on the board and add any other characteristics that identify an 'intelligent person' which students suggest. Are there any characteristics which nobody thinks are a sign of intelligence? Are there any which the majority agree are a sign of intelligence?

2 Students work individually matching the words to the definitions.

ANSWERS
1 e); 2 g); 3 c); 4 b); 5 h); 6 a); 7 d); 8 i); 9 f)

3 Set a time limit of three minutes for this gist reading task.

ANSWER
e) *old age* is not referred to.

4 Students work individually before comparing answers with a partner and then with the rest of the class.

ANSWERS
1 C; 2 F; 3 A; 4 B; 5 G; 6 D

5 Students make a note of two things and compare answers with a partner. Get each pair to tell you what things they both learnt. Make a note of them on the board and see how many things the class learnt as a group.

6 Students work on the puzzles in class or at home.

FURTHER PRACTICE: First Certificate Gold Exam Maximiser Unit 6, p.48.

Vocabulary: word formation p.60

1 Students work individually to find the words in the text before checking with the whole class.

ANSWERS
1 intelligence 2 differ 3 similarity 4 calculation
5 useful 6 health 7 energy 8 scientific

2 Students mark where they think the stress falls and check their answers in English–English dictionaries.

ANSWERS
2 'different/'differ (*same*); 3 'similar/simi'larity (*different*);
4 'calculate/calcu'lation (*different*); 5 'useless/'useful
(*same*); 6 'healthy/'health (*same*); 7 ener'getic/'energy
(*different*); 8 'science/scien'tific (*different*)

3 Students fill in the gaps individually before checking with a partner and the whole class.

ANSWERS
1 energetic 2 miscalculation 3 differently 4 similarity
5 healthily 6 scientist 7 intelligence 8 useless

Speaking p.60

1 Encourage students to help one another to say more by asking follow-up questions and showing an interest in what their partner says. Demonstrate this by asking a student some of the questions and responding in an interested manner. They work in pairs taking it in turns to ask and answer the questions. Pairs who do the task well can repeat their discussion in front of the rest of the class.

2 Students discuss the questions in groups of three or four and compare their lists with the rest of the class.

ALTERNATIVE PROCEDURE: put some characteristics on the board e.g. *obedient, hard-working, beautiful, cheerful, strict, cooperative, punctual, patient, well-organised, kind, intelligent, tidy, honest, young, knowledgeable, funny,* etc.

Students decide which characteristics should ideally apply to teachers, which apply to students and which do not apply to either of them.

Vocabulary: education pp.60–61

1 Students work individually before comparing their answers in pairs and then with the whole class.

ANSWERS
1 correct/give 2 cheat/headmaster 3 playground/break
4 report/hard/term 5 university/degree 6 board/heart
7 absent/truant

2 Give students five minutes to decide on their answers. Ask a student to read out her/his version of the text and discuss the answers, explaining the difference between the words when necessary.

ANSWERS
1 primary school 2 classes 3 teachers
4 secondary school 5 subjects 6 marks 7 teach
8 revising 9 pass 10 failed 11 retake 12 career

Watch Out! take/pass/fail

He *took* the exam first. If he *passed* the exam, it is a good result; if he *failed* it it is a bad result.

3 Students work in pairs matching the verbs to the definitions.

ANSWERS
1 f); 2 g); 3 d); 4 i); 5 h); 6 c); 7 b); 8 e); 9 a)

EXTRA ACTIVITY: students suggest a context for each of the sentences, e.g.:

1 Someone who is sitting at the back of a room listening to a speaker.
2 A student to another student who is always asking her what words mean.
3 A child complaining to a parent about unfair treatment.
4 A teacher writing in a school report or talking to a parent.
5 A teacher writing a comment or speaking to a student about her/his written work.
6 A teacher talking to another teacher about a particularly bright student.
7 A teacher talking to two pupils who have been caught fighting.

8 A younger sister/brother asking an older sister/brother for help with homework.
9 A woman telling a friend how her husband learnt a language.

4 Students work in pairs talking about their school lives.

ALTERNATIVE PROCEDURE: students prepare two-minute talks on their school lives which they present to the rest of the group.

FURTHER PRACTICE: First Certificate Gold Exam Maximiser **Unit 6, p.45.**

Listening: exam fever p.61

1 Play the cassette once and elicit answers to the gist questions.

TAPESCRIPT

1 I've always been terrible in exams, which is probably why I can't stand them! I don't know what it is exactly, but I just seem to go to pieces. I forget everything I've learnt. I think it's really unfair because I write really slowly – when I look around the exam room, everyone else has usually written twice as much as me! The other thing is that it all depends on luck. I mean, it's all right if the questions you have revised come up, but sometimes they don't and then it's a disaster. I must say I hate revising – it's so boring!

2 I think exams are much better in a way than coursework. I'd prefer to just have exams at the end of the year. As far as I'm concerned, the problem with coursework is that the pressure is on you all the time and nearly everything you do counts towards your final result, whereas with exams you can pace yourself and work really hard in the final stages. I think exams are okay … in the end I think they generally give a pretty accurate picture of how much you know about a subject. In fact I quite like revising for exams. I find it brings together all the different things I've been learning and I suddenly begin to understand what the teachers have been going on about. I like to get up early and go through my notes on the day of the exam. That way everything is fresh in my mind.

3 In my country we have to repeat our school year if we fail the end-of-year exams, so they are pretty serious. In fact most people repeat a year at some point or other. Something which is a bit different to England is that we quite often have oral exams where you see your question a few minutes in advance and then you have to go and speak your answer to a group of professors, for example. Another thing which

happens sometimes is that exams can be competitive, so only a certain percentage will pass. That makes it hard if you happen to be taking the exam at the same time as a lot of very good students!

ANSWERS

1 Student 2   2 Student 1   3 Student 3

2 Allow a minute for students to look at the questions before playing the cassette again. Students compare answers in pairs.

ANSWERS

(see underlined sentences in tapescript)

a) Student 3   b) Student 2   c) Student 3   d) Student 1
e) Students 1 and 2   f) Student 3

3 Play the cassette a third time so that students can take notes. Emphasise that they do not have to write complete sentences, just a few words. Check the answers to Exercises 1 and 2 again if necessary by playing the cassette and pausing after the relevant sections.

POSSIBLE ANSWERS

a) they quite often have oral exams
b) with coursework the pressure is always on
c) sometimes exams can be competitive, only a percentage of students pass
d) writes very slowly, others write much faster
e) hates revising; likes revising, it helps understanding
f) have to retake if fail end-of-year exams

Function: giving opinions, agreeing/disagreeing p.62

1   **1** Elicit the missing words from the class.

ANSWERS

In my opinion … ; *From* my point of view … ; As *far* as I'm concerned …

2 Tell the students to say the phrases quietly to themselves and to mark where they think the main stress falls before comparing their answers with a partner.

3 Play the cassette while students check their answers. Play the sentences again if necessary before getting the students to repeat them individually or as a whole class.

ANSWERS

I think that exams are a good thing.

In my opinion exams are a good thing.

From my point of view exams are a good thing.

As far as I'm concerned exams are a good thing.

2   **1** Students work in pairs putting the phrases in order before checking their answers with the whole class.

ANSWERS

AGREEMENT	I couldn't agree more./I completely agree.
	That's right.
	I agree up to a point, but …
	I don't really agree.
DISAGREEMENT	I don't agree at all.

2 Play the cassette pausing after each dialogue and getting the class and individuals to repeat.

TAPESCRIPT

1 A: I think people who smoke in restaurants are so thoughtless.
  B: *I couldn't agree more.*

2 A: As far as I'm concerned it's always a mistake to hit children.
  B: *I completely agree.*

3 A: In my opinion more people should start worrying about the state of the planet.
  B: *That's right*, they certainly should.

4 A: From my point of view TV is getting worse and worse these days.
  B: *I agree up to a point, but* there are some very good children's programmes.

5 A: All politicians are the same. You can't believe anything they say.
  B: *I don't really agree.* Some of them are honest.

6 A: Isn't the new Tom Cruise film good?
  B: *I don't agree at all.* I think it's absolute rubbish!

Watch Out! *agree*

Agree is a verb (not an adjective) and must be used with the auxiliary *do* in questions and negative sentences e.g. *I'm sorry, but I don't agree with you.*

3 Check understanding of *smacking, banning* and *quality*. Students work in pairs giving their opinions and saying if they agree/disagree with one another and why.

Before they start, tell students to use the phrases from Exercises 1 and 2 where appropriate.

ALTERNATIVE PROCEDURE: students give opinions and reasons round the class until everyone has expressed their opinion about each issue.

4   Students work in groups of three or four discussing the issues. Go round monitoring and make a note of any errors they make with the language of agreeing/disagreeing to go through at the end.

ALTERNATIVE PROCEDURE: students work in pairs preparing arguments for or against one of the statements. Then hold a series of mini-debates in which each pair argues their case. Finally the class votes in favour or against the statement.

Writing: article p.63

Read the exam information aloud to the class and ask students to read the sample question.

1   Elicit the names of the punctuation marks from the class.

ANSWERS
capital letter, inverted commas, question mark, speech marks, apostrophe, comma, full stop, hyphen, exclamation mark

Check that students understand the uses of the various punctuation marks.

2   1 Students work in pairs finding and correcting the mistakes.

CORRECTED VERSION
More and more in my country, student achievement is being based on a mixture of continuous assessment and end-of-year exams. Some people claim that this is leading to lower standards in schools, but I don't believe this is true.

In my opinion, it is much fairer to allow the work students do during their school year to count towards their final result for various reasons. Firstly, it is possible to have a bad day when you take your exams and not show your true ability. Secondly, exams don't encourage real learning as students just memorise lots of information for the exam and then immediately forget it all. As well as this, it is much more realistic to spend time thinking about a question or problem, discussing it with other people and researching it in books. This is, of course, something you cannot do in an exam.

2 Students rewrite the third paragraph individually, before comparing answers in pairs and then with the whole group.

CORRECTED VERSION
In conclusion then I believe that we should make coursework an increasingly important part of students' final marks. This will give a fairer and more accurate picture of each student's real ability.

3 1 Give students two minutes to re-read the text before eliciting the purpose of each paragraph.

ANSWERS
Paragraph 1: statement of situation and opinion about situation.
Paragraph 2: reasons for opinion
Paragraph 3: conclusion – restating opinion.

2 Ask for a show of hands from those who agree and those who disagree.

4   Pair students according to the topic they have chosen to write about and get them to brainstorm ideas. Students can write the rough draft at home and then swap answers in the next class. The final version can be written in class. Use the correction code in the *Introduction* on pages 7–8 to mark their work. As you mark students' work focus particularly on errors connected with expressing opinion and agreement/ disagreement.

FURTHER PRACTICE: First Certificate Gold Exam Maximiser **Unit 6, pp.46–47.**

Exam focus: Paper 1 Reading: Part 2 (multiple choice) pp.64–65

Read the exam information aloud to the class.

Students work in pairs putting the advice in a sensible order. Go through the answers as a class.

ANSWERS
2, 3, 7, 6, 5, 4, 1 (or the teacher's own interpretation)

1   Ask students what they do when they want to avoid studying. Set a three-minute time limit for the gist reading task and discuss the gist question with the class.

2   Students work individually before comparing answers with a partner and then with the whole class.

ANSWERS

1 B (*giving himself time to complete the first <u>excuse</u>: he recalls that in the morning he <u>did not have quite enough time to read all items of interest in the newspaper.</u>*)

2 C (*He also realises that if he is going to study it is best to have such small items completely out of the way <u>before settling down to the task at hand.</u> He therefore leaves his desk, browses through <u>the newspaper</u>*

At this point <u>it will seem like a good idea to plan for the evening's first break</u> – perhaps an interesting half-hour programme between 8 and 8.30 pm.)

3 B (*At this stage, he still hovers over his desk tapping his book reassuringly as he remembers that phone call to friend which, <u>like the articles of interest in the newspapers, is best cleared out of the way before the serious studying begins.</u>*)

4 B (*…. he experiences <u>the first pangs of hunger and thirst</u>. This is disastrous because he realises that <u>the longer he waits to satisfy the pangs, the worse they will get, and the more interrupted his study concentration will be.</u> The obvious and only <u>solution</u> is a light snack. … Having <u>removed this final obstacle.</u>*)

5 C (*….<u>he will think that things have not gone too badly</u>, for after all he has had a good rest, a good meal, watched some interesting and relaxing programmes, fulfilled his social commitments to his friends, digested the day's information, and got everything completely out of the way <u>so that tomorrow, at 6 o'clock….)</u>*

6 B (*<u>The Six-o'clock-In-The-Evening-Enthusiastic-Determined-And-Well-Intentioned-Studier-Until-Midnight</u> the <u>intrepid studier</u> finds himself back at his desk at about 8.30 p.m.*)

7 A (*The Six-o'clock-In-The-Evening-Enthusiastic-Determined-And-Well-Intentioned-Studier-Until-Midnight <u>is a person with whom you are probably already familiar.</u>*)

Grammar: gerunds and infinitives p.66

1 Check that students understand the terms *gerund* and *infinitive*. They work individually before comparing answers with a partner and then with the whole class.

ANSWERS

The sentences that are grammatically incorrect are:

1 He decided *planning* his first break. (He decided **to plan** his first break.)

4 She wants *buying* a good dictionary. (She wants **to buy** a good dictionary.)

7 Have you considered *to leave* school at sixteen? (Have you considered **leaving** school at sixteen?)

2 Check that students understand the three columns in the table before they work with a partner classifying the verbs.

ANSWERS

Verbs + infinitive: want, promise, decide.
Verbs + -*ing*: keep, consider, admit.
Verbs + -*ing* or infinitive: hate, like, begin.

3 Students classify the verbs in pairs. When they have finished, refer them to page 167 of the *Grammar reference* so that they can check their answers.

ANSWERS

Verbs + infinitive: agree, arrange, choose, expect, fail, hope, manage, offer, plan, pretend, promise, refuse, seem.
Verbs + -*ing*: avoid, deny, enjoy, mind, suggest.
Verbs + -*ing* or infinitive: can't stand, continue, intend, prefer, remember, stop, try.

Watch Out! *to mind*

B is happy to close the window.

4 Work with the whole class, asking individual students to read each pair of sentences aloud and discussing the differences. Refer students to the *Grammar reference* on page 167 once again to check their answers.

ANSWERS

1 The first sentence means that she stopped some activity she was engaged in so as to have lunch; the

second means she gave up the habit of having lunch, perhaps because she was on a diet.

2 The first sentence means on a particular occasion; the second means as a general rule.

3 No significant difference in meaning.

4 The first sentence means it was in your mind that you had to lock the door and you did, that is you remembered before you locked. The second means that you locked the door and you remember the actual experience of locking it, that is you locked then you remembered.

5 No significant difference in meaning.

6 The first sentence means he tried to learn ten new words as an experiment in order to see what would happen; the second means that he made an effort to learn ten new words without necessarily succeeding.

5 Students work individually writing sentences. Go round checking their work and drawing their attention to any errors. Get individuals to read out their sentences to the rest of the class.

6 Decide with the class what name to use and write the first sentence on the board. Put students in groups of four or five and give each group a piece of paper. Student 1 writes a sentence and passes the paper on to Student 2. S/he also writes a sentence and passes the paper on to Student 3 and so on until everyone has written a sentence. The group then decides on an ending and appoints a representative to read the story aloud to the class. The class decides which is the best story.

ALTERNATIVE PROCEDURE: you will need an overhead projector, a transparency and felt tip pens. Go round the class eliciting a sentence to add to the story from each student and writing them on the overhead transparency (you may need more than one). When you have finished, ask if the class want to make any changes to the completed story.

FURTHER PRACTICE: **First Certificate Gold Exam Maximiser Unit 6, p.42.**

Unit 6 Review

ANSWERS

1 1 truant 2 degree 3 terms 4 nursery school 5 pick up 6 cheat 7 let off

3 1 unhealthy 2 energetic 3 useless 4 dissimilar 5 childhood 6 intelligence 7 cleverest 8 scientist 9 calculators 10 competitive

4 1 We need eggs, tomatoes and some rice.
2 How do you say 'teacher' in Italian?
3 'Do you think he's good looking?' she asked.
4 First of all, in my opinion, we should ban smoking in all public places.
5 Sarah has lived in Argentina since she was a child.
6 'Don't give him the gun!' she screamed.

5 1 promised to send (us/them/her etc.) 2 you mind helping me 3 refused to speak 4 denied (ever) having seen
5 agreed that we should 6 considered getting 7 offered to look after 8 avoid giving 9 admitted he had been going/admitted (to) going 10 expect to pass

Now your students are ready to do the test for Unit 6 on page 128.

UNIT

7 The price of fame

Reading pp.68–69

1 Discuss the questions with the whole class, encouraging students to answer as fully as possible.

Jodie Foster – Anna & the King; Macauly Culkin – Home Alone 1 & 2; Alex D Linz – Home Alone 3.

2 Pre-teach the meaning of the key words: *on demand, talent spotters, predecessor, show off, (make) a fuss, wardrobe, entourage, publicist* by writing the following definitions on the board in scrambled order and asking students to match the words to the definitions.

on demand: as soon as someone asks you to do something

talent spotter: a person who finds potential stars for the film, music or sports industries

predecessor: a person who held a position before someone else

show off: behave so as to get attention or admiration for oneself

make a fuss: pay a lot of attention to

wardrobe: a collection of clothes

entourage: all the people who surround and follow an important person

publicist: a person whose business it is to bring something, especially products, to the attention of the public.

Tell students to read the text. Ask three or four students what surprised them most.

3 Explain that this task is like Paper 1, Part 2 and that they can use the procedure suggested for sentences on p.23 of the Coursebook for paragraphs as well. Go through this procedure with the class. Students work individually, comparing their answers in pairs and then open-class

ANSWERS

1- E; 2 - A; 3 - H; 4 - G; 5 - D; 6 - B; 7 - C
Paragraph F is not used.

4 Remind students to use the language of agreeing and disagreeing they practised on page 62 of the *Coursebook*. Students discuss the questions in groups before reporting back to the whole class.

ALTERNATIVE PROCEDURE: lead a whole-class discussion of the questions.

FURTHER PRACTICE: First Certificate Gold Exam Maximiser Unit 7, pp.54–55.

Vocabulary: entertainment p.69

1 Students work individually to complete as many words as they can. They then compare answers with a partner before checking with the whole class. Check spelling and understanding of each word.

ANSWERS

1 row/screen 2 scene 3 director/actors 4 plot/ending 5 play/theatre 6 audition/part/rehearsals 7 performance 8 critics/reviews/audience/applauded 9 concert/symphony/composer/conducted/orchestra 10 group/cassette/singer/guitarist

2 Students answer the questions in pairs. They should talk for at least three minutes each before reporting back to the class.

FURTHER PRACTICE: First Certificate Gold Exam Maximiser Unit 7, p.50.

Function: giving advice p.70

1 Focus attention on the sentence from the text and elicit what actual words/phrases would be used to give advice. Write these up on the board and then direct students to the table in their books. Students work individually before comparing answers with the whole class.

ANSWERS

Possible direct speech answers are:
You ought to ..., If I were you, I would ..., You really must ...

Corrected items are:
You **should** pursue ...; You **had better** pursue ...; It would be a good idea if you **pursued** ...

2 Students work individually writing sentences. Go round helping with vocabulary and pointing out any errors related to the function of giving advice.

POSSIBLE ANSWERS

1   You should find an English-speaking girlfriend/
    boyfriend and spend as much time with her/him as
    possible.
    You should go to an English-speaking country and
    do a language course.

2   If I were you, I would eat exactly half what I eat now.
    You had better stop eating chocolate, sweets, bread
    and fatty foods.

3   You really must make sure she has a normal home
    life.
    If I were you, I would make sure she keeps up with
    her school work.

3   Students work in pairs before comparing answers with
the whole class.

ANSWERS

accept advice: That's a really good idea./Yes, you're
quite right, I should.

reject advice: Actually, I've already tried that./I'm not
sure that's such a good idea./I couldn't possibly do that!

4   Students rehearse their roleplays in pairs before
performing them in front of the rest of the class.

Grammar: Present Perfect pp.70–71

1   Demonstrate the activity to the students by doing it
yourself. The Present Perfect should naturally occur in
responding to questions 1 and 2 e.g.

*Someone I really admire is X. S/he has worked hard all
her/his life ...*

The most famous person I have ever met is ...

Question 3 should provide a contrast between the Past
Simple and the Present Perfect e.g.

*I haven't seen many films recently, but one film I saw a
couple of months ago really impressed me.*

Allow a few minutes for students to think about the task
before answering the questions in pairs. Ask two students to
report back to the whole class.

ALTERNATIVE PROCEDURE: pairs of students interview each
other in front of the rest of the class.

2   Read the information about the Present Perfect to the
students. They work individually matching the examples to
the rules before comparing their answers with a partner and
then with the whole class.

ALTERNATIVE PROCEDURE: students check their answers by
looking at the *Grammar reference* on page 175.

ANSWERS

1 c); 2 f); 3 a); 4 d); 5 e); 6 b)

3   Students work in pairs finding the mistakes and
correcting them before comparing their answers with the
whole class.

CORRECTED VERSION

Dear Robin,

*Well, as you can see, I finally got to England. I <u>have
been</u> here now since January 10th and it <u>has all been</u>
wonderful!*

*I <u>am staying</u> with a very nice family who are looking
after me very well. I <u>have</u> my own room with an ensuite
bathroom and a comfortable chair, a desk to work at
and even a TV (very good for my English!).*

*I <u>have done</u> lots of things since I arrived. <u>I have visited</u>
Buckingham Palace, been to Camden Market (where I
bought lots of clothes!) and seen the waxworks at
Madame Tussaud's, which were incredible (so life-like!).*

*The other great thing is the school where <u>I am studying</u>.
My teacher is very friendly and the other students are
also very nice. We have all been out together a couple
of times to a restaurant, which was great.*

*<u>I have watched</u> TV every night since I arrived. It's quite
difficult to understand but I'm getting used to it.
Something I am not getting used to is the weather,
which <u>has been</u> crazy. One minute it is raining, the next
minute, brilliant sunshine. You never know what to
wear!*

Well, that's about it for now. I'll write again soon.

Best wishes,

Ahmet

4   Divide the class into groups of four. Half the groups
should look at the instructions for Student A on page 201 and
the other half at the information for Student B on page 205.
Allow five to ten minutes for the groups to study the
instructions and write their answers. Go round checking they
know what they have to do. Pair a Student A with a Student
B. As students do the task, go round making a note of any
errors you hear with the Present Perfect. Go through the errors
later with the whole class, but do not say who made them.

5   Ask students if they watched the news last night or
have read a newspaper today. Conduct this as a whole-class
discussion. Encourage students to answer with more than
single sentences.

6 Give students two minutes to read through and think about the sentences before eliciting the difference in meaning from the whole class.

ANSWERS

The basic difference in meaning is that the Present Perfect Simple often emphasises result and completion, whereas the Present Perfect Continuous emphasises the activity.

1 a) Implies that you have finished reading the book.
  b) Implies that you are currently reading it, but have not yet finished it.
2 a) He has finished cutting down one tree.
  b) Refers to repeated actions leading up to the present.
3 a) They live in Athens permanently.
  b) They live in Athens, but it may only be temporary.
4 a) You have finished writing six letters. (This emphasises the result of the morning's work.)
  b) Refers to repeated actions leading up to the present. (This emphasises the activity.)

7 Discuss which rule is not true with the whole class.

ANSWER

We do not use the Present Perfect Continuous for d) to describe a completed action (something that has finished).

8 Students work in pairs deciding which verbs to change before comparing their answers with the whole group.

ANSWERS

What have you been doing? I've been working; I've been playing; I've been trying

EXTRA ACTIVITY: give students a few minutes to study the dialogue silently. Tell them to close their books. Read out the beginning of each line (e.g. *Oh, not much, but ...*). Students complete the line (e.g. *I did get a job!*). It is not important that they are word perfect, but that they convey the general meaning.

9 Pair two Student A's and two Student B's together and give them one minute to prepare what they are going to say. Then pair Student A with Student B and let them act out the roleplay. One or two pairs can perform for the rest of the class.

ALTERNATIVE PROCEDURE: divide the class into two groups A and B. Students in each group appoint a representative and prepare things for her/him to say. The two students do the roleplay in front of the rest of the class.

FURTHER PRACTICE: First Certificate Gold Exam Maximiser **Unit 7, p.51.**

Exam focus: Paper 2 Writing: Part 2 (a report) pp.72–73

1 1 Read the exam information and advice aloud before doing Exercise 1 with the whole class. Elicit the rules and refer students to the relevant sections of the *Grammar reference* on page 169 (9.4/9.5/9.6).

ANSWERS

He is rich and famous, *but* he isn't happy.
Even though/Although he is rich and famous, he isn't happy.
He is rich and famous. *However*, he isn't happy.
In spite of/Despite being the fact that he is rich and famous, he isn't happy.
On the one hand he is rich and famous, *but on the other hand* he isn't happy.

2 Students work individually before comparing their answers in pairs and then with the whole class.

POSSIBLE ANSWERS

a) The seats in the theatre were comfortable, but *we were too far from the stage to see the actors well*.
b) He wanted to be a famous actor. However, *his parents persuaded him to study to be a lawyer*.
c) She refused to star in his new film despite the fact that *she had worked with him so successfully before*.
d) On the one hand he enjoyed being recognised in the street, but *on the other hand he didn't like having his photograph taken*.
e) Although the film received good reviews in the press, *it was a box office disaster*.
f) In spite of needing a holiday, she decided to *go on working until she had finished the project*.

3 Students work individually before comparing answers with the whole class.

2 Students read the question and sample answer before filling in the gaps individually. They then compare answers with a partner and with the whole class. Focus students' attention on the layout of the report.

ANSWERS

1 However 2 Even though/Although 3 despite/in spite of
4 however

3 Students write their reports for homework. Mark them using the correction code on pages 7–8 of the *Introduction*, paying particular attention to layout, verb tense and linking words. Give the following grades:

Excellent: for a report that follows the layout conventions, covers the key points, uses a range of vocabulary and structure and is generally accurate.

Good: for a report that shows sensitivity to layout conventions and attempts to cover the key points, but has a more limited range of language and a higher degree of error.

Satisfactory: for a report that shows some attempt to follow layout conventions and cover the key points, but has a somewhat limited range of language and one or two basic errors.

Unsatisfactory: for a report that makes little or no attempt to follow the layout conventions or cover the key points, uses a very limited range of language and has a large number of basic errors.

FURTHER PRACTICE: **First Certificate Gold Exam Maximiser Unit 7, pp.52–53.**

EXTRA ACTIVITY : students visit a museum or local tourist attraction in the area and write a similar report.

Listening: The psychology of fame p.74

1 Get students to work on the questions in groups of four or conduct an open-class discussion. Make a note of students' ideas on the board.

2 Play the tape once through to see if any of the ideas were mentioned.

3 Focus attention on the True/False statements. Ask students to see if they can remember any of the answers. Play the tape a second time. Students work individually before comparing their answers in pairs and then open-class. If necessary, play the relevant sections of the tape again. (see underlining in tapescript)

TAPESCRIPT

P = Presenter O = Olga S = Simon

P: Well, what is it that makes people want to become famous in the first place? Olga, as the professional psychologist perhaps we'd better start with you.

O: Well, sadly, <u>people who have had unhappy childhoods are often deeply insecure and go on to want to be publicly adored.</u> There are numerous

---

examples including Jack Nicholson and of course Marilyn Monroe.

P: Well Simon, you're the manager of a number of aspiring young rock stars, what do you think?

S: When it comes to rock musicians, <u>it definitely goes back to insecurity during childhood.</u> In ninety-nine per cent of cases real stars have been desperate to be famous from an early age.

P: And then someone discovers them, I suppose.

S: Not necessarily. I've met people who'll do anything just to become famous. If they can't sing well enough they'll jump off the Eiffel Tower.

P: But, surely talent comes into it?

S: Talent? Actually, <u>I don't think it's got much to do with success in rock music. It's certainly nothing like as important as that total obsession with being famous that so many big stars have.</u> I wouldn't take on anyone without that.

P: But is this obsession with being famous good for people?

O: No. It most certainly is not. For the kind of personality that desperately wants to become famous, actually <u>giving them fame can be very dangerous. It's like a drug. They become addicted to being the focus of attention</u> and when the situation changes, they get terribly depressed.

S: Sure, sure … but the <u>one thing you mustn't do when managing a star is to help them become more balanced,</u> because pretty soon you won't have a star on your hands any more. I've seen it happen. The star meets a nice girl or boy and settles down and all of a sudden he or she can't be bothered to get out there and behave outrageously in press conferences or whatever. Once they're normal, they're just not star material.

O: <u>That's ridiculous! As I see it, these people need help and I think it's the responsibility of those close to them – particularly their managers – to see that they get that help.</u> A lot of stars would still be alive today if someone had stepped in and helped them to see that being famous isn't the same as being truly loved and that it doesn't bring happiness.

S: Come on Olga. <u>A lot of them have a great time … travelling all over the world, staying in the best hotels … and wrecking their hotel rooms!</u> I mean, it can be a lot of fun.

P: Okay. Now what about the role of the media in all this. How important is it for a star to have a high public profile?

S: It's everything ... but the problem is that the media aren't generally interested in the music; they're only interested in your personal life, so to get onto the front page you have to do something shocking.

P: So, if they want this attention, why do so many celebrities react so negatively, even violently, to the press?

O: Well, it's a love-hate relationship basically. As Simon says, stars need the press to remain in the public eye but they resent the invasion of privacy.

P: And how do they cope?

O: A lot of them don't!

ANSWERS

See underlined sentences in tapescript
1 True   2 False   3 False   4 True   5 True
6 False   7 False

4 Begin by telling students about an occasion on which you met or nearly met a famous person. Ask if anyone else has met someone famous. Say what you would do if you met a famous person and ask a couple of students to say what they would do.

Writing p.74

Ask if the students have access to e-mail and what differences if any there are between e-mail and letters. If students have never used e-mail and are unlikely to have access to it, change the task and tell them to write an informal letter to a friend. Students work in pairs drafting their messages.

EXTRA ACTIVITY: If students do have access to e-mail they could send you their writing exercise and you could respond (with corrections) on line.

Use of English p.75

1 Students work in pairs describing the photos. Encourage them to keep talking for as long as possible.

2 Set a two-minute time limit for the gist reading task. Ask if anyone has visited Madame Tussaud's and what they thought of it. Ask what they know about the people mentioned in the text.

BACKGROUND INFORMATION

Marie Antoinette: the wife of Louis XVI of France who was guillotined in 1789 at the beginning of the French Revolution.

Bob Geldof: lead singer of the Boomtown Rats and TV personality. He is well known for his work with the charity Live Aid', which involved musicians playing for free at large concerts in the 1980s. The proceeds of these concerts were used to provide food and other aid to African countries suffering a famine.

the Dalai Lama: the leader of Tibetan Buddhists who lives in exile in India.

John Haigh: murdered twelve people in the 1930s and tried to dissolve their bodies in acid.

Lenny Henry: a popular comedian who began his career at a club in London and is now often seen on TV in the UK.

3 Point out that students have some but not all of the words they need to complete the text. Students work individually filling in the gaps before comparing answers with a partner and then with the whole class.

ANSWERS

1 most   2 on   3 despite   4 with   5 it   6 has   7 Either
8 are   9 as   10 enough   11 by   12 are   13 the   14 had
15 to

Listening: stagefright p.76

1 Ask if anyone has ever given a speech, performed in a play or played a musical instrument in front of a large audience. Ask how they felt before they went on stage. Elicit or tell students the meaning of *stagefright*.

Focus students' attention on the names and statements, reminding them there is one extra statement that they do not need to use. Play the cassette once straight through. Students compare their answers in pairs. Play the cassette again and check the answers through with the whole class, pausing the cassette after the relevant underlined sections in the tapescript.

TAPESCRIPT

**P = presenter   HB = Helen Brannington
KG = Kathleen Griffen   SS = Steve Sutcliffe
GC = Gavin Cartwright   CV = Colin Vickers
GW = Glen Wilson**

P: And now on this week's edition of *Fears and Phobias* we're going to be hearing about the problem of stagefright. By some it has been called 'the wall of terror' and many famous names have fallen victim to it. Reporter Kathleen Griffen has been in search of the psychological roots of stagefright. How bad can it be? Here's Helen Brannington, currently with the Royal Shakespeare Company.

HB: ... and I could not remember what the next line was and I had just done it in the dressing-room. I literally thought, 'I'm going to go out there and apologise to the audience and say, "I made a mistake."' I literally did. I thought I was going to do that. I've never been so frightened in my life.

KG: When the house lights go down and the curtain rises, a paralysing fear can grip the most experienced of performers. Here's how Steve Sutcliffe, a regular face on our TV screens, describes it.

SS: I would be standing in the wings and my heart rate would reach something like 130, 135 a minute. I would seriously consider not going on stage. I remember in one production on about the five-minute call, looking for fire alarms 'cos I thought if I went to a fire alarm and stuck the hammer in it and the fire alarms went off, then the production, the show, would have to be cancelled that night.

KG: And it can bring out quite strong physical reactions as Gavin Cartwright has found.

GC: I sweat, my palms sweat, I feel cold and shivery. My stomach is churning, and basically I just want to be sick. It's awful.

KG: And of course the results of the fear can take a number of other forms as Colin Vickers, a drummer for a well-known rock group, found out.

CV: And there's one performance that I just can't remember at all. I have a distinct memory of sitting behind the drumset as the other musicians walked in ... erm ... and the audience was filing in and that's it – I don't remember after that really what happened. I don't remember the beginning, the middle or the end of it. I just froze.

KG: Helen, Steve, Gavin and Colin, professional performers, reliving their own personal nightmares on stage. Now, we have in the studio Dr Glen Wilson, senior lecturer in psychology at the Institute of Psychiatry in London, who specialises in just this area.

GW: The symptoms of anxiety are very much the same as fear, panic or any other kind of phobia. The palpitations, the sweaty palms, the racing heart beat and the feeling of terror ...

ANSWERS

(see underlined sentences in tapescript)

1 Colin 2 Helen 3 Gavin 4 This statement does not apply to any of the speakers. 5 Steve

2 Students complete the sentences individually before comparing their answers with a partner and then with the whole class.

ANSWERS

1 terror 2 psychological 3 anxiety 4 frightened
5 production 6 performer 7 professional 8 froze

Speaking p.76

If possible, begin by talking about what you are afraid of and frightening experiences you have had. Students then discuss the questions in groups of three or four.

ALTERNATIVE PROCEDURE: conduct a whole-class discussion.

Unit 7 Review

ANSWERS

1 1 B; 2 A; 3 C; 4 D; 5 A; 6 B; 7 C; 8 C; 9 C; 10 A; 11 C; 12 B; 13 A; 14 D; 15 B

2 1 although 2 but 3 However 4 In spite of

3 1 have been 2 played 3 been playing 4 has not given 5 visit 6 have been lifting

4 1 Her father will not let her go to an event of some kind because she will arrive home very late.

2 The following lines are incorrect:
   line 2 – delete *of*
   line 4 – delete *so*
   line 6 – delete *be*
   line 7 – delete *to*
   line 10 – delete *being*
   line 11 – delete *well*
   line 12 – delete *if*

Now your students are ready to do the test for Unit 7 on page 129.

8 Looking good

Speaking p.78

1 Focus students' attention on the photos and conduct a class discussion on the styles of clothes the people are wearing. Ask which styles people still wear and which ones the students would consider wearing themselves. Give students two minutes to match the photos to the following decades: the 1920s, the 1940s, the 1950s, the 1970s, and the 1990s. Check the answers open-class and see if everyone agrees.

ANSWERS

A the 1990s B the 1940s C the 1920s
D the 1950s E the 1970s

2 Play the cassette. Students answer the questions open-class. Ask if they know who the original singer was (*Elvis Presley*) and if they know any other famous songs from the fifties.

TAPESCRIPT

Verse 1

Well, it's one for the money,
Two for the show,
Three to get ready,
Now go, cat, go.
But don't you step on my blue suede shoes.
Well, you can do anything,
But stay off my blue suede shoes.

Verse 2

Well, you can knock me down,
Step on my face,
Slander my name all over the place.
Well, do anything that you want to do,
But uh-huh, honey, lay off them shoes.
And don't you step on my blue suede shoes.
Well, you can do anything,
But stay off my blue suede shoes.

ANSWERS

1 the 1950s photo (D) 2 *Blue Suede Shoes*

3 Point out that the meanings of *lay off* and *slander* appear below the lines of the song. Students read through the jumbled lines and then number the lines as they listen to the song. They compare answers with a partner before listening to the song again to check and clear up any doubts. Play the song once more and discuss whether the students liked it, etc.

ALTERNATIVE PROCEDURE: write the jumbled lines out on a piece of paper leaving plenty of space between each line. Make enough photocopies so that every two students will have a copy. Cut the copies into strips with one line of the song on each strip. Put the strips into envelopes. Students work in pairs putting the strips in order as they listen to the song.

4 Elicit some clothing vocabulary, particularly for items that you or your students are actually wearing. Begin by telling the class about your tastes in clothes so that they can see that they are expected to speak at some length. Students discuss the questions in pairs. Ask two students to report back to the class about their partners' tastes in clothes.

Vocabulary: clothes p.79

1 Explain the meaning of *accessories* and *patterns*. Tell students to classify as many words as they can individually before checking with a partner and/or in their dictionaries. Remind students about recording vocabulary systematically and point out that classifying words in certain ways is a useful approach.

ANSWERS

Types of clothes: jacket, anorak, pullover, skirt, cardigan, T-shirt, vest, tights, socks, shorts, waistcoat, suit, raincoat, blouse, dress, dungarees, sweatshirt, leggings, pyjamas.
Types of shoes: sandals, trainers, slippers, Wellington boots, high-heeled shoes.
Accessories: belt, brooch, earrings, bow-tie, bracelet, braces, scarf.
Patterns: plain, striped, checked.

2 Students work in pairs taking it in turns to describe and name the item.

ALTERNATIVE PROCEDURE: do this round the class.

3 Do this open-class asking individuals to describe what other students are wearing.

ALTERNATIVE PROCEDURE: pair students and get them to sit back to back. Each student tries to remember and describe in as much detail as possible what the other student is wearing.

Watch Out! *suit/fit/go with*

1 This coat doesn't *suit* you. It's the wrong colour. (*suit* = look good on someone)
2 The tie doesn't *go with* this shirt. It needs to be plain. (*go with* = match or look good with another item of clothing)
3 The sweater doesn't *fit* me. I need a larger size. (*fit* = be the right size)

4 This information gap activity must be done in pairs.

FURTHER PRACTICE: **First Certificate Gold Exam Maximiser Unit 8, pp.56–57.**

Reading p.80

1 Focus attention on the photo and ask the class if they know who she is and why she is famous. Ask if the class know any other top models (Claudia Schiffer, Kate Moss, Christy Turlington, etc.).

> **ANSWER**
> Naomi Campbell, supermodel.

2 Focus attention on the headline and the introduction in bold. Allow half a minute for the class to read it and answer the question.

> **ANSWER**
> She has written a novel and made an album.

3 Tell students to look at the questions with a partner and try to predict the answers. Divide the class into two groups, if possible of equal size. Pre-teach *pushy, fiery, work the system, know-how,* and *long-held celebrity*. Point out that they will not find *all* the answers in their part of the text. As students read they see how accurate their predictions were.

> **ANSWERS**
> 1 15 (Text A) 2 How hard they work. (Text B) 3 She is so famous that she is known by her first name only. (Text A) 4 Since she was at school. (Text B) 5 Cooking, having friends over and going to clubs. (Text B) 6 She is always late, she is stupid, she is pushy. (Text A)
> 7 Because she knows how to 'work the system' (get the best out of the system for herself). (Text A) 8 She had to learn to cope on her own in the New York fashion world very quickly when she was very young. (Text A)
> 9 Because she doesn't want to give up travelling yet. (Text B.) 10 Being a normal teenager. (Text A)

4 Students work in pairs telling each other about the answers to the questions before reporting back to the whole class.

ALTERNATIVE PROCEDURE: work with the whole class. Ask students from Group B for their predictions for the questions answered by Text A and vice versa. Then get a student who has read the text to tell them if their prediction was accurate or not.

5 Remind students that pronouns can refer back not only to the previous sentence, but to elements much earlier in the text, to things 'outside' the text itself, that is to the reader or the writer, or to something not specifically mentioned in the text at all. Students work individually before comparing answers with a partner and then with the whole class.

> **ANSWERS**
> **Text A**
> *I* = James Collard; *they* = women so famous and so talked about…; *her* = Naomi Campbell; *She* = Naomi Campbell; *that* = have no brains at all, no intelligence, that we can't make decisions, we can't even speak …;
> *it* = Swan (the novel); *it* = having to get used to the New York fashion business when she was so young
> **Text B**
> *it* = the working life of a supermodel; *it* = performing arts; *it* = travelling.

6 Discuss the questions with the whole class. Ask for students to justify their answers by quoting from the text.

> **ANSWER**
> The writer is sympathetic.

Vocabulary: phrasal verbs (*give*) p.81

1 Students work individually before comparing their answers with a partner and then with the whole class.

ANSWERS

1 e); 2 a); 3 g); 4 d); 5 f); 6 b); 7 c)

2 Students work with a partner before comparing answers open-class.

ANSWERS

1 give off 2 give in 3 give away 4 give out
5 give away 6 give up 7 give back

Writing: describing people p.81

1 Read the exam information and the instructions aloud to the class. Students work individually before checking their answers open-class.

ANSWERS

para. 1 line 5 – delete *much*
para. 1 line 6 – delete *some*
para. 2 line 2 – delete *of*
para. 2 line 6 – delete *to*
para. 2 line 8 – delete *as*
para. 3 line 7 – delete *to*
para. 4 line 5 – delete *am*

2 Students work individually before comparing answers with a partner and then with the whole class.

ANSWERS

1 quite 2 particularly 3 comments 4 great 5 a little
6 first 7 seems 8 loves 9 lots 10 actually

3 Do this writing task in class or for homework.

FURTHER PRACTICE: *First Certificate Gold Exam Maximiser* **Unit 8, pp.58–59.**

Grammar: *used to/would* p.82

1 Students work individually before comparing answers with a partner and then with the whole class.

ANSWERS

1 Dance *used to* be my main subject.
2 Did you *use* to play basketball?
3 I am not used to *working* such long hours.
4 He is getting used *to* living in the city.

5 My father *used to/would* **play** football with me every weekend.
6 I *would walk* to church with my parents every Sunday.
7 I *used to* really love playing tennis when I was younger.

2 Do this exercise with the whole class. Refer students to the relevant section of the *Grammar reference* on page 177 (18.1/18.2).

ANSWERS

1 a) and c); 2 a); 3 b)

3 Students work individually before comparing answers with a partner and then with the whole class.

ANSWERS

1 to 2 going 3 get 4 would 5 am 6 didn't 7 would

4 Do this orally yourself first so that students get some ideas. They work individually before comparing answers open-class.

5 Students work individually making notes on the routines. Go round helping where necessary. They work with a partner describing the process of getting used to the new routine.

ALTERNATIVE PROCEDURE: students choose famous people only e.g. Janet Jackson, Macaulay Culkin, Naomi Campbell. They do not say who they have 'life-swapped' with. The rest of the class listen to them describing trying to adjust to the famous person's routine and try to guess who the famous person is.

FURTHER PRACTICE: *First Certificate Gold Exam Maximiser* **Unit 8, p.57.**

Exam focus: Paper 3 Use of English: Part 3 (key word transformation) p.83

Read the exam information and procedure aloud to the class.

Students work individually before comparing answers in pairs and then open-class.

Note: If you think your students will have difficulty with this exercise, indicate the number of words missing from each sentence like this:

1 _ _ _   2 _ _ _ _ etc.

If the exercise as a whole or some of the items are still

causing problems, give a further hint by providing the first word or the first few letters of the first missing word like this:

1 Many people *are* _ _ flying.

2 I *hardly* _ _ _ the cinema.

5 He *lo*… _ his father.

ANSWERS

1 Many people **are afraid of** flying.
2 I **hardly ever go to** the cinema.
3 You haven't done **as much work as** Jim.
4 There were **far fewer people than** I had imagined.
5 He **looks like** his father.
6 My doctor advised me **to take up** swimming.
7 He **accused me of stealing** the money.
8 I thought **I ought to go** home.
9 I **have lived here since** 1984.
10 The teacher **gave out** the examination papers.

---

*FURTHER PRACTICE: **First Certificate Gold Exam Maximiser** **Unit 8, p.62.***

Listening: designer row p.83

1 Focus attention on the picture and ask students to describe the people, their clothes and appearance as well as what seems to be happening. Play the cassette once and elicit the answer to the gist question.

ANSWER

The mother bought the wrong brand of trainers.

TAPESCRIPT

M = Mum J = Julie D = Dad

M: Hi! I'm home.

J: Hi! Everything all right? Did you get them okay?

M: Yes, it was fine. Now, come and help me put all this stuff away.

J: Can I just see them first? I just want to have a look.

M: In a minute … take these bags into the kitchen first.

J: I only want to see … Oh no! Oh, Mum! You got the wrong ones.

M: What do you mean 'the wrong ones'? I got exactly what you asked me for … the right colour, the right size, all the various bits and pieces you wanted. <u>I couldn't believe I was so lucky and at £30 cheaper</u>

<u>than you said they would be!</u> Oh, look, come on, they're fine, just try them on …

J: <u>They are not fine. They're not the right make. I told you which make to get. Who's ever heard of 'Runwear'?</u>

D: Hi, love. Everything all right?

M: Apparently not!

J: She bought the wrong make. Look. <u>I'll be the laughing stock at school. No one will talk to me.</u>

D: Come on Julie, don't take it so seriously. No one will care at school. After all they're only a pair of …

J: They *will* care. It's really important …

M: Well, I'm sorry, but if you think I'm going to pay an extra £30 just so you can parade around with a different name on your trainers, you'll just have to think again.

D: Surely, love, it's not so important to have a particular make …

J: Oh yeah, <u>so how come you always have to have those jumpers with the little crocodile on?</u> They're much more expensive than ordinary ones and there's never any arguments then. It's just not fair. It's always the same. One rule for grown-ups and another for kids.

---

2 Tell students to take notes in answer to the questions while they listen to the cassette again.

ANSWERS

(see underlined sentences in tapescript)

1 She paid £30 less for the trainers than she had expected to pay.
2 They were not the make Julie wanted.
3 She is worried that everyone will laugh at her and refuse to talk to her.
4 Because she thinks he is being hypocritical since he wears a particular make of jumper.

---

3 Students discuss the questions in groups of three or four and appoint a spokesperson to report back to the whole class.

Vocabulary: body and health p.84

1 Set a time limit of one minute for students to write down parts of the body. Write the words that students come up with on the board.

ALTERNATIVE PROCEDURE: students initially only write words for parts of the body with three letters, then with four letters, with five letters, etc. Give occasional hints if they are having problems.

2 Students work in pairs before comparing their answers with the rest of the class.

ANSWERS

1 time on his <u>hands</u>: *a lot of free time*
2 put words in my <u>mouth</u>: *anticipate what someone is going to say*
3 on the tip of my <u>tongue</u>: *can't quite remember it*
4 a sweet <u>tooth</u>: *likes sweet things*
5 have/has (got) a <u>cheek</u>: *is rude or disrespectful*
6 get off on the wrong <u>foot</u>: *start a relationship or conversation badly*
7 get it off your <u>chest</u>: *tell someone else about a worry or problem*
8 his <u>heart</u> is in the right place: *has good intentions*

3 Students work individually before comparing their answers with a partner and then with the rest of the class.

ANSWERS

1 surgery 2 pain 3 prescription 4 heal 5 temperature
6 twisted 7 injections 8 sore 9 stretcher 10 over
11 bruises 12 plasters

4 Students work in groups of two or three. Remind them to say as much as possible when answering the questions.

Reading pp.84–85

1 Focus attention on the photos and ask if students know the famous comedians shown in the pictures. Ask which comedians in their country they really like and why. Discuss the title of the article open-class.

2 Students work in pairs matching the words to the definitions before checking their answers with the rest of the class.

ANSWERS

1 g); 2 e); 3 a); 4 h); 5 b); 6 f); 7 c); 8 d)

3 Set a three-minute time limit for students to answer the questions. Students compare answers with a partner and then open-class

ANSWERS

1 no *(but how it works is still being puzzled out)*
2 less *(paragraph 4)*
3 yes *(paragraph 9)*

4 Refer students to the procedure on page 23 in Unit 2 of the *Coursebook*. Draw attention to the fact that this time there is an extra sentence that they do not need to use. Set a fifteen minute time limit for the task.

ANSWERS

1 H; 2 D; 3 G; 4 A; 5 B; 6 E; 7 C

FURTHER PRACTICE: First Certificate Gold Exam Maximiser Unit 8, p.60.

EXTRA ACTIVITY: if you have access to videos of *Fawlty Towers* or other comedy programmes, the class could watch part of or an entire episode.

Grammar: *can, could, may, might* p.86

1 Do this exercise open-class.

ANSWERS

1 ... are losing our ability to laugh.
2 ... to provide a kind of pain relief.
3 ... able to tolerate the discomfort for much longer.
4 ... to attend the workshop.

2 Students work individually before checking their answers with the rest of the class.

ANSWERS

1 It is possible that you are right.
2 You are allowed to go now if you wish.
3 It is possible that they are in the kitchen.
4 You are not allowed to smoke in here.
5 It is possible that he will be home late tonight.

6 It is possible that it will rain this evening.

7 I am able to swim.

8 It is possible that Paul knows the answer.

9 It is not possible that he is still at the office.

10 I was able to play the piano when I was much younger.

3 Remind students to use *may/might/could* and demonstrate the task yourself first. Students work in pairs before reporting their speculations back to the class.

ALTERNATIVE PROCEDURE: do this round the class with individuals speculating about what the objects are.

ANSWERS

A a pair of glasses B a bath plug C a hairbrush
D a remote control E the heel of a shoe F the side of a coin G a can opener H the handset of a telephone

4 Begin by telling students about your own abilities before getting them to work in pairs or open-class.

5 Students rehearse their roleplays in pairs. A couple of pairs can perform their roleplays for the rest of the class.

ALTERNATIVE PROCEDURE: divide the class into two groups, Group A (Parents) and Group B (Teenagers). Each group appoints a representative and prepares things for her/him to say. The two representatives act out the roleplay in front of the rest of the class.

*FURTHER PRACTICE: **First Certificate Gold Exam Maximiser** Unit 8, p.62 (Grammar).*

Unit 8 Review

ANSWERS

1 1 who 2 able 3 had 4 her 5 to 6 few 7 the 8 being 9 was 10 the 11 aged 12 of 13 to 14 for 15 at

2 1 used to 2 would 3 get 4 am used 5 spend 6 could 7 might 8 may 9 can't 10 Could

3 1 up 2 away 3 off 4 in 5 out 6 away 7 back

5 Direct students to the relevant pages in the *Coursebook*. Students work together writing sentences. Go round checking that their sentences make sense and that there are no mistakes with word order. They form groups of four and rewrite the second group of sentences using the phrasal verbs. Get each group to read their sentences aloud. Write them on the board. Elicit one word equivalents from the other groups.

Now your students are ready to do the test for Unit 8 on page 130.

9 Too much of a good thing

Grammar: countables/uncountables p.88

1 Check that students understand the concepts *countable* and *uncountable*. Give an example to illustrate the difference in meaning between *cheese* as a countable and uncountable noun e.g. *The French produce some of the best cheeses in the world.* (= 'varieties of cheese') and *My brother is allergic to cheese.* (= the substance). Students work individually before comparing lists with a partner and then with the whole class.

ANSWERS

(the meanings of words which can be both countable and uncountable are indicated in italics)

countable: an apple, a wood *(a small forest)*, an iron *(the implement)*, a headache, a business *(a company)*, a chicken *(the whole animal)*, a coffee *(a cup of coffee)*, a country *(a nation)*, a chocolate *(an individual sweet)*, a hair *(an individual strand)*, a trip, a work *(a work of art)*, a cold *(the illness)*, a toast *(e.g. to the bride and groom at a wedding)*, a fruit *(a variety of)*.

uncountable: apple *(the substance)*, wood *(the substance)*, bread, travel, flu, furniture, iron *(the metal)*, information, business *(the activity)*, chicken *(the meat)*, luggage, coffee *(the substance)*, advice, country *(land outside the city)*, news, weather, chocolate *(the substance)*, hair *(a mass)*, work *(the activity)*, cold *(the sensation)*, toast, fruit *(the foodstuff)*, equipment, rubbish.

2 Focus attention on the cartoon and elicit the answer to question 1 with the whole class. Students work in pairs before comparing their answers with the whole class.

ANSWERS

1 Wrong. *He's got **short black hair** and a beard.* (The use of the indefinite article would imply that he only had one hair growing on his head and was otherwise bald.)

2 Unlikely. *I'd like **chicken** to start with, please.* (The use of the indefinite article would imply that she wanted a whole chicken to eat.)

3 Wrong. *The news **is** very bad.*

4 Wrong. *My trousers **haven't** been cleaned yet.*

5 Wrong. *Let me give you some **advice**.*

6 Wrong. *The police **were** very helpful.*

7 Wrong. *Can I have some more/another **piece/slice of** bread, please?*

8 Wrong. *Let's go for a walk in **the** country.*

9 Wrong. *I'd like to make **a toast** to the bride and groom.*

3 Check that students understand the meanings of *sheet*, *lump* and *slice*. They work individually before comparing answers with a partner and with the whole class.

ANSWERS

1 lots 2 many 3 piece/slice/bit 4 lots 5 bit/piece 6 little
7 bit/piece/sheet 8 lump/bit/piece 9 some 10 few
11 deal 12 lot 13 bit/piece/slice 14 some 15 much

FURTHER PRACTICE: **First Certificate Gold Exam Maximiser Unit 9, p.64.**

Reading pp.88–89

1 Tell students to work in pairs. Focus attention on the illustration and the information about the extract. Ask them to decide as they read which of the characters in the illustration is George and which is Montmorency. Set a three-minute time limit for this and the gist task.

ANSWER

Yes, they did enjoy the meal.

2 Remind students to follow the procedure described in Unit 6, page 64. Set a ten-minute time limit. Students compare answers with a partner before checking with the whole class.

EXTRA ACTIVITY: ask students to describe in pairs the first meal they ever cooked.

ANSWERS

1 B; 2 B; 3 D; 4 B *(the ingredients are: potatoes, a cabbage, peas, half a pork pie, a bit of boiled bacon, half a tin of potted salmon, eggs and a dead water-rat);*
5 D; 6 D; 7 A

Vocabulary: phrasal verbs (*put*) p.90

1 and **2** Focus attention on the sentence taken from the text and elicit the meaning of the phrasal verb *to put up* (= *to stay*). Students work in pairs before comparing their answers with the whole class.

ANSWERS
1 e) *(tolerate)* 2 h) *(kill an animal humanely)* 3 a) *(save)*
4 g) *(make somebody feel ashamed or foolish)*
5 c) *(connect by telephone)* 6 i) *(increase)*
7 f) *(postpone)* 8 b) *(accommodate)* 9 d) *(extinguish)*

3 Students work in pairs and continue the conversations. Once they have completed one, get them to change partners and choose another pair of sentences and do the same thing. As they work, go round and make a list of errors that they make in the use of the phrasal verbs. Go through the errors with the whole class at the end.

POSSIBLE CONTEXTS FOR CONVERSATIONS
1 e) Two women talking about the reasons why one of them has split up with her boyfriend.
2 h) A vet talking to a pet owner about a beloved pet, probably a horse.
3 a) Friend talking to someone who has had her/his house repossessed because s/he couldn't meet the payments.
4 g) A couple driving home from a party.
5 c) A salesman ringing a company and talking to the switchboard operator.
6 i) Two people in business together discussing profits.
7 f) A reluctant bride/bridegroom talking to her/his fiancé(e).
8 b) An acquaintance talking to someone s/he met on holiday.
9 d) An official talking to the head of the fire brigade.

EXTRA ACTIVITY: students act their conversations out in front of the class.

FURTHER PRACTICE: **First Certificate Gold Exam Maximiser Unit 9, p.66.**

Vocabulary: food and cooking p.90

1 Do this with the whole class, explaining any unknown items as you do the exercise.

ANSWERS
1 peas *(the other items are herbs)*
2 a penknife *(the other items are specifically kitchen utensils)*
3 to grate *(the other items are all ways of cooking rather than preparing food)*
4 a cook *(the other items are all items of kitchen equipment whereas 'a cook' is a person)*
5 to roll *(the other items all involve knives)*
6 a sieve *(the other items are all receptacles used for cooking food, not for preparing it)*
7 to sprinkle *(the other items all involve turning the ingredients)*
8 hard *(the other items are flavours)*
9 a course *(the other items are all receptacles for serving food)*
10 tough *(the other items are all ways in which people request their meat to be cooked)*
11 a second helping *(the other items are all stages in the meal where different dishes are served)*
12 to fold *(the other items are all things you do with eggs)*

2 Students work in groups of three or four. Explain that they may not be able to add to all the categories. Provide vocabulary for any ideas they have where necessary.

POSSIBLE ANSWERS
1 oregano, tarragon, thyme, rosemary
2 carving/bread knife, slotted spoon
3 to grill, to sauté, to boil
4 a microwave, a rotisserie
5 to peel
6 a bain-marie, an ovenproof dish
7 to beat
8 salty, hot, spicy, bitter
9 a side plate, a casserole dish, a platter
10 medium-rare
11 a first course, hors d'oeuvre, a pudding
12 to fry, to poach

3 Students work individually before comparing their answers in pairs and then with the whole class.

4   Students discuss the questions in pairs and then open-class. Any new vocabulary items should be written up on the board. Remind students to record their vocabulary systematically.

FURTHER PRACTICE: **First Certificate Gold Exam Maximiser Unit 9, p.63.**

Watch Out! *lay/lie* p.91

Number 3 is incorrect. It should be *lay*.

lie – lied – lied (regular verb) = to say untrue things

lie – lay – lain (irregular intransitive verb) = to be in a flat position on a surface

lay – laid – laid (irregular transitive verb) = to put someone or something in a flat position on a surface. It is used in the phrase *to lay the table* meaning to arrange knives, forks plates and other things on a table ready for a meal.

5   Divide the class into two groups, A and B, and get them to turn to the relevant pages. Check that students in each group understand the vocabulary, but do not let the students in the other group hear. Students work in A/B pairs miming the actions for their partners.

Exam focus: Paper 4 Listening: Part 2 (note taking/blank filling) p.91

Read the exam information aloud to the class. In order to help students to predict what they are going to hear, focus attention on the illustration and ask them to write three wh- questions about pizzas e.g. *Where was pizza invented? Who invented pizza? How many pizzas are sold each year? How is pizza made?* Put the questions up on the board and see if the class can answer them.

Focus attention on the note-taking task and get them to match as many questions as possible to the gaps. For the other gaps, get them to work out possible questions and to suggest how each gap might be filled. Play the tape once straight through while students work individually filling in the gaps. Allow time for them to compare answers before playing the tape again and checking the answers open-class. If necessary, play the relevant sections of the tape again (see underlining in tapescript)

TAPESCRIPT

What's your favourite kind of food? Hot dogs and hamburgers? Or maybe you like Greek foods, such as gyros and pizza. Pizza? Greek? Well, believe it or not, pizza was actually invented by the Greeks.

The early Greeks turned their bread into a main course by topping it with cheese, oil, onions, garlic, herbs, olives, and vegetables. These early pizzas were flat and round with a rim of crust that people used as a handle. When the Greeks colonized the southern part of Italy, they brought the idea of the edible plate with them. And in 1830, the first pizzeria was opened in Naples. It was the Neapolitans who began putting tomato sauce on pizza.

Many credit Raffaele Esposita with inventing the tomato and cheese pizza. In 1889, this pizzeria owner baked a special pizza in honor of the queen of Italy, Marguerita Teresa Giovanii. Pizza Marguerita had the colors of the Italian flag: red tomatoes, white mozzarella, and green basil leaves.

During the late 1800s, many Italians emigrated to the United States. Some started their own bakeries where they sold groceries and pizza. But it wasn't until 1905 that Gennaro Lombardi opened the first pizzeria in America. By the early 1920s, this thin-crusted, Neapolitan pizza was very popular in the northeastern states. Twenty years later, deep-dish pizza was invented by Ike Sewell and Ric Riccardo in Chicago. Pizza's popularity continued to grow. Finally, during the early sixties, pepperoni-sausage-covered pies could be found all over the country.

What is America's favourite pizza topping? You guessed it – pepperoni. Last year, Americans ate four million pounds of it! Other countries like more exotic toppings. In Japan, favourite toppings include eel and squid. Costa Ricans like coconut on their pizzas. In Russia, people top their pies with red herring, while Australians like seafood and pineapple.

If you order a plain cheese pizza you'll be eating from three major food groups: the crust is from the grain group, the tomato sauce is from the fruit and vegetable group, and the cheese is from the dairy group. Pizza also provides a fair amount of vitamins and calcium. Top it with vegetables such as green peppers, onions, tomatoes or olives, and it becomes an even more healthful and delicious meal.

Pizza has come a long way from its humble beginnings. So far in fact that the Naples Pizza Association would like the European Union to set down laws about what you can put on top of a pizza. It doesn't look as if they'll be able to convince many people to limit the topping to cheese and tomato, because pizza has become a global favourite and we're putting everything on top from fruit to seaweed. Nowadays you can order your pizza from your favorite pizzeria and unlike the ancient Greeks, you'll be eating it in thirty minutes or less!

ANSWERS

(see underlined sentences in tapescript)

1 *The Greeks* 2 *flat and round* 3 *1830* 4 *queen of Italy* 5 *1905* 6 *America* 7 *seafood and pineapple* 8 *food groups* 9 *vitamins* 10 *put on top*

EXTRA ACTIVITY: if your students are all the same nationality, ask them how they or their parents cook a well-known national dish. You may find there is considerable disagreement on what exactly goes in. They can bring a sample of their version of the dish for another class or for you and some other teachers to try. You act as judges and select the best version. In multilingual classes students can bring a typical dish to class for the others to try. The class try to guess the ingredients.

***FURTHER PRACTICE: First Certificate Gold Exam Maximiser* Unit 9, p.64.**

Reading p.92

1 Elicit a dictionary-type definition of *addict* e.g. *a person who is unable to free themselves from a harmful habit, especially of taking drugs.* Students discuss their answers in pairs and then open-class. Tell students some of your own addictions, if you have any (e.g. coffee, chocolate).

2 Set a three-minute time limit for the gist task. Students discuss their answers in pairs and then open-class.

3 Remind students not to worry about unknown vocabulary for the moment as they will do an exercise to help them work out meanings from context later.

Students read through the statements before re-reading the text. Remind them that there is one sentence they do not need to use. Set a ten-minute time limit for this task. Students discuss their answers in pairs and then open-class.

ANSWERS

1 Anne (*When her cash ran out, she stole money from the elderly patients in her care and was charged with theft.*)
2 Janine (*My husband said that I didn't have time for him, and he was right. But I couldn't believe it when*

he left me.)
3 Anne (*Her home was soon an Aladdin's cave of household goods and trendy clothes she didn't need.*)
4 This sentence does not apply to any of the people.
5 Becci (*Towards exam time, Becci feels she has to increase her intake to cope with all the work.*)
6 Janine (*Now, I'm seeing a counsellor and gradually reducing the amount of exercise I do.*)
7 Tony Benn (*... his addiction has raised concern about his health. When he collapsed recently, some people blamed his excessive tea drinking.*)
8 Becci (*..., but I have no plans to give it up. If I like it so much, why should I?*)

4 Students work individually before comparing their answers with a partner and then with the whole class.

ANSWERS

1 odd one out 2 an urge 3 to make up for 4 to melt 5 to ruin 6 to come to one's senses 7 to get out of hand 8 to raise concern 9 to collapse 10 excessive 11 agonising 12 trendy 13 ran out

5 Students discuss the questions in groups of three or four before reporting back to the whole class.

ALTERNATIVE PROCEDURE: students act out a roleplay in pairs, one of them is one of the characters from the text, the other is a good friend trying to give some advice.

***FURTHER PRACTICE: First Certificate Gold Exam Maximiser* Unit 9, pp.66–67.**

Grammar: future forms p.93

1 Do this exercise with the whole class.

ANSWERS

a) 1; b) 4; c) 6; d) 3; e) 5; f) 7; g) 2

2 Elicit the names of the different forms from the class. Refer students to the relevant section in the *Grammar reference* on pages 176–177 (17.8).

ANSWERS

a) Future Simple *will* b) Future Simple *will* c) *going to* future d) Present Continuous e) *going to* future f) Future Continuous g) Future Perfect

3 Emphasise that students should choose the most appropriate answer, although sometimes more than one answer may be possible. Students work individually before comparing their answers with a partner and then with the whole class.

ANSWERS

1 am going to apply 2 will leave 3 is going to fall
4 will be lying 5 is going 6 will have finished 7 'll get

4 Demonstrate this by telling the class about your own future plans. Allow a few minutes for students to write their responses. Emphasise that they should write them in any order. Go round checking and pointing out any errors. Students work in pairs trying to guess which category each activity comes under.

5 Explain *resolutions* and that we traditionally make them on New Year's Eve (and often break them the next day!). Tell the class about any resolutions you have made and whether or not you stuck to them. Allow a minute or two for students to think of resolutions and write them down. They work in pairs comparing resolutions.

ALTERNATIVE PROCEDURE: students tell the whole class about their resolutions. Have any students made the same 'resolutions'? How are they going to stick to them?

FURTHER PRACTICE: **First Certificate Gold Exam Maximiser Unit 9, p.68.**

Listening: an addict's story p.94

1 Focus attention on the gist questions. Play the cassette once straight through and elicit the answers.

TAPESCRIPT

RP = radio presenter L = Lawrence

RP: Now, Lawrence, you've described yourself as a 'shopaholic', haven't you?

L: Yes, well, in fact, we don't much like that term. We prefer to be called 'over-spenders'.

RP: But whatever you call it, <u>it's a very common impulse, isn't it? I mean, we all have bad days and at the end of them think ... oh well, to heck with that, I'm off down to buy myself something to make myself feel better.</u>

L: Oh agreed, but you don't do it 365 days a year. Erm ... and it's a case really of physically buying ten or twenty of everything.

RP: Ten or twenty of everything?

L: ... to start with, and not even remember doing it.

RP: So, what sort of things are you buying by the dozen?

L: <u>Anything. It can be ... er ... it can be food, it can be tapes, clothes. It can be dolls' houses. It can be anything.</u>

RP: So, when you get home, I mean, do you enj-, do you get any fun out of twenty pairs of shoes or twenty CDs or whatever? Or did you yourself go away and hide them because you were ashamed of them? I mean did you enjoy it at all?

L: <u>Well, at first, you enjoy the experience, er, you know, you get the famous 'buzz'...</u>

RP: So what happens when the bank statements arrive?

L: Oh, that's easy – erm, you hide them. <u>You just pretend they're not there. They haven't arrived. They've just got lost in the post.</u>

RP: So how bad did it get for you then?

L: Me? I went into about £30,000 of unpaid ...

RP: <u>£30,000 worth of debt?</u>

L: Yeah.

RP: And were you married?

L: Yes. I had a long suffering wife who could not understand what was going on until 1993 when she found a threatening letter from our bank.

RP: And have you ever really found out why you did it?

L: Oh yes, yes. <u>In my case it was my childhood ... where I was constantly ... er ... doing without,</u> and being envious and jealous of other kids. And then when I was fifteen, I discovered I could spend and my parents couldn't stop me. All you had to do was to sign on the dotted line.

RP: So, how did you manage to stop it then?

L: Well, it was quite simple really. When Marlene, my wife, found out, <u>she said, either I had to see someone or she would leave. So I started seeing a hypnotherapist, which really helped, and Marlene became like my manager ... and together we started to sort things out.</u>

RP: So, what did you do with all the stuff in the house?

L: <u>Gave it away to charity.</u> I gave away over 3000 records and tapes at one point and that was just the beginning ...

ANSWERS

1 He was addicted to shopping. 2 Yes.

2 Tell students to read through the True/False statements and check understanding of key vocabulary e.g. *bank statements, compensating, professional help*. Play the cassette again. Let students compare their answers before listening for a second time. Again allow comparison of answers and then check them by replaying the relevant sections of the cassette to the whole class.

ANSWERS

(see underlined sentences in tapescript)
1 True 2 False 3 True 4 False 5 True 6 True 7 False
8 True 9 False 10 False

Vocabulary: shopping p.94

1 Do this exercise with the whole class, explaining any unknown vocabulary as you go along.

ANSWERS

1 g); 2 a); 3 d); 4 c); 5 f); 6 e); 7 b)

2 Students work individually before comparing their answers with a partner and then with the whole class.

ANSWERS

1 bargains/sales 2 queue/value 3 loose/size
4 assistant/change 5 refund/receipt 6 charge/delivered
7 suits/matches 8 label/silk 9 stock/order
10 wallet/credit 11 wrong/guarantee

3 Students discuss the questions in pairs. Remind them to answer in more than single sentences.

ALTERNATIVE PROCEDURE: conduct an open-class discussion.

FURTHER PRACTICE: First Certificate Gold Exam Maximiser Unit 9, p.68.

Listening: a complaint p.95

1 Focus attention on the pictures and ask students to describe each one.

Play the cassette through once while students put the pictures in order. They compare answers in pairs and then open-class.

TAPESCRIPT

SA = shop assistant C = customer

SA: Yes, can I help you?

C: Yes, I hope so. You see I bought this personal stereo here last week, and I'm afraid it hasn't really matched up to what I was told about it.

SA: I see. What exactly is the matter?

C: Well, first of all, can you see there's this large scratch across the front of it?

SA: But you should have noticed that when you bought it.

C: But it was in the box and all sealed up.

SA: Well, I'm sorry but it really is your responsibility to check the goods when you buy them. How are we to know that it wasn't you who made the scratch?

C: That's ridiculous. But anyway, it's not the most important thing.

SA: Yes ...?

C: Well, you know it's not supposed to need new batteries for ten hours, well it definitely does.

SA: Can I ask what batteries you have been using?

C: Surely that shouldn't make any difference?

SA: I think you'll find you'll have no problems if you use the batteries that we sell here.

C: But these are twice as expensive as the batteries I normally use.

SA: But you will find they are worth it because you get so much more playing time out of them.

C: But the whole point was supposed to be that I could buy ordinary batteries ... oh, never mind. But look, I really am not happy about this other thing.

SA: And what is that?

C: Look, it says here that the noise from it should be undetectable by other people.

SA: Yes, that's right.

C: But, people *can* hear it and it's really embarrassing on the bus and the underground. People keep giving me funny looks.

SA: Well, I'm sorry, but it must be the way you are wearing the headphones. We've certainly never had any complaints like this before.

C: Look, I know how to put earphones in my ears,

thank you very much. But what I want to know is what you are going to do about it all.

SA: Well, I suppose we could exchange it for another model if you really aren't happy with it.

C: No, I certainly am not.

SA: Well, if I could just have the receipt ...

C: Ah yes, well, there is a slight problem about the receipt ...

ANSWERS

1 personal stereo; 2 batteries; 3 noise; 4 receipt

2 Play the cassette again, pausing after each section for students to note down what is said.

ANSWERS

1 Batteries don't last long, customer doesn't want to buy batteries sold in shop because too expensive
A scratch on front of the personal stereo, shop assistant says he should have seen it when he bought it
A problem with the receipt
People can hear noise from the personal stereo on the bus, etc.

2 c)

3 Students work in pairs trying to remember who said what and to complete the sentences from memory. Play the cassette again for them to check their answers and fill in any missing words. Pause after each sentence if necessary.

ANSWERS

1 I see. *What exactly is the* matter? (shop assistant)

2 But you should *have noticed that when you* bought it. (shop assistant)

3 That's ridiculous. But anyway, *it's not the most important* thing. (customer)

4 Well, you know it's *not supposed to need new batteries* for ten hours. (customer)

5 Look, it says here *that the noise from it should be* undetectable by other people. (customer)

6 We've certainly never *had any complaints like this* before. (shop assistant)

7 Well, I suppose *we could exchange it for another* model. (shop assistant)

8 Well, if I *could just have the* receipt. (shop assistant)

Speaking p.95

1 & **2** Students practise roleplaying the situation on the cassette. A strong pair could act out their roleplay in front of the rest of the class. In pairs they practise two of the other situations. Go round checking that they have sufficient vocabulary for their particular role. Let them write if they want to, but encourage them to learn their parts. They need not memorise word for word. Get a couple of pairs to act out their roleplay for the rest of the class. They then practise and act out the roleplay(s) in 2.

ALTERNATIVE PROCEDURE: divide the class into two teams. Students from each team mime the situations for the other team. The team have to work out what the situation is and exactly how to make the complaint in correct English. If they do this within a three-minute time limit, they win a point. If they don't, the mimer's team wins a point.

Writing: a letter of complaint p.96

1 Students work in pairs classifying the phrases/sentences.

ANSWERS

1 F; 2 I; 3 I; 4 F; 5 F; 6 F; 7 I; 8 F

2 Students work in pairs completing Mike's letter.

POSSIBLE ANSWER

... that the personal stereo had a scratch across the front. The shop assistant I spoke to said it was my responsibility to check for scratches before leaving the shop. This would, however, have been impossible as the personal stereo was in a plastic-covered box.

A more serious problem is the fact that although your advertisement says that the personal stereo will run for ten hours on the same batteries, this is not the case. I had to change the batteries after only five hours of use. Once again the shop assistant was very uncooperative when I mentioned this and told me that I should buy the extremely expensive batteries you sell.

I also pointed out that although the personal stereo was supposed to be completely inaudible to those around me, I had noticed that people on the bus and train often looked at me. I am sure they were irritated by the noise. The shop assistant tried to convince me that I was not using the headphones properly.

He finally agreed to exchange the faulty personal stereo for another one as long as I could provide the receipt. When I explained that I had accidentally thrown it away, he refused to exchange the personal stereo, which I think was very unfair since he knew very well that I had bought it in your shop.

3 **1** Students work individually before comparing answers with a partner and then with the whole class.

ANSWERS

1 e); 2 c); 3 g); 4 b); 5 d); 6 h); 7 f); 8 a)

2 Students brainstorm, plan and draft their letters with the partner they worked with in the **Speaking** activity on page 95. The writing itself can be done in class or for homework. Use the correction code on pages 7–8 of the *Introduction* to mark students' work. Allow time in the next class for students to work on the errors you have marked.

Unit 9 Review

ANSWERS

1 *The kitchen contains the following objects:* cooker, grill, oven, saucepan, frying pan, spatula, sieve, cheese-grater, chopping board, knife/chopped onion, herbs and spices, knives/forks/spoons, napkins, salt and pepper, plates, vegetable dishes, serving spoons.

2 a) *a ladle* is used for serving soups and sauces or transferring them from one saucepan to another; *a spatula* is used for turning over eggs or other fried foods.
b) *to fry* involves the use of fat or oil; *to boil* involves water or some other liquid.
c) *a bowl* is rounded and will hold liquids; *a plate* is flat and will not hold liquids.
d) *a cooker* includes an oven, a grill and gas burners or hot plates; *an oven* is the part of the cooker (or possibly a separate item) used for roasting and baking.
e) *well-done* means cooked for a long period of time generally applied to meat; *tough* is sometimes the result of meat being over-cooked, so that it becomes hard to chew.
f) *tight* means too small and close fitting; *loose* the opposite of *tight*.
g) *a bargain* is an individual item bought for less than the normal price; *a sale* is a number of items offered for sale at a reduced price.

h) *to suit* means to look good on someone; *to fit* means to be the right size for someone.
i) *a receipt* is a piece of paper listing goods and the amount paid for them; *a recipe* is a list of instructions on how to cook a dish.

3 1 up 2 with 3 down 4 out 5 off 6 by 7 down 8 through 9 up

4 1 the 2 bit 3 the 4 lots/plenty 5 pieces 6 other/fourth 7 information 8 advice 9 a 10 pair 11 bed 12 a 13 my 14 a 15 waste

Now your students are ready to do the test for Unit 9 on page 131.

UNIT

10 How to make a fortune

Reading p.98

1 Provide a brief explanation of the headline of the article, it is a play on the word *pack*. (*Pack* here is a novel spelling and shortened form of the word *packaging*.) There was a hit song in the 1960's called *Leader of the Pack* about a girl whose parents didn't want her to go out with a boy who was the leader of a motorcycle gang or 'pack'. Lead an open-class discussion in which you encourage students to speculate about the questions. Don't indicate whether their answers are right or wrong.

2 Set a time limit for the gist task.

ANSWERS

Erik Wallenberg, a scientist who says he actually designed the first TetraPak for Ruben Rausing.

3 Remind students about the suggested procedure on p. 23. They work individually before comparing their answers with a partner and then open-class.

ANSWERS

1 H; 2 C; 3 F; 4 B; 5 G; 6 D; 7 A; Sentence E is not used.

Grammar: relative clauses and pronouns p.99–100

1 Tell students to spend five minutes studying the information on defining relative clauses and to refer to the relevant section in the *Grammar reference* on page 173 (14).

Students work individually before comparing their answers with a partner and then with the whole class.

ANSWERS

1 i) *where* 2 h) (*which/that*) 3 a) *whose* 4 g) *where*
5 d) *who/that* 6 b) *where* 7 c) *which/that*
8 e) *who/that* 9 f) (*which/that*)

2 Tell students to spend five minutes studying the information on non-defining relative clauses and to refer to the relevant section in the *Grammar reference* on page 173 (14).

Students work individually writing the sentences. Go round checking and helping where necessary. Go through the answers with the whole class.

ANSWERS

1 We went to Spain, *where* there are fantastic beaches.
2 I'm looking forward to my birthday, *which* is next month.
3 My present car, *which* is three years old, is a grey Saab.
4 I'm seeing Carol, *whose* parents are on holiday, this evening.
5 My boss, *who* I don't get on with, wants to see me.
6 I read that new book by Iain Banks, *which* Pete lent to me, and I enjoyed it.
7 Matt, *who* I've been friends with since university, is going to be best man at my wedding.
8 Thank you for the birthday card, *which* I got on Friday.

3 1 Give students a few minutes to think about the relative pronouns and then do the exercise round the class.

ANSWERS

a) essential b) essential c) essential d) can be omitted
e) can be omitted

2 Demonstrate this first by telling students about yourself referring to the underlined words. Students work in pairs and report back to the rest of the class on what their partner told them.

*FURTHER PRACTICE: **First Certificate Gold Exam Maximiser** **Unit 10, p.72.** (Students should do the Reading on pp.70–71 first.)*

Vocabulary: do/make p.100

1 Focus attention on the sentence from the text and elicit other nouns that go with *make*. Tell students to make two columns headed *do* and *make* in their notebooks. Students work individually before comparing answers with a partner and then with the whole class.

> **ANSWERS**
>
> **do:** business, homework, the washing-up, a favour, one's best, harm, a test.
>
> **make:** an arrangement, a mistake, money, a decision, the bed, a noise, a complaint, sure, fun of, an excuse, a choice, an effort, a phone call, a profit, peace.

2 Students work in pairs writing their stories. If possible, get them to write their final versions on an overhead transparency so that they can be displayed and read by the rest of the class, or ask them to write on sheets of paper so that you can display them on a noticeboard.

ALTERNATIVE PROCEDURE: students write their stories individually for homework. In the next class they read their stories aloud while the class notes all the instances of *do* and *make* to see who used these verbs the most.

FURTHER PRACTICE: First Certificate Gold Exam Maximiser **Unit 10, p.70.**

Vocabulary: money p.101

1 Group the students so that stronger members of the class are evenly distributed through the three groups.

Students should refer to dictionaries for words they do not understand. Monitor and give help where necessary.

2 Make sure that each group has a representative from Groups A, B and C. They explain their words to one another.

3 Students discuss the questions in pairs or groups. Tell them to use the vocabulary they have just studied as much as possible.

Watch Out! *earn/win/gain*

> **ANSWERS**
>
> 1 won 2 gained 3 earn

win = to be the best or first in a struggle or competition
gain = to have an increase, to get something useful or wanted or to become stronger or more popular
earn = to get money by working or something that you deserve because of your qualities or actions
You **win** competitions and contests, contracts, someone's approval, arguments or someone's heart.

You **gain** weight and strength, an advantage, someone's support or someone's attention.
You **earn** money or someone's respect.

4 Focus students' attention on the sayings and elicit possible paraphrases e.g. *Money is the cause of all the problems in the world./We couldn't function without money.* and conduct a discussion with the whole class. Ask students if they know any other sayings related to money in English e.g. *Look after the pennies and the pounds will look after themselves.* (Be careful with spending small amounts and you will be able to save money easily.); *Money doesn't grow on trees.* (There isn't a limitless supply of money available.); *There's no use throwing/Don't throw good money after bad.* (Don't waste more money on something that has already cost too much as you risk losing again.) Discuss equivalent sayings in students' language(s) or whether they know other sayings connected with money.

EXTRA ACTIVITY: conduct a class debate on the topic of money. Divide the class into two groups. One group should prepare to argue for the motion *Money is the root of all evil*, the second group for the motion *Money makes the world go round*. Each group chooses a representative to argue their case. If possible, invite other classes to join your group to listen to the debate and finally vote in favour of one of the motions.

FURTHER PRACTICE: First Certificate Gold Exam Maximiser **Unit 10, p.73.**

Speaking p.102

Read the situation aloud to the class or get students to read it silently. Set a time limit of three minutes for them to read the information about each of the candidates. Check that they understand key vocabulary e.g. *fluent, charity, refugee*. Refer them to *Functions: giving opinions agreeing/disagreeing* on page 62. They work in pairs and agree on two candidates to select. Go round monitoring and making a note of any errors with the language of expressing opinions and of agreeing and disagreeing to go over when students have finished. Discuss students' decisions with the whole class. How many pairs chose the same candidates? Is there a candidate that no one chose? Draw their attention to any errors you heard without saying who made them.

ALTERNATIVE PROCEDURE: do this as a pyramid discussion. Once a pair have agreed on two candidates, they make a group of four with another pair with whom they must also come to an agreement. The groups of four combine and once more reach an agreement and so on until the whole class has agreed to send the same candidates. Throughout the discussion monitor errors as above.

Writing: an application p.103

1 Read the exam information aloud to the class. Students read the application and discuss with a partner which of the applicants it is from. How would this application influence their decision to choose this candidate or not?

ANSWER
It is from Javier.

2 Students work individually before comparing their answers in pairs and then with the whole class. If possible, write the corrected version on an overhead transparency so that students can correct their versions.

CORRECTED VERSION

I arrived in London <u>three months ago</u> with my wife and <u>two young children</u>. Since then I <u>have tried very hard</u> to get a job (in my country I was a lawyer). However, <u>my English isn't very good</u> and I think this is the reason why I <u>haven't found a job yet.</u> I <u>always seem</u> to have problems when I have to speak at interviews. I am sure that if I could improve my <u>spoken English</u>, I would <u>be able to get a job</u> and <u>support my family</u>.

I have done my best to improve my English since I arrived. I have studied <u>grammar books</u> and listened to the radio, but <u>it is quite difficult</u> to meet people so that I can practise my speaking. I think that having <u>regular language classes</u> would really help me and I am very keen to start <u>as soon as possible</u>. I know what a <u>good reputation</u> <u>your school has</u> and <u>I would be very grateful</u> if you would <u>seriously consider</u> my application.

3 Students write their applications for homework. Mark them using the correction code and paying particular attention to word order.

Vocabulary: numbers p.103

1 Emphasise the structure of the pyramid: tens, hundred, thousands, tens of thousands, hundreds of thousands, millions, tens of millions, before students write their own pyramids for their partners to say. Monitor and corrrect pronunciation of the numbers.

2 Check that students understand the words or tell them to use a dictionary. They work individually before checking their answers in pairs

ANSWERS
a) 10; b) 4; c) 11; d) 12; e) 3; f) 5; g) 8; h) 2; i) 6; j) 7; k) 1; l) 9

3 Get individual students to say the items. Correct, if necessary, before getting the whole class to repeat.

ANSWERS/TAPESCRIPT
a) a quarter
b) nought point two five
c) three nil
d) forty fifteen
e) oh one seven one four nine one two five nine eight
f) thirtieth of the sixth ninety-five
g) one metre sixty-five centimetres
h) eighty-five kilos
i) seventy-eight per cent
j) thirty-two degrees centigrade
k) eighty-five miles per hour
l) fourteen pounds five pence

4 This information gap activity must be done in pairs.

Watch Out!: '0'

football = nil; *tennis* = love; *telephone numbers* = oh; *decimal numbers* = nought; *percentages/temperatures* = zero

FURTHER PRACTICE: **First Certificate Gold Exam Maximiser Unit 10, p.76.**

Exam focus: Paper 5 Speaking: Part 3 (collaborative task) p.104

ADVANCE PREPARATION: Make copies of the interlocutors' scripts and assessors' check lists.

Read the exam information and advice aloud to the class.

1 Focus attention on the descriptions of candidates' use of language. Explain that for item 1 there is only one example on the tape whereas for the others there are several. Play the tape. Students work individually noting examples, before checking answers open-class. Point out that agreeing can be achieved by saying 'no' and that disagreement is usually prefaced by token agreement, e.g. *yes, but…*

ALTERNATIVE PROCEDURE: Give students copies of the tapescript and ask them to underline the examples.

TAPESCRIPT

I = Interlocutor   M = Maria   A = Ana

I: I'd like you to imagine that you are trying to raise money for an 'end-of-year' trip for your English class. Here are some ideas for fund-raising activities. Talk to each other about the various suggestions, saying how effective you think they would be, and then choose one activity from each group. All right? You have about three minutes for this, so don't worry if I stop you and please speak so that we can hear you.

M: Shall we start?

A: Umm. Can I just check something? Are we supposed to talk about all the activities or just the ones we choose?

I: You can talk about all the activities and then choose one from each group.

A: Okay. Thank you.

M: Right. A Karaoke night would probably be quite good fun, don't you think?

A: Yeah, it would, but I'm not sure that we would make much money from it. Those machines are quite expensive to hire.

M: Are they? I didn't know that. Perhaps we could have a fashion parade instead. Lots of people in the FCE class have very fashionable clothes.

A: Yes, that's a good idea. They could just wear their own clothes. You know, new clothes they've just bought or their favourite outfit.

M: Yes, exactly. That way it wouldn't cost very much at all and we could charge for other students to come along and watch the parade.

A: I think it would be more fun than the second-hand book sale, don't you?

M: Yes. Much more fun. Anyway, a lot of people don't like to sell their old books.

A: No, I like to keep my books. Well, what about a fund-raising activity for outside school? I mean for members of the public. I don't think a fun run is a very good idea. It's too hot at this time of year.

M: Mmm, I suppose so, but if we have it in the evening it would be much cooler.

A: Yes. It sounds a bit difficult to organise. I like the idea of a street stall. We could make some snacks and sell them, could we?

M: Yes and some people might have old CDs or magazines that they want to sell or even things that they have made themselves, clothes or furniture.

A: And, there are a couple of people who paint and they might like to sell their paintings. Anyway, it sounds better than cleaning windows. That sounds like too much hard work to me.

M: Yes, to me too. Anyway, I don't think offering that kind of thing would work here do you?

A: No. Most people either do those kind of jobs themselves or pay someone to do it professionally.

M: So let's go for the fashion parade and the street stall.

A: Yeah, I agree.

I: Thank you.

ANSWERS
(see underlined answers in typescript)
1 Can I just check something?
2 … don't you think?/… could we?
3 Yeah/Are they?
4 Perhaps we could/what about
5 Yes, that's a good idea/Yes, exactly/Yeah, I agree
6 … but I'm not sure that/I suppose so, but

2 Ask the interlocutors and examiners to come to the front of the room so that you can give them their instructions: Give each 'interlocutor' a slip of paper with the following script:

This is what you must say to the two candidates. Do NOT show them this piece of paper.

I'd like you to imagine that you are trying to raise money for an 'end-of-year' trip for your English class. On page 104 there are some ideas for fund-raising activities. Talk to each other about the various suggestions saying how effective you think they would be and then choose one activity from each group. All right? You have about three minutes for this, so don't worry if I stop you and please speak so that we can hear you.

Tell them to stop the two candidates when they have been speaking for three minutes by saying **'thank you'**.

Tell them that they should think about how well each candidate communicated and how well they performed the task and give them a mark out of five for Part 3.

Give the 'assessor' the following checklist:

Explain that they should give each candidate a mark out of five in each category:

	Candidate A	Candidate B
Grammar and vocabulary		
Pronunciation		
Discourse management*		
Interactive communication**		

* Did the candidate express her/his ideas and opinions clearly? Did s/he do what the interlocutor told her/him to do?

** Did the candidate respond to the other candidate naturally? Did s/he ask the other candidate for her/his opinion, suggestions and ideas? Did s/he let the other candidate speak?

Explain that the assessors can take notes of performance. any good use of vocabulary, any errors or anything that particularly impressed them about the 'candidates'.

Tell the two 'examiners' that they can compare marks before explaining their assessment to the two candidates.

Move around the room monitoring the task and noting any good use of language, any errors or anything that particularly impresses you.

When all groups have finished, conduct a de-briefing session in which you write up your notes on the board and allow students to raise any problems they encountered in performing the task.

3   Follow the same procedure with the new examiners.

Give each new interlocutor a slip of paper with the following script:

I'd like you to imagine that you have been given the task of furnishing a one bedroom flat for students, spending no more than £1000. At the bottom of page 206 there are some things you might buy. Talk to each other about how important some of these things might be and decide which three you would not buy. All right? You have about three minutes for this, so don't worry if I stop you and please speak so that we can hear you.

Tell them to stop the two candidates when they have been

speaking for three minutes by saying **'thank you'**.

Explain that they should give each candidate a grade out of five for communication and task performance.

Give the assessor her/his instructions and the assessor's checklist.

Once again, move around the room monitoring the task and noting any good use of language, any errors or anything that particularly impresses you.

Finally, when all groups have finished, conduct a de-briefing session in which you write up your notes on the board and allow students to raise any problems they encountered in performing the task.

Listening: inventors p.105

1   Focus attention on the photos and ask students if they are familiar with these two inventions. What do they know about them? Which one do they think has made the most money?

Students work individually putting the numbers into the texts before discussing their answers in pairs and then with the whole class.

ANSWERS

1) 55 million 2) 15/9/79 3) 45 4) 6 5) 120 billion

2   Play the cassette through once so that students can answer the question.

TAPESCRIPT

RP1 = first radio presenter RP2 = second radio presenter DP = Dick Payne

RP1:   Good evening and welcome to this week's edition of *Money Matters*, the programme that takes a closer look at issues of finance that matter to you. And this week we look at how you can invent your way to riches.

RP2:   'Make a better mousetrap,' said the American writer Ralph Emerson, 'and the world will make a beaten path to your door.' But sadly this isn't true, as hundreds of inventors find out every year. Making a commercial success out of your back-of-an-envelope ideas is by no means an easy process. However, for some, the rewards are clearly worth the effort. The creators of Trivial Pursuit and Post-It notes among others, all became multi-millionaires – eventually. So, what are the secrets of successful invention? We spoke to Dick Payne, marketing manager of Inventorlink, the only company that specialises in matching inventors to firms with a need for their invention.

DP: Well, ideally you shouldn't start with the invention at all. You should look for a gap in the market, and then come up with the idea to fill it. We receive over a thousand ideas every year and we see about 300 inventors to take ideas further.

RP1: And what are the hallmarks of a successful invention?

DP: Really, that first it's original and secondly that it's wanted.

RP1: Unfortunately, even when an invention is original and it's wanted, some inventors never see any of the profits that come from the commercial exploitation of their ideas. The creator of the first wire coat-hanger didn't receive a cent for his ingenious invention. In 1903, Albert J. Parkhouse was working for a company in Jackson, Michigan, manufacturing wire lampshade frames. The firm was too mean to provide enough hooks for its employees to hang up their coats, so one day, rather than throw his coat on the floor, Parkhouse twisted a piece of wire into the now familiar shape of a hanger. His employer noticed what he'd done, immediately understood its potential and patented the idea. Parkhouse just went on working on the shop floor of the factory.

RP2: And then of course there was the case of John Styth Pemberton, an Atlanta pharmacist. A self-styled inventor his previous work had included Globe of Flower Cough Syrup and French Wine Coca, but in 1886 he put together and brewed a mix of cola nuts, coca leaves, caffeine and other unlikely ingredients in an old iron bath in his backyard. He stirred it all together with a wooden oar from an old boat and called it Coca-Cola. His bookkeeper, Frank Robinson, who was very good at calligraphy, drew up the logo that Coke uses to this day. Pemberton saw his invention not as the refreshing thirstquencher that the world has come to love, but as an effective tonic for hangovers and other ills of the upper body. It was also suggested that it was a powerful aphrodisiac. Unfortunately Pemberton failed to see Coca-Cola's true potential. In 1887, he sold a two-thirds interest in the company for the sum of $283.29 cents. It took another Atlanta pharmacist, Asa G. Candler, to capitalise on Coca-Cola's true possibilities as a money-making refreshment. Just before the turn of the century he bought the formula from its new owners for $2,000 and with clever marketing turned his investment into a fortune. By 1919,

when the company was sold again, Candler's $2,000 investment had grown in value to $25 million.

ANSWERS

Trivial Pursuit, Post-it notes, coat hangers and Coca-Cola are all mentioned.

3 Give students time to read through the sentences they have to complete. Emphasise that they only need to write a few words and that they don't always have to write exactly what is said on the cassette.

ANSWERS

1 It is not easy to **make money** out of an invention.

2 Richard Payne's company specialises in **matching inventors** to companies.

3 The first thing he says you should do is to find **a gap in the market**.

4 The two things that make an invention which makes money are that it is **original and it's wanted**.

5 In Parkhouse's office there was nowhere for employees to **hang their coats.**

6 Pemberton created Coca-Cola in the year **1886**.

7 The original Coca-Cola logo was drawn by **Frank Robinson**.

8 Pemberton sold his claim to the Coca-Cola fortune for **$283.29**.

9 Candler made Coca-Cola into a huge success through (**clever) marketing.**

4 Students work in groups of three or four.

ALTERNATIVE PROCEDURE: give students time to decide individually on the invention they regard as most significant and then conduct an open-class discussion. Are there any other significant and useful inventions that are not illustrated?

Exam focus Paper 3 Use of English: Part 1 (multiple choice cloze) p.106

Read the exam information and advice on procedure aloud to the class. Focus attention on the images of coins and ask the students if they recognise any of them. Ask if they know where and when the first coins were used and what metals have been used most often for minting coins. Put their ideas up on the board. Tell them to read the text quickly to see if they were right.

ANSWERS

1 A; 2 B; 3 C; 4 A; 5 B; 6 C; 7 C; 8 C; 9 B; 10 D; 11 D; 12 C; 13 A; 14 B; 15 D

Units 6–10 Progress check

ANSWERS

1 1 C; 2 A; 3 D; 4 A; 5 D; 6 B; 7 A; 8 B; 9 D; 10 C; 11 C; 12 D; 13 D; 14 B; 15 A

2 1 When I leave school, **I will/am going to** look for a job in a hotel.
2 I think **I'll go** to bed now, I'm very tired.
3 I promise **I'll phone** you tonight.
4 I can't come this Tuesday because **I'm playing** volleyball.
5 If **I see** her, I will give her your love.
6 **Will you make** my bed for me this morning? I'm too tired.

3 1 way 2 some 3 start/begin 4 recipes 5 Make 6 make 7 everything 8 than 9 something 10 important 11 times 12 should 13 will/might/may/could 14 which 15 who

4 1 I *did my best*, but I still didn't pass.
2 My parents *have known each other since* 1970.
3 I *don't agree with* you about military service.
4 He has too much *time on his hands* since he retired.
5 I don't think I will ever *get used to driving* on the left.
6 Can you *work out* the answers to these sums?
7 She promised *not to tell* anyone about what happened.
8 The operator had trouble *putting me through* to the sales department.
9 I *used to live* in London as a child.
10 Would you *mind sharing* your book with me?

5 1 B: Yes, of course you **can**.
2 Her parents gave a party when they heard she had successfully **passed** all her exams.
3 My family **have lived** in the city since 1963.
4 You **lay** the table while I finish cooking the dinner.

5 He **won** a really big prize in the National Lottery.
6 I **finished** school two years ago.
7 I'm sorry. I **do not agree** with you.
8 You ought **to take** up jogging.
9 **From** my point of view, spending a lot of money on expensive clothes is stupid.
10 You really **should go** and see that film. It's fantastic.

6 1 playground/hurt 2 headmaster/cheating 3 row/group 4 plot/characters 5 pyjamas/slippers 6 temperature/prescription 7 healed/bruises 8 scrambled/boiled/fried 9 Pour/sprinkle/grated 10 suits/bargain 11 assistant/order/size 12 withdraw/account/cheque

7 *line 3:* delete *have*
line 4: delete *going*
line 5: delete *do*
line 7: delete *would*
line 8: delete *for*
line 9: delete *it*
line 11: delete *they*
line 12: delete *than*
line 15: delete *got*

8 1 competitive 2 athletics 3 energetic 4 distance 5 performance 6 preparation 7 unnecessary 8 Successful 9 psychological 10 strength

9 1 keep up with 2 put up with 3 put off 4 gave back 5 give out 6 gave away 7 speak up 8 give up 9 put me up 10 gave in 11 put up 12 put by

Now your students are ready to do the Progress test for Units 6–10 on pages 132–134.

UNIT
11 The planet Earth

Reading pp.110–111

1 Elicit descriptions of the photos and the picture open-class.

2 Students work in pairs using their dictionaries to find definitions of words they do not know.

3 Divide the class into two groups, A and B. Students read their text silently before discussing what information is missing with other members of the group. Check that each group is focussing on the right kind of missing information.

4 Students discuss what questions are needed with other members of the group and write their questions down. Go round helping where necessary and pointing out any errors with question form.

5 Pair a student from Group A with a student from Group B. Seat them so that they will not be tempted to show each other their texts. Encourage students to ask for spelling of any new/unfamiliar words in the answers so as to practise the pronunciation of the letters of the alphabet.

POSSIBLE QUESTIONS AND ANSWERS
Group A

1) What is the study and forecasting of weather called? *Meteorology.*
3) What did it rain on Paris in AD 582? *Blood.*
5) What had the red dust done to the rain? *It had dyed it.*
7) How many kilometres away did the tornado put the children down? *Twenty.*
9) Who believed that the Earth lay on the back of a giant tortoise? *The Algonquin Indians.*
11) What did the ancient Japanese legend say caused earthquakes? *The movement of a vast underground spider.*
13) How many tornados on average strike the USA each year? *Seven hundred and eight.*
15) How many people died in the tornadoes in 1974? *Three hundred and fifteen.*
17) What should you get rid of during a thunderstorm? *Any metal you are carrying.*
19) In what year was the woman struck by lightning in her kitchen? *1982.*

Group B

2) Which great philosopher and scientist had the idea about how meteors were formed? *Aristotle.*
4) What is the name of the wind that blows from the Sahara across the Mediterranean and Europe? *The sirocco.*
6) Who/What was sucked up by a tornado in west China? *Twelve school children.*
8) Where have the highest wind speeds occurred? *At the top of Mount Washington in New Hampshire, USA.*
10) What did the Algonquin Indians believe about the Earth? *That it lay on the back of a giant tortoise.*
12) Who/What did the ancient Greeks think were wrestling underground? *Huge giants.*
14) In what year did 148 tornadoes hit the United States? *1974*
16) What shouldn't you shelter under if you're stuck out in a storm? *A tall isolated tree.*
18) What should you do if you're with other people? *Spread out.*
20) What was the woman holding? *A tea strainer.*

Grammar: the article pp.112–113

1 Tell students to read through the rules and examples silently. Students work individually matching the rules before checking the answers with the whole class.

ANSWERS
1 j); 2 e); 3 d); 4 b); 5 c); 6 k); 7 h); 8 i); 9 a); 10 g); 11 f)

Remind students to look at pages 163–164 of the *Grammar reference* to see if there are any other instances of article use not specifically highlighted here.

2 Students work individually before comparing their answers with a partner and then with the whole class.

ANSWERS
1 the 2 a 3 the 4 a 5 the 6 (–) 7 (–) 8 the 9 (–) 10 (–) 11 the 12 the 13 the 14 (–)

Ask students to match each of the sentences to the rules in Exercise 1. Allow a minute or so for students to work individually before checking through with the whole class.

ANSWERS

1 f); 2 i); 3 e); 4 i); 5 g); 6 k); 7 j); 8 f); 9 k); 10 k); 11 a); 12 c); 13 d); 14 j)

3 Tell students to check their record of mistakes and check yours as well. Write up some examples of mistakes you and your students have noted. In a monolingual class draw students' attention to any L1 interference errors with the article. Go over the rules for the article which students have broken in their errors.

4 Students work in pairs before checking their answers with the whole class.

ALTERNATIVE PROCEDURE: do this round the class with each student reading a sentence and saying whether the articles need to be added anywhere.

ANSWERS

The Dead Sea, which lies between Jordan and Israel, is the lowest lake in the world. It is about 397 metres below sea level and it contains the saltiest water in the world. This is because several rivers carrying minerals (including salt) flow into the lake, but none flow out of it. The surface water evaporates, but all the minerals remain behind. The salt makes it easy for swimmers to float – you can even read a book while floating on your back. In fact the lake contains six times more salt than ordinary sea water, so a swimmer's body is six times more buoyant than usual.

FURTHER PRACTICE: First Certificate Gold Exam Maximiser **Unit 11, p.79.**

Vocabulary: weather p.113

1 Tell students to make headings in their notebooks and ask if they know any weather words that would fit into these categories before they look at the words in the box. Do the exercise round the class, explaining any items that cause difficulty and providing grammatical information about the words as you go along.

ANSWERS

rain: drizzle (verb = *to rain very lightly; can also be used as an uncountable noun*), pour (verb = *to rain very heavily),* shower (noun = *a short period of light rain*),

hail (noun = *uncountable, small drops of ice that fall from the sky; can also be used as a verb*)

wind: breeze (noun = *a light gentle wind*), gust (noun = *a sudden strong rush of wind*), gale (noun = *a strong wind*)

heat: boiling (adjective = *extremely hot*), warm (adjective = *pleasant but not strong enough to be hot*), sunny (adjective = *full of bright sunlight*), mild (adjective = *not extremely cold or extremely hot*)

cold: freezing (adjective = *extremely cold*), cool (adjective = *slightly cold*), chilly (adjective = *quite cold*), frost (noun = *uncountable, a white powdery substance formed of tiny drops of water that is found on surfaces on very cold days*), snow (noun = *uncountable, also a verb: water frozen into soft white pieces that falls like rain on very cold days*)

wet: damp (adjective = *also an uncountable noun: rather wet often in an unpleasant way*), humid (adjective = *having a lot of wetness in the air and usually very hot*)

2 Students work in pairs before reporting back to the whole class.

ALTERNATIVE PROCEDURE: students prepare mock weather forecasts for their town or region for the times mentioned and the months.

3 Emphasise that students should answer this with more than a single sentence. Ask individuals to tell the class about their weather likes and dislikes and what they like doing during these particular weather conditions e.g. sitting by the fire on a cold wet day; going to the beach when it's sunny.

4 Do this with the whole class.

ANSWERS

1 under the weather = *not very well and/or unhappy*
2 Make hay while the sun shines. = *take advantage of favourable conditions*
3 It never rains but it pours. = *events of the same bad kind seem to come together*
4 as right as rain = *perfectly healthy; quite well*
5 a storm in a teacup = *a lot of worry and nervous annoyance over something insignificant*
6 put the wind up someone = *make someone afraid or anxious*

ALTERNATIVE PROCEDURE: students work individually or in small groups using their monolingual dictionaries to find a definition of *one* of the items only. They also find another weather idiom to teach to the rest of the class e.g. 'I'll be there *come rain or shine.*' 'It really *took the wind out of her sails.'* (Most English – English dictionaries list more idioms under *rain* and *wind*.) Students read out the definitions for the idioms only while you write them on the board. The class matches the definitions to the idioms. Each student or group then 'teaches' the rest of the class one other weather idiom.

5 1 Students work individually before comparing their answers with the whole class.

ANSWERS

heavy: *rain, traffic, smoker, accent*
strong: *wind, tea, opinion, accent*
hard: *winter, bed*
thick: *fog, skin, accent*

---

2 Students work individually before comparing sentences with a partner.

*FURTHER PRACTICE: **First Certificate Gold Exam Maximiser** Unit 11, p.79.*

Pronunciation: homophones p.114

1 Point out that where there are more than two words, two may be the same and the third (and fourth) word(s) the ones which is/are pronounced differently. Students work in pairs before checking their answers with the whole class.

ANSWERS

Note the transcriptions used are phonemic transcriptions based on Received Pronunciation. If you have a different accent (e.g. Scottish, Midlands, New Zealand), teach *your* pronunciation, but point out to students that the phonemic transcriptions in the dictionary represent another variety.

1 different: wind /wɪnd/; (to) wind /waɪnd/
2 same /weðəʳ/
3 same /mɪst/
4 same /pɔː/
5 same /wʌn/
6 same /ðeəʳ/
7 same: bear/bare /beəʳ/
    different: beer /bɪəʳ/
8 different: bird /bɜːd/; beard /bɪəd/
9 same /səʊ/
10 same: wait/weight /weɪt/
    different: white /waɪt/
11 different: hat /hæt/; hate /heɪt/; height /haɪt/
12 same: flower/flour /flaʊəʳ/
    different: floor /flɔːʳ/

---

13 same: wear/where /weəʳ/
    different: were /wəʳ/
    different: we're /wɪəʳ/
14 different: hurt /hɜːt/; heart /hɑːt/
15 same /kɔːt/
16 same /həʊl/
17 different: won't /wəʊnt/; want /wɒnt/
18 same /saɪt/
19 same /sɔː/
20 same: (to) row (a boat)/row (a line of chairs) /rəʊ/
    different: row (an argument) /raʊ/

---

2 Play the cassette or say the words so that students can change any answers they were unsure of. If students know phonemics, write up the transcriptions to illustrate the differences.

3 Pause after each sentence and get students to repeat chorally and individually.

Exam focus: Paper 1 Reading: Part 3 (gapped text) pp.114–115

Read the exam information aloud to the class.

1 Give students time to read the suggested procedure on page 23 and then discuss this and other possible approaches open-class.

2 Students discuss the photos in pairs and compare answers with the whole class. Do not tell them the answers at this stage.

3 Set a three-minute time limit for the gist task.

ANSWERS

1 Easter Island 2 enormous stone statues to be found on the island

---

4 Set a ten-minute time limit for this task. Students compare their answers with a partner before checking with the whole class.

ANSWERS

1 F; 2 C; 3 A; 4 G; 5 B; 6 D

---

5 Check, elicit meanings for or explain the items the students are to consider. They work in groups of three or four discussing the issues. They should appoint a spokesperson to report back to the rest of the class.

ALTERNATIVE PROCEDURE: conduct an open-class discussion.

EXTRA ACTIVITY: students prepare poster presentations on these issues to present to the rest of the class. They choose one of the topics and depict their views in words and pictures.

FURTHER PRACTICE: First Certificate Gold Exam Maximiser **Unit 11, p.78.**

Grammar: modals of deduction/criticism (past) p.116

1 Focus students' attention on the sentences and elicit the answers from the whole class.

> **ANSWERS**
> 1 certainty: *They must have moved ...*
> 2 impossibility: *They can't have moved ...*
> 3 criticism: *They shouldn't have destroyed ...*
> 4 possibility: *They might/could have moved ...*

2 Students work individually before comparing their answers with the whole class. Practise the pronunciation of *must have been/must've been, could have been/could've been,* etc. focussing on the weak form /əv/. Students read the dialogue in pairs paying particular attention to the weak forms. Good pairs can read the dialogue aloud to the rest of the class.

> **ANSWERS**
> 1 have been ill 2 have been ill 3 have forgotten about it 4 have done 5 have stayed at home to work 6 have told me

EXTRA ACTIVITY: tell students to close their books. See how much of the dialogue they can remember. Prompt them by saying the first few words of each sentence: *Do you know ...? Oh no, he ...,* etc.

3 Focus students' attention on the examples. Students work in pairs writing sentences. Go round helping and pointing out any errors particularly of modals of deduction. Get some students to read their sentences out to the rest of the class.

> **POSSIBLE ANSWERS**
> 2 He *must have decided* to work in his father's firm because there were no other possibilities.
>
>   He *might have decided* to work in his father's firm because his father promised him a good job.
>
> 3 He *can't have started* going out with Sophie because he was after her money.
>
>   They *could have started* going out together because they liked each other.
>
>   She *might have started* going out with him because she knew he was the boss's son.
>
> 4 He *can't have loved* Sophie very much if he decided to leave his job and go abroad.
>
>   He *might have decided* to leave his job and go abroad because she started seeing another man.
>
>   He *might have decided* to leave his job and go abroad because he wasn't enjoying the job very much.

4 Demonstrate the task yourself with one of the photos. Students work in pairs before reporting their speculations back to the rest of the class. Whose ideas/speculations are the most interesting?

5 Once again demonstrate the task yourself before giving students a few minutes to make a list of people and criticisms. Students compare answers in pairs and open-class.

FURTHER PRACTICE: First Certificate Gold Exam Maximiser **Unit 11, pp.80–81 (Grammar).**

Vocabulary: problems/disasters p.117

1 Ask students if there have been any major natural disasters in the news recently. Do they remember any major natural disasters in their country? What do they think are the most serious problems threatening the Earth? Supply vocabulary as needed. Check understanding of the words in the box, many of which should have come out in the lead-in. Students complete the sentences individually before comparing their answers with a partner and then with the whole class.

> **ANSWERS**
> 1 famine 2 earthquake 3 emergency 4 refugees 5 charity 6 aid 7 injuries 8 disease 9 drought 10 floods

EXTRA ACTIVITY: ask students which of the sentences would not occur in a news report *(3 and 5)*. Students work in groups of three or four preparing a mock news report including the sentences in Exercise 1. They appoint someone to act as news reader and read their news to the other groups.

2 Students work individually before comparing answers with the whole class. Check that students pronounce the words with correct word stress.

ANSWERS

1 destruction 2 starvation 3 solution 4 demonstration
5 poverty 6 extinction 7 pollution 8 survival

FURTHER PRACTICE: ***First Certificate Gold Exam Maximiser***
Unit 11, p.83.

Listening: Biosphere 2 p.117

1 Focus students' attention on the photo and discuss it with the whole class. Get individual students to describe it, reminding them to answer in more than one sentence. Encourage speculation as to the purpose of the building, where it is, etc. Then tell them about the photograph. It shows Biosphere 2, an experiment by a group of scientists to build a new planet Earth (the scientists regard the Earth as Biosphere 1). Biosphere 2 was completely sealed off from the outside world. It was intended to imitate exactly the functioning of the Earth and as a prototype for communities that could be built on other planets. Explain to the class that the project had many critics and ask what kinds of criticisms they think were made. Ask what kinds of things could go wrong with a project like this.

ANSWER

The photo was taken in the Arizona desert in the USA.

2 Play the cassette once and discuss the gist question with the class.

ANSWER

Generally the experiment has been a failure.

3 Play the cassette again so that students can take notes. Allow two minutes for them to compare answers with a partner before playing the cassette again. Then get individual students to read out their answers before playing the relevant section again so that everybody can check their answers.

TAPESCRIPT
RP = radio presenter JP = Jane Poynter

RP: It was supposed to be the greatest adventure since the Moon landing, a model for the future village on Mars. And 700 days ago, 31-year-old British ecologist Jane Poynter locked herself away in a giant glass bubble in the Arizona desert to become one of the world's first eight 'bionauts'. The group shared a home with 4,000 plants, fish and animals and dreamed of breathing unpolluted air as they grew their own fruit and vegetables in the £100 million Biosphere 2. But as their re-entry into the Earth's atmosphere approaches, the Biosphere is anything but a paradise. Giant insects have invaded the fields and the bionauts are desperately short of food. The pigs were killed after they ate some of the bionauts' chickens. And then the chickens refused to lay any eggs. And the health of the bionauts has suffered badly. At times, the oxygen level fell so low that Jane had to use an oxygen tank to breathe. Thin and pale, she spoke for the first time yesterday about the fight for survival. We contacted her over a phone link through the Biosphere's glass.

JP: At one point, it was so bad that it became very difficult to speak a sentence without panting for breath. At first the hunger was really dreadful, too. I'd go to bed hungry. I'd be hungry at the end of a meal. We just couldn't grow enough.

RP: Now the colour of her skin is orange because of the sweet potatoes they eat.

JP: They're one of the basic foods the insects haven't destroyed. For breakfast today we had them with pinto beans. At the worst moments, I tell myself, 'Imagine what it would be like on Mars. You couldn't leave.'

RP: Jane lives in a two-storey apartment with an electronic system that allows her to contact the outside world. Today, as usual, she was up at dawn to harvest peanuts. In the Biosphere, she is surrounded by a series of microcosmic worlds – a desert, prairie, jungle, marsh, and ocean, complete with a wave machine. Despite the problems, the group in the Biosphere has set a world record for living inside a sealed environment. They don't believe in using pesticides, so they used hairdryers to blow away the insects that destroyed their crops.

The four men and four women originally planned a diet rich in vegetables, jungle fruit, pork, fish, chicken and eggs, with milk from a herd of goats, the only animals to survive. But disaster followed disaster in the project. Jane and Sally both lost more than seven kilos. Jane's boyfriend, Taber

MacCallum, the project's laboratory manager, lost more than twenty kilos. Now Jane cannot wait to be free to enjoy the simple pleasures of life – like country walks and shopping. But like a prisoner released from jail, she wonders if she will ever adjust to the ordinary world again.

ANSWERS

(see underlined sentences in tapescript)

1 The Biosphere cost £100 million.
2 They killed the pigs because they had eaten some of the chickens.
3 Jane sometimes had to use an oxygen tank to breathe.
4 The sweet potatoes turned her skin orange.
5 Instead of insecticides they used hairdryers to stop insects eating their crops.
6 The goats are the only animals that survived.
7 Jane's boyfriend lost twenty kilos.

Speaking p.117

Demonstrate the task yourself by saying what you would take with you and why. Students work individually before comparing answers in groups of two or three.

Writing: transactional letter (2) p.118

Students work in pairs noting down any problems they find with the letter. Discuss the answers with the whole class before asking students to work together to rewrite it. If possible, get students to write their versions on overhead transparencies so they can be read by others.

ANSWERS

The basic problem with the letter is that it is too informal and chatty in style. It is more like a letter to a friend than to an organisation.

POSSIBLE IMPROVED VERSION

Dear Sir/Madam,

I am writing in reply to your advertisement in yesterday's Eco Magazine. I would be very interested in taking part in the voyage you describe, but I have several questions I would like to ask.

I am not a marine biologist, anthropologist or geologist and wonder if any special qualifications are required for crew members. I would also like to know whether crew members have to pay anything towards the cost of the

voyage and what we would be expected to bring with us.

Would it be possible to give an exact date of return? I am starting university in October and need to be sure I will be back before the term begins.

I look forward to receiving your reply.

Yours faithfully,

Dieter Schmidt

FURTHER PRACTICE: *First Certificate Gold Exam Maximiser* **Unit 11, p.77.**

Unit 11 Review

ANSWERS

1 1 C; 2 B; 3 A; 4 A; 5 A; 6 C; 7 B; 8 C; 9 A; 10 D; 11 D; 12 B; 13 D; 14 B; 15 D

2 1 You **shouldn't have sat** in the sun for so long.
2 He **can't have gone** far because the car is still here.
3 The cat **might have scratched** the table
4 She **must have been** here earlier because she's left her umbrella.
5 We **shouldn't have bought** that car.
6 He **could have phoned**, but I haven't been in.
7 She **can't have taken** the money. I've been with her all the time.
8 She **must have gone** to play tennis. She's taken her racket.

Now your students are ready to do the test for Unit 11 on page 135.

U N I T

12 The great persuaders

Reading pp.120–121

1 Check that everyone understands what and where the Eiffel Tower is. Focus on the illustration and ask a student to describe what is happening. Discuss the title, encouraging students to speculate as much as possible.

2 Students work individually before comparing answers with a partner and then the whole class.

ANSWERS

1 g); 2 a); 3 f); 4 h); 5 b); 6 e); 7 d); 8 c)

Ask students if they have any more ideas about what might have happened now that they have looked at these words from the text.

3 Students read the text and discuss whether their speculations were right or wrong open-class. Encourage them to react to what is described in the text.

4 Explain that though this is not an exam-accurate task in that the text is shorter and only five sentences have been removed, they should still follow the procedure for 'Gapped text' outlined on p. 23. Students work individually before checking their answers open-class.

ANSWERS

1 B; 2 D; 3 F; 4 A; 5 E

5 Students work in pairs referring to a dictionary if necessary. Go through the answers open-class.

ANSWERS

2 invitation 3 secret 4 danger 5 explanation
6 unavoidable 7 introduction 8 smooth 9 suspicious
10 repetition

Vocabulary: phrasal verbs (*get*) p.121

1 Focus attention on the sentence from the reading text. Elicit a meaning for 'to get away with something' *(to avoid being caught or punished)*.

Students work in pairs before comparing their answers with the whole class.

ANSWERS

1 b); 2 f); 3 h); 4 a); 5 c); 6 d); 7 e); 8 g)

2 Students work individually before comparing answers with a partner and then with the whole class.

ANSWERS

1 away 2 on 3 up 4 by 5 down 6 over 7 round
8 through

3 Students work individually before checking answers with the whole class.

ANSWERS

1 Why don't you get on with your sister?
2 I've got enough Spanish to get by in everyday situations.
3 How long will it take him to get over this illness?
4 I can always get round her by buying her flowers.
5 What have you been getting up to while I've been away?
6 It is time to get down to business.
7 He is not going to hurt me and get away with it.
8 I phoned the hospital and got through to Dr Jones easily.

FURTHER PRACTICE: **First Certificate Gold Exam Maximiser Unit 12, p.86.**

Grammar: *have to/don't have to/must/need* pp.122–123

1 Discuss the question open-class.

ANSWERS

The Eiffel Tower { ***needs to be*** pulled down
must be pulled down

2 Students discuss the questions in pairs and then open-class.

ANSWERS

1 I had to tell John about the party.

2 a) I must take a holiday …
   b) I have to take a holiday …

3 Sentences a), c) and d) are good English. Sentence b) is not good English because the verb *have* when used in *have to* is not usually contracted. Sentence e) is not good English because *have got to* is not used to describe routines.

4 Sentences a), b) and c) all imply a lack of obligation to wait; sentence d) implies an obligation <u>not</u> to wait.

5 Sentences a) and b) prohibit smoking; sentence c) implies that smoking is not obligatory.

6 Sentence b) implies that he did his homework; in sentence a) we are not sure whether he did or not.

Watch out! *supposed to*

1 You *should speak* English in class.
2 You *shouldn't speak* Greek in class.

3 Students work individually before comparing their answers with a partner and then with the whole class.

ANSWERS

1 I **must write** to my brother.
2 They **needn't have** cooked so much food.
3 They **had to do** their homework before they went out.
4 You **can't/cannot take photographs** in here.
5 You **needn't have** come.
6 You **are not supposed to** talk while the teacher is speaking.
7 I**'ve got to** work late tonight.
8 You **didn't need** to wait for them.

4 Students complete the sentences individually before comparing answers with a partner and then with the whole class.

ANSWERS

1 Do you have to
2 Is there anything/What do I need to
3 You don't have to
4 You mustn't
5 You don't have to/You don't need to/ You needn't
6 Do I have to/Must I/Do I need to/Need I
7 I don't need to/I don't have to

EXTRA ACTIVITY: students add two or three lines of dialogue to each A/B sequence. They can write their extra lines either before or after each A/B sequence.

5 Students write two or three sentences about their chosen activity in pairs before reading them out to the rest of the class. Does everyone agree?

FURTHER PRACTICE: **First Certificate Gold Exam Maximiser Unit 12, pp.86–87.**

Listening: radio advertisements p.123

1 Play the cassette once through. Play it a second time to check the answers.

TAPESCRIPT

1 Stratford Cars, approved Mercedes Benz dealer. Stratford Cars 983 5555. Just minutes from the centre of the city, with an extensive range of new Mercedes in stock ready for you to test drive. Stratford Cars really do care about the service they provide. Stratford Cars, Mercedes Benz – 0181 983 5555.

2 A: Now let's see – tablecloth, flowers, soft music, candles ... I'm sure something's missing ... Darling! You look wonderful! Come in, let me take your coat.

   B: Thanks. Oh, this looks fantastic! Oh, you shouldn't have gone to so much trouble. What are we having to eat?

   A: Oh no! I knew I'd forgotten something! Fancy a MacBurger Superspecial?

   MacBurger Superspecial meals. Something special at a moment's notice. Two quarter-pounders, onion rings, fries and two large drinks, all for under £10. MacBurger Superspecial meals won't let you down!

3 During May Netcom dealers are offering you a special challenge. If you spend more than £30 a month on your mobile phone bill calling local and national numbers, Netcom will save you money. Call free on 0700 822222 with details of last month's bill to see how much you would have saved and whether you qualify for a free car stereo worth up to £300. For full details call 0700 822222 now!

4 From the makers of *Manhattan Express* and *The Fourth Amendment* comes *True Dirt*, the fastest, most action-packed evening of your life. Starring Angela

Dawn, Sandra Stones and Kurt Hegel as you've never seen him before. Seductive, powerful, gripping – *True Dirt*, at a cinema near you from Monday. Don't miss it!

5 At Weatherout we've got a really crazy offer for you – seven windows, any size from only £1,450. Yes, seven double-glazed windows installed and fully guaranteed for just £1,450. Phone Weatherout for full details on 0171 805 2777. That is 0171 805 2777. And take us up on our offer before they take us away. Weatherout – where quality costs less.

ANSWERS

1 Stratford Cars, a Mercedes Benz dealer
2 a MacBurger Superspecial meal 3 Netcom, a mobile phone company 4 *True Dirt*, an action film
5 Weatherout, a double-glazing firm

2 Students discuss the questions in pairs.

EXTRA ACTIVITY: make video recordings of between five and ten English language advertisements and prepare tapescripts for each one. Half the class watch the video without the sound and try to work out what is said. The other half of the class (working in another room) have the tapescripts and try to work out what images appear on the screen. The two groups then compare their answers and watch the advertisements with sound.

Speaking pp.123–124

1 Focus students' attention on the cartoon. Ask an individual to describe the people and the situation. Students work in groups of three or four appointing a spokesperson to report their discussion to the whole class. Note the skills/qualities on the board. How many groups mentioned the same ones?

ALTERNATIVE PROCEDURE: write a list of possible and unlikely skills and qualities on the board e.g. *intelligence, patience, shyness, belief in what you are selling, an attractive appearance, university qualifications, ability to put yourself in the customer's position, a friendly manner, a driver's licence, a good sense of direction, a knowledge of foreign languages, ability to make people trust you, honesty, etc.* Students decide in pairs or groups which of the skills and qualities are important and add others of their own. Follow this with a whole class discussion.

2 Check understanding of the genre 'product presentation' and the context: in-company to sales representatives. The presentation needs to highlight all the qualities of the product the sales representatives themselves can later use in their own pitches to potential customers. Emphasise that the grammar work that follows is essential for the product presentation.

A Grammar: modifiers/intensifiers

1 Students work in pairs.

ANSWERS

Sentences c), e) and j) are not possible.

In sentences c) and e) the adjective is not gradable as it refers to an absolute quality. It is therefore not possible to put an adverb that suggests gradability before these adjectives.

In sentence j) *good* is a gradable adjective and cannot be premodified by *absolutely,* which collocates with absolute adjectives only.

Refer students to the relevant section of the *Grammar reference* on page 171 (11).

2 Demonstrate the task yourself first before getting students to work in pairs.

***FURTHER PRACTICE: First Certificate Gold Exam Maximiser* Unit 12, p.86.**

B Writing and speaking: linkers (addition)

1 Draw attention to the inversion of subject and operator after *not only*, the use of the *-ing* form after the other two linkers and the punctuation with *Moreover/Furthermore.*

ANSWERS

i) mainly in writing: *In addition to + -ing* and *Moreover/ Furthermore;*

ii) mainly in speaking: *and* by far the most common speaking linker though it is also used in writing; *What's more;*

iii) in both writing and speaking: *Not only... but also* and *As well as + -ing.*

3 Students work individually before comparing answers with a partner and then with the whole class.

POSSIBLE ANSWERS

a) *As well as being* very good-looking, he is very intelligent.

b) *Not only was* the room in the hotel dirty, *but* it was *also* cold.

c) *In addition to* wanting us to start working half an hour earlier, they also say they can't pay us any more.

d) The weather in Cairo is fantastic. *Furthermore*, the people are incredibly friendly.

e) He did all the washing *and* he ironed all my shirts.

f) The volume control on the personal stereo was faulty. *What's more* the headphones were very uncomfortable.

4 Students work individually planning and writing their presentations. They can then rehearse their presentation with a partner before going on to deliver it to a larger group (either the whole class or a group of four).

FURTHER PRACTICE: **First Certificate Gold Exam Maximiser Unit 12, p.84.**

Vocabulary: media p.124

1 Students work individually before comparing their answers in pairs and then with the whole class.

ANSWERS
1 headlines 2 journalist 3 crossword/cartoons
4 circulation 5 editorial 6 gossip/scandal 7 frequency
8 station/broadcasts 9 channels 10 aerial
11 remote control 12 soap

2 Students discuss the questions in pairs and then open-class. How many people read the same newspaper, listen to the same radio station, have the same favourite/worst TV programme?

EXTRA ACTIVITY: bring in enough British newspapers (preferably broadsheet) or colour supplements for each pair to share one paper/supplement (it doesn't matter if the papers are from different dates). Prepare five scanning questions for each paper e.g. *Who won the semi-final in the Monte Carlo tennis championship? What was the temperature in Karachi? What's on Channel 4 at 9.00 tonight? Where was the president of the USA on Thursday?* Set a time limit of five minutes for the questions. Students then work in groups of four finding the answers to their questions. Ask students what, if any, differences they notice between the British papers and the papers in their country. Do their papers have the same sections e.g. Home News, International News, Editorial and letters, Columnists, Business, Sport, etc.? Are these sections in the same order? Are their papers the same size? Do their papers come with supplements, special sections on education, etc.? Do they have papers like the tabloids which are concerned mainly with gossip and scandal about celebrities, crime and sport? Are there special Sunday papers in their country? If there are, in what ways are they different to the daily papers?

FURTHER PRACTICE: **First Certificate Gold Exam Maximiser Unit 12, p.89.**

Exam Focus: Paper 5 Speaking (a complete interview) p.125

1 Go over the criteria with the class explaining and clarifying where necessary.

2 Students evaluate the interview individually before comparing their answers with a partner and then with the whole class.

TAPESCRIPT

(Complete interview)

I = Interlocutor J = Juliette M = Mohamed

Part 1

I: Good morning. Could I have your mark sheets please? Thank you. My name is Pauline Stephens and this is my colleague Jan Graham. She is just going to listen to us. So you are Juliette and Mohamed?

J/M: Yes/Yes, that's right.

I: First of all we'd like to know something about you so I'm going to ask you some questions about yourselves. Juliette, where are you from?

J: I'm from Paris.

I: And where do you come from Mohamed?

M: I'm from Cairo, in Egypt.

I: Were you born there?

M: No. I was born in Alexandria but my parents moved to Cairo when I was very young so for me Cairo is my home.

I: And Juliette, have you always lived in Paris?

J: Yes, I have.

I: Now, you are both learning English. Juliette, do you speak any other languages?

J: I speak French, of course, and a little little bit of German.

I: What about you Mohamed?

M: I speak Arabic and a little French in fact.

I: Mohamed, how do you think you will use English in the future?

M: I think it will help me to get better job. I work for a bank and I often must to speak to people from other countries and we must to use English. If I speak English well, it is also possible that I can work for my bank in other countries.

I: And what about you, Juliette?

J: I will use it for many things. You must speak English for communicate with the other peoples.

I: Now, we'd like to know something about your daily routine. Juliette what do you normally do at the weekend?

J: I like to go out with my friends. We go to a café and have a coffee or sometimes we go to a club for dancing. Often I just want to be alone. I like to read and listen classic music. I never play sport. I hate sport.

I: And you Mohamed? What do you do at the weekend?

M: I play football for a team. We practise in the week and then play matches at the weekend. I also like going to the cinema. I often go with my friends.

Part 2

I: Now, I'd like each of you to talk on your own for about a minute. I'm going to give each of you two different photographs and I'd like you to talk about them. Juliette, here are your two photographs. They show different ways of communicating. Please let Mohamed see them. Mohamed, I'll give you your photographs in a minute. Juliette. I'd like you to compare and contrast these photographs saying how you think the people are feeling. Remember you only have a minute for this, so don't worry if I interrupt you. All right?

J: In the first picture I can see a woman who reads a letter. There are different things on the table. I think there is a book and there are some flowers. Maybe she received a letter from her son or daughter. Yes? I think so.

I: And what about the other photograph?

J: Oh yes? It's a businessman who speaks on the telephone. He looks very? very? I don't know the word. He has a lot of work to do. There are many papers on the table.

I: Thank you. Mohamed, which way of communicating do you prefer?

M: Well, I prefer to speak to my friends on the telephone, I like to hear what they think immediately. When I write I must wait for them to reply.

I: Thank you. Now Mohamed, here are your photographs. They show people travelling in different ways. Please let Juliette see them. Mohamed, I'd like you to compare and contrast these photographs saying what you like or don't like about these different ways of travelling. Remember, you only have about a minute for this, so don't worry if I interrupt you. All right?

M: Okay? Well? In the first picture there is a family in a car. They looks as if they are on quite a long journey. Children look bored and unhappy and the parents as well. There is a big problem with cars these days. There are more and more cars on the roads and it can take a lot of time to go from one place to the other. There is, this actually is also true in my country.
The other picture has a very different feeling. It is a very nice train. There is space for people to move. The people in the picture looks as if they are comfortable and enjoying the journey. There is a man who brings drinks and sandwiches for everyone. This looks a much more comfortable way to travel than the first. So, I think for long journeys, I prefer to travel by train, it is more comfortable. But, of course, when you only want to go a short way, you can't have a train.

I: Thank you. Juliette, which of these ways of travelling do you use more often?

J: More often I go in my car. I like because I am free. I can go the way I want and I can listen to my stereo.

I: Thank you.

Part 3

I: Now, I'd like you to talk about something together for about three minutes. I'm just going to listen. I'd like you to imagine that a local school is considering adding two new subjects to its curriculum. First talk about the different subjects. Then decide which two you would choose and why. You have only about three minutes for this, so, once again, don't worry if I stop you. Please speak so that we can hear you. All right?

M: Okay. I think it is very important that children learn how to swim at school. If they can't swim, they will always be in danger when they are near water. Maybe they fall in water from a boat. They will also be afraid in water and they can't enjoy when they have a holiday by the sea, for example. Do you agree, Juliette?

J: I don't know. Yes, it is important to know how to swim, but I think the parents can teach the children. Maybe it is better if the school teaches computers to the children because this is difficult for parents to do in the home.

M: That's true and it is very useful to know how to use computers. I think almost every kind of job will need computers in the future. So … we agree about computers. We need one more subject. What do you think about teaching pupils about cars?

J: No, I think that is stupid. It is not interesting and if you have problem with a car you can take it to the mechanic.

M: Okay … so … what other subject do you think is important to learn at school?

J: Perhaps … er … cooking … everyone must know how to cook. It is something you must do every day.

M: I think learning to repair car is also important.

J: Mmm. Maybe but you can take it to a mechanic and he will fix for you, no?

M: I suppose so. Photography. Mmmm. That would be very enjoyable.

J: But not so important as to cook and computer, I think. I like very much but I do not think it is important to learn at school.

M: No? And I think to be an actor is also not so important. It is something you can do at a special school or in your spare time. But make things with wood? Ah? Carpenter? Ah? I think this is a good thing to learn, don't you?

J: Yes, it is very nice, but I still think if we have to only choose two subjects we should have to cook and computer.

M: Yes, I agree, because they are both things you need in for your work and your life after school.

I: Thank you.

Part 4

I: Mohamed, how important do you think it is for schools to prepare pupils for life as well as teaching them academic subjects? Do you think that school education should be more practical than it is now?

M: In my opinion, it is important that school does both things. I think it is important that students learn subjects like Maths, History, English and so on. This teaches them how to think and be logical, but also

I think there must be time to prepare pupils to get jobs and live in the world. It is no good if pupils know all these things, but then they can't get a job and they have no money for their family.

I: Do you agree with that, Juliette?

J: Yes, but I think it is much more important to study things like Maths and History than to go swimming or do cooking. If you are not good in Mathematics and things like this, you will not pass your exams and then you will not go to the university. It is very important to go to the university, to get a good job.

I: And do you think that pupils should go straight from school to university or should they have time off in between?

J: I think it is not important.

M: I think it can be good for pupils to do something different before university.

I: And why do you think that?

M: Well, maybe they can travel or have a job, then they will be older when they go to university and maybe they will appreciate more what they study.

I: Okay. Juliette, what do you think is a good size for a class at school?

J: You mean in secondary school?

I: Yes, that's right.

J: I don't know. I think maybe twenty-five or thirty.

I: Is that how many you had in your classes at school?

J: Yes.

I: And you didn't think it was too many?

J: No … the teacher talked to us and we write down what he said.

M: Yes … it was the same for me. Sometimes it was even more in the class. It was okay, but it is difficult if you have a problem, or you don't understand. I have studied English in private classes and it was only eight students. This is much better.

I: Juliette, why do you think some teachers have problems keeping control of their classes at school?

J: It is because they are not strong with their pupils. They try and be nice, but children do not understand this. You know, they play and do not listen. The teacher must be in control of the class.

M: I think also that maybe it is because the lessons are not interesting. The pupil are bored and so they don't pay attention.

I: Fine ... and lastly, Mohamed, at what age do you think pupils should be free to leave school?

M: That is a difficult question. For some families it is necessary for the children to work and to get money. If they must stay at school for a long time, they cannot earn the money. But I think also it is important for all children to have education. I don't know ... maybe fourteen?

J: This is very young to leave school. They must stay until they are sixteen, I think. It is not enough time to learn to leave when you are fourteen.

I: Thank you both very much. That's the end of the test.

3 Give Student A in each pair a copy of the following instructions:

After you have asked the Part 1 questions on p. 92 move on to Part 2. This is what you should say to the candidates:

Now, I'd like each of you to talk on your own for about a minute. I'm going to give each of you two different photographs and I'd like you to talk about them. (Name of Candidate A), here are your two photographs. They show different ways of communicating. Please let (name of Candidate B) see them. (Name of Candidate B) I'll give you your photographs in a minute. (Name of Candidate A), I'd like you to compare and contrast these photographs saying how you think the people are feeling. Remember you only have a minute for this, so don't worry if I interrupt you. All right?

After Candidate A has been speaking for one minute say **'thank you'** *to indicate that they should stop.*

Ask Candidate B this question:

(Name of Candidate B), which way of communicating do you prefer?

After 20 seconds, say **'thank you'** *to indicate that they should stop.*

Now (Name of Candidate B), here are your photographs. They show people travelling in different ways. Please let (Name of Candidate A) see them. (Name of Candidate B), I'd like you to compare and contrast these photographs saying what you like or don't like about these different ways of travelling. Remember, you only have about a minute for this, so don't worry if I interrupt you. All right?

After Candidate B has been speaking for one minute say **'thank you'** *to indicate that they should stop.*

Ask Candidate A this question, **(Name of Candidate A),** *which of these ways of travelling do you use more often?*

After 20 seconds, say **'thank you'** *to indicate that they should stop.*

Now move on to Part 3. This is what you should say to the candidates:

Now, I'd like you to talk about something together for about three minutes: I'm just going to listen. I'd like you to imagine that a local school is considering adding two new subjects to its curriculum. First talk about the different subjects. Then decide which two you would choose and why. You have only about three minutes for this, so, once again, don't worry if I stop you. Please speak so that we can hear you. All right?

When the candidates have been speaking for three minutes say **'thank you'** *to indicate that they should stop speaking and move on to Part 4.*

Ask Student A in each group to pass the sheet to Student C.

Reading p.126

1 Focus attention on the definition of 'ration' before discussing the question with the whole class.

2 Set a three-minute time limit for the gist task.

3 Students work individually before comparing their questions with a partner and then with the whole class.

> **POSSIBLE ANSWERS**
> 1 How does the television ration box work?
> 2 What do the children do instead of watching TV?
> 3 Who invented the gadget?
> 4 Why did he invent it?
> 5 What happens when the child's viewing time runs out?
> 6 How much does it cost in Britain?
> 7 How does Moss Levenson think TV rationing has affected him?
> 8 Who asked Mr Levenson to make units for them?
> 9 How many gadgets have been sold so far?
> 10 How long does it take children to accept the situation?

4 Students discuss the questions in pairs.

ALTERNATIVE PROCEDURE: conduct a whole class discussion.

Exam focus: Paper 2 Writing: Part 2 (discursive composition) pp.126–128

1 Play the cassette through once and then again to check answers, pausing after each relevant section.

TAPESCRIPT

A: Did you see that, that article about the TV, TV ration box in the paper today?

B: Oh, yes.

A: Wasn't it amazing? I mean … isn't it … don't you think it's just so great? I mean, the problem with …

C: But why?

A: Well, with my kids … don't you find that they, they just can't stop themselves watching TV. They go in, they sit down in front of the box and it just goes on and on and on and on. And really, the thing about this box is that it stops them watching all the time and then they can start thinking about doing other things – they have to actually go out and meet friends …

C: You mean like go and play in the garden …

B: And actually talk to people.

A: Yeah, that's right.

D: I'm sorry, I think it's a dreadful idea. I think surely it's up to the parents to take on that responsibility of telling them when they can or can't watch television. They don't need a box for that.

C: Obviously, you aren't a parent, Roger.

D: No, I'm not a parent, but I don't see why you should give up that responsibility.

B: It is a bit like, yeah, being controlled by a machine, isn't it? It's a bit robotic, isn't it?

D: Exactly.

A: But you say 'controlled by a machine'. Think about the power of television. I mean television controls children. Think about the way it brainwashes our kids into thinking all sorts of things which really may not be good for them at all.

D: But don't you think that … the kids … without this box the kids have to decide what they watch. I mean that, that's part of growing up as it is, you have to decide what you want to watch and have the discipline yourself to turn it off when you don't want to watch it.

B: But even with the box you have to decide what you watch, don't you? You just have less things you're

---

allowed to watch, but you still have to make decisions.

D: Yes, except you have more pressure, because you know you can only watch a certain amount of time, which to me is … limiting.

C: But this way, so far as I can understand it, is a way of allocating your viewing time so a child can actually choose what they're going to watch. For instance if they want to see *Blue Peter* and they want to watch *Jimbo and the Jet Set* they can't watch both, they can only watch one of them and so they can choose. And so everyday they can choose what they're going to watch.

D: Do you think then that they will make the choice of watching one of them? I don't think so. They'll watch one of them, use up some of their time on their ration box then go round to their neighbours and watch it there. All they'll do is lie to their parents.

A: You have a very cynical view of children.

C: I'm talking about young children.

D: Children are far cleverer than that, they won't just settle for that.

C: But, Roger, the point is, I'm talking about four, five, six year olds. They don't go off and play with neighbours. I mean they do when they're twelve and thirteen …

B: Well, that's because they're watching television all day!

ANSWERS

In favour: children can't limit themselves; they should be encouraged to develop other interests; TV brainwashes kids and needs to be controlled.

Against: it isn't right to limit children's freedom of choice like this; it doesn't let children learn to decide for themselves how much TV they should watch; because children can't watch TV all the time, they'll want to watch it more when they do.

2 **1** Give students one minute to read through the exam information and sample task. Go through the various categories with the class. Students work individually before comparing their views with a partner and then with the whole class.

ANSWERS

Length: the answer is longer than the upward word limit (217 words). This would probably not matter, but students should be encouraged to write within the 180 word limit.

Grammar: the writer uses a wide range of structures very accurately. (EXCELLENT)

Spelling: there are sixteen spelling mistakes. (POOR)

Handwriting: clear and easy to read. (GOOD)

Vocabulary: there is a good range of vocabulary: *range, watch rubbish, involved in the decision, addicted.* (EXCELLENT)

Organisation of ideas/paragraphing: there is a clear progression from one idea to another, but the composition is written as one paragraph. (POOR)

Use of linking expressions: the writer uses a good range of linking expressions accurately and appropriately. (EXCELLENT)

Logical order of argument: there is clear development of an argument. (EXCELLENT)

Appropriacy of language for context: the writer has chosen an appropriate style for an article. (EXCELLENT)

2 Students work with a partner before comparing answers open-class.

ANSWERS

a) impor*tant*, *quality*, pro*grammes*, *suitable*, in*terests*, coun*tries*, rub*bish*, ob*viously*, con*trolled*, a*gree*, in*volved*, de*cision*, al*lowed*, *their*, pre*pared*, un*healthy*.

b) There should be four paragraphs beginning: *First of all ...*; *As well as this ...*; *I do think, however, ...*; *To sum up then, ...*

3 **1** Discuss the answers to the questions open-class.

ANSWERS

- as well as this
- on the other hand, however
- therefore

2 Students work individually before comparing answers open-class.

ANSWERS

a) although b) In addition to c) so d) Furthermore
e) Not only f) despite

give more information: sentences b), d) and e).
introduce a contrasting idea: sentences a) and f).
explain the consequence of something: sentence c)

3 Students work in pairs before comparing answers open-class.

ANSWERS

a) Furthermore b) so c) in spite d) However
e) in addition to f) Despite g) although h) despite
i) therefore

4 Students work in groups of three or four preparing a plan and then writing a draft. The final version can be written for homework.

Speaking p.128

1 Focus students' attention on the pictures. Students work in pairs, with one student describing one of the pictures in as much detail as possible. The other student should try to work out which picture is being described. They should then change roles before discussing which picture is most like their own family.

ALTERNATIVE PROCEDURE: get individuals to describe one of the pictures without saying which one, while the rest of the class try to work out which picture is being described. Say which picture is most like your family and why and get individual students to do the same.

2 To give students some ideas tell them about your ideal TV channel. Students work in pairs before comparing their answers with another pair. Get feedback from each pair open-class. What kinds of programmes are most popular?

Unit 12 Review

ANSWERS

1 1 C; 2 B; 3 D; 4 A; 5 C; 6 D; 7 C; 8 A; 9 D; 10 A;
11 B

2 1 giving him a bribe 2 explanation 3 wisdom
4 get over 5 headline 6 gossip 7 an aerial
8 remote control

3 **Possible answers**
1 ... visit my grandmother. 2 ... smoke.
3 ... practise as much as possible. 4 ... putting on my mother's make-up. 5 ... we went to this absolutely fantastic discotheque. 6 ... very pretty.
7 ... the fact that Nigel was going to be there.
8 ... sat around by the pool.

Now your students are ready to do the test for Unit 12 on page 136.

UNIT

13 It's a mad world

Reading pp.130–131

1 Give students a minute to look at the photos before asking individual students to describe them. Encourage students to react to the people in the photos.

2 Set a four-minute time limit for the gist task. Discuss open-class students' reactions to the people described in the text and whether or not such things could happen in their country.

3 Set a ten-minute time limit for students to do the task individually before comparing answers with a partner.

ANSWERS
1 C); 2 F); 3 A); 4 E); 5 B); 6 G)

4 Students work individually before comparing answers with a partner and then with the whole class.

ANSWERS
2 unbelievable 3 strengthened 4 refusal 5 unhealthy
6 theoretical 7 prove 8 creation 9 variety

Vocabulary: phrasal verbs (*out*)

1 Do this exercise with the whole class.

ANSWERS
1 c); 2 b); 3 d); 4 a); 5 e)

2 Students work individually before comparing answers with a partner and then with the whole class.

ANSWERS
1 b); 2 e); 3 a); 4 c); 5 d)

3 Give students time to look over the previous units and the *Phrasal verbs reference* on pages 196–198 of the *Coursebook* to refresh their memories about the phrasal verbs they have studied so far. They may find it helpful to

note down the phrasal verbs they want to use as they tell their story. Get a couple of students to describe their week for the whole class.

Speaking p.132

1 Students answer the questionnaire individually before discussing their answers with a partner. Go round monitoring and noting down any errors. Put these up on the board at the end of the Speaking activities and discuss them with the whole class without saying who made the errors.

2 Tell the class about something eccentric you have done or an eccentric person you know before they work in pairs discussing the questions.

Listening: vampire woman p.132

1 Discuss the questions open-class, eliciting as much information as possible from the class about vampires e.g. they hate the light of day, they sleep in coffins, they hate garlic, they are actually dead but continue to 'live', they have long fangs (long sharp teeth like those of a cat or wolf) instead of incisor teeth, they can be killed by running a stake through their heart, etc.

2 Focus attention on the pictures and get individual students to describe each one and to point out the differences between them. Play the cassette once while students answer the question.

ANSWER
Picture B

TAPESCRIPT

RP = radio presenter   CB = Carole Bohanon
PM = Paul Maloney

RP: Carole Bohanon could easily be mistaken for a vampire. She has wild hair, ice-white skin and pale, glittering eyes that look right through you. She mostly dresses in Gothic black and when she laughs, two long pointed fangs appear and make your blood run cold. Her fingernails are sharpened into two inch points and look like cats' claws. Carole has been fascinated by vampires since she was a child. She spoke to our reporter, Paul Maloney.

CB: I know I'm not one because I'm alive, but I'd like to come back to Earth as a vampire. I believe in them, and my interest in vampirism takes up most of my time and all my money.

PM: Carole, twenty-five, works as a graphic artist. She is an only child.

CB: From the age of about four I've been obsessed with horror stories. I like the idea of corpses rising from the grave and have never been frightened by the supernatural. I've always been fascinated by blood. I love the colour and texture, and as a young child I'd watch hospital operations on TV. I've never drunk anyone's blood, but the idea doesn't shock me. My parents have always thought I'm weird. Dad used to call me a witch, and I'm sure in a past life I was one.

PM: Carole's flat gives plenty of signs of her obsession. Her bedroom is full of bats, skulls, masks and signs of death. As she says:

CB: If I had the money, I'd sleep in a coffin and drive a hearse. I saved up to have my fangs made. My canine teeth never grew properly, so I had to have my teeth fixed. I asked the dentist if I could have any shape of teeth fitted, and when he said 'Yes', I asked for long, pointed ones. It took months before he would believe me. It's against all dental rules to make fangs.

PM: She confesses that she has always felt different.

CB: At school I tried to be like everybody else, but I felt inhibited and unhappy. Now, I'm just not interested in everyday conventions and I don't feel the need to fit in. In fact if I didn't have to work, I'd sleep all day and get up at night.

PM: Last year Carole formed the Vampire Society with a friend and they produce a regular newsletter and magazine.

CB: It's amazing how quickly the group has grown. I think if we'd realised how many people were interested, we would've started the Society much sooner.

PM: Although Carole is in perfect health, she admits to classic vampire symptoms.

CB: I can't bear sunlight – it gives me headaches if I stay out too long. I love cold windy nights, and can see much better in the dark.

PM: True to form, garlic makes her ill and she is sick if she eats flesh. All her money goes on vampire books and objects, and as she says:

CB: If I manage to save enough money, I'll go on a trip to Transylvania next year. They still believe in vampires there, so there's always the chance that I'll be staked.

3   Students read through the questions. Check that they understand *reincarnation* before playing the cassette. Students compare answers with a partner before they listen to the cassette again. Check answers open-class, replaying relevant sections if necessary.

ANSWERS

(see underlined sentences in tapescript)

1 Since she was a child.

2 No.

3 No.

4 Red.

5 Yes.

6 No.

7 No.

8 No.

9 Transylvania.

Grammar: conditionals pp.133–134

1   Play the cassette or read the sentences to the class. Get individual students to read their answers aloud to the class while you write them up on the board.

ANSWERS

1 If *I had the money, I'd sleep* in a coffin and drive a hearse.

2 If *I didn't have to work, I'd sleep* all day and get up at night.

3 If *we'd realised how many people* were interested, we *would've started the Society* much sooner.

4 I can't bear sunlight – it *gives me headaches if I stay out* too long.

5 She *is sick if she eats* flesh.

6 If *I manage to save enough money, I'll go on* a trip to Transylvania next year.

2   Students read the information silently and label the conditional sentences. Go through the answers highlighting the form. Refer them to the relevant section of the *Grammar reference* on page 165.

ANSWERS

1 second 2 second 3 third 4 zero 5 zero 6 first

3 Students work individually before comparing their answers with a partner and then with the whole class.

ANSWERS

1 If I **come** to the party, will you give me a lift home?
2 He definitely **won't** pass the exam unless he does a lot more work.
3 I **would have** a couple of days in bed if I were you.
4 You can borrow the car tonight provided that **you take** good care of it.
5 I wouldn't have cooked so much food if I **had known** they weren't coming.
6 If you **press** that button, you get extra sugar.
7 He **might have stayed** if you hadn't shouted at him.
8 As long as you have enough money, I'm sure you **will have** a good time when you go to New York.
9 We won't be able to buy it unless our parents **lend** us some money.

4 Students work individually. Go round checking and pointing out any errors. Get individuals to repeat their sentences for the rest of the class.

5 Follow the same procedure as for Exercise 4.

6 1 Check that students understand the meaning of *regret*. Play the cassette once whilst students make notes. Play the cassette a second time before going through the answers open-class.

TAPESCRIPT

1 No, really, it was very stupid of me. I suppose it was 'cos I wanted to get away from exams and the whole school thing, the thought of university at the time seemed like a nightmare, but now, thinking about it, I really can't get the kind of job I want to do. I know now that I should've gone.

2 In the end it came down to a kind of choice, I think. I mean, I knew they both fancied me, but Derek, well, to be honest, then I felt he was a bit boring. I mean, don't get me wrong, I really liked him and he was really nice, but ... well, you know. Anyway, Matthew, he was something else, it was always exciting with him, you never knew quite what was going to happen. So, in the end we got married, but it was then that everything started to go wrong and really I've been pretty miserable ever since. Oh, if only I'd gone for Derek ...

3 I'm sorry I got so angry. I know I shouldn't have shouted at her like that. It was just that she was my only daughter and when I thought of her ... getting married to that ... well, I mean, he didn't have a job, they had nowhere to live, it was all so ridiculous. Okay, so I said some very hurtful things, but I don't deserve this. She hasn't been in contact with us for nearly five years. I don't know where she is, what she's doing or anything.

4 It was really stupid, but I was desperate for money and then this guy I knew a bit asked me if I wanted to make some extra cash really quick. Of course I was interested ... and by the time I knew what it involved it was all too late. I can't believe how stupid the whole thing was ... neither of us really knew what we were doing. We were caught almost immediately. A neighbour had noticed us breaking in and phoned the police. I did two years – it was awful and now no one'll give me a job because of my criminal record.

5 It was all my fault really. The score was level and there were only a couple of minutes left. Then what happened was that I tackled someone on their team who pretended that I'd really hurt them, that it was some kind of terrible foul, but it was all just acting. Anyway, the referee came over and started warning me about dangerous play and I tried to tell him what had happened. The next thing I knew he'd sent me off. I couldn't believe it. And then, of course we were one player down and they scored and we lost the match. I feel really sick about the whole thing!

ANSWERS

2 She is sorry that she married Matthew instead of Derek.
3 She is sorry that she had a row with her daughter and that they have lost touch.
4 He is sorry that he broke into someone's house.
5 He is sorry that he tackled a player from the other team and that he had a misunderstanding with the referee.

2 Students work in pairs writing sentences about each person.

POSSIBLE ANSWERS

a) If he had gone to university, he would have got a better job.
b) If she had chosen Derek instead of Matthew, she would have been happier.
c) If she hadn't shouted at her daughter, she wouldn't have lost contact with her.

d) If he hadn't tried to break into someone's house, he wouldn't have gone to prison.

e) If the player in the other team hadn't pretended to be hurt, his team wouldn't have lost the match.

3 Students work in pairs before feeding back to the whole class.

7 Look at the cartoon with the whole class and discuss the question.

ANSWER

The last sentence is an example of a Mixed Conditional.

8 Students work individually before comparing answers with a partner and then with the whole class.

ANSWERS

1 a) and c); 2 a) and b); 3 b) and c); 4 a) and c); 5 a) and b); 6 b) and c)

*FURTHER PRACTICE: **First Certificate Gold Exam Maximiser** Unit 13, pp.92–93.*

Vocabulary: animals p.134

1 Check students understand the words in the box and the animals listed. Students work individually before comparing answers with the whole class.

ANSWERS

1 wings/claws 2 hooves/a horn/a tail 3 fur/paws/a tail 4 a trunk/a tail 5 hooves/a tail 6 a fin/a tail 7 fur/paws/a tail/a mane/claws 8 hooves/a tail/a mane 9 fur/claws/paws/a tail 10 wings/feathers/a beak 11 wings 12 hooves/a tail/a hump 13 a tail

2 This information gap activity must be done in pairs.

3 Do this exercise with the whole class.

ANSWERS

a) cat b) dog c) cow d) lion e) snake f) horse

4 Students work in pairs trying to guess the meanings of the idioms and referring to their dictionaries where necessary.

ANSWERS

1 *let the cat out of the bag:* tell a secret

2 *kill two birds with one stone:* get two results with one action

3 *the rat race:* endless competition for success among fellow-workers in business

4 *plenty more fish in the sea:* many other young men/women available for you to go out with

5 *have kittens:* get very upset and angry

6 *take the bull by the horns:* face difficulties without fear

7 *put the cat among the pigeons:* create chaos and confusion

8 *straight from the horse's mouth:* something is told to you directly by the person concerned and not via someone else

*FURTHER PRACTICE: **First Certificate Gold Exam Maximiser** Unit 13, p.91.*

Exam focus: Paper 3 Use of English: Part 2 (open cloze) p.135

Read the exam information and suggested procedure aloud to the class.

1 Ask students why they think people are often afraid of bats. Tell them to read the text through to see if any of their reasons were mentioned.

2 Focus attention on gap 1. Ask what the main verb is. Ask what tense it should be and if it is in active or passive form. Ask if it is singular or plural. Ask what auxiliary verb should be used. Students work individually to fill in the remaining gaps before comparing answers with a partner and then open-class.

ANSWERS

1 are 2 have 3 from 4 in 5 making 6 no 7 Among 8 than 9 why 10 but 11 of 12 addition 13 bring 14 fact 15 that

*FURTHER PRACTICE: **First Certificate Gold Exam Maximiser** Unit 13, p.93.*

Vocabulary: places pp.136–137

1 Focus students' attention on the photos and get individual students to describe them in as much detail as possible. Students discuss the questions in groups of three or four, appointing a spokesperson to report back to the whole class. Encourage students to speculate as much as possible as they may have to do this in Paper 5. How many people agree on the place they would like to live?

2 Students work in pairs, using English – English dictionaries where necessary before comparing their answers with the rest of the class.

ANSWERS

2 1 *a terraced house* is attached on both sides to other houses; *a semi-detached house* is attached to another house on one side only; *a detached house* is not attached to any other houses.

2 *a bungalow* is a single storey free-standing house; *a flat* is a set of rooms usually on one floor; *a bedsit* is a single room used for both living and sleeping in.

3 *a cottage* is a small house, especially in the country; *a hut* is a small simply-made building often made of wood.

4 *a caravan* is a vehicle that can be pulled by a car with cooking facilities and places to sleep; *a tent* is a moveable shelter made of cloth supported by poles.

5 *a town* is a large group of buildings and houses where people live and work; *a city* is usually larger and more important than a town; *a village* is usually in the country and is smaller than a town; *a suburb* is an outer area of a town or city where people live; *the capital* is the most important city in a country or area.

6 *a county* is a region of a country which is divided from other regions for the purpose of local government; *a country* (countable) a nation or state with its own land; *a continent* is one of the seven major land masses on Earth.

7 *a skyscraper* is a very tall modern city building; *a penthouse* is a small house or set of rooms on top of a tall building, often considered very desirable to live in.

3 1 Students work individually using a dictionary where necessary before comparing their answers with a partner.

ANSWERS

A hedge B pavement C gate D drainpipe E porch
F roof G chimney H TV aerial I attic J cellar K patio
L pond M shed N fence O lawn P flowerbed

2 Students discuss the questions in pairs before reporting back to the whole class.

Watch Out! *country*

In the first sentence it is the uncountable noun and means 'an area outside a city or town'. In the second sentence it means 'a nation or state with its own land'.

4 1 Students discuss the questions in pairs and then open-class.

ANSWERS

a) *a theatre*: to see concerts or plays

b) *a cathedral*: to attend a religious ceremony

c) *a market*: to shop for food or other goods

d) *a stadium*: to watch a sporting event

e) *a museum*: to look at exhibits of historic, artistic or scientific interest

f) *a gallery*: to see art exhibitions

g) *a factory*: to work

2 Students discuss the questions in pairs, possibly feeding back to the whole class.

FURTHER PRACTICE: **First Certificate Gold Exam Maximiser Unit 13, p.94.**

Use of English p.137

Ask students what they know about Romania: the landscape, the language, anything it is famous for. Focus attention on the photos and ask individual students to describe them in as much detail as possible.

Students work individually before comparing answers with a partner and then with the whole class.

ANSWERS

line 1; suggests <u>that</u> *line 2;* <u>the</u> Imperial Rome
line 3; <u>as</u> like Italian *line 4;* <u>where</u> is *line 5;* <u>there</u> are
line 6; <u>a</u> summer *line 7;* <u>very</u> marvellous *line 8;* <u>be</u>

mention *line 9;* <u>so</u> impressive *line 10;* <u>of</u> century
line 11; <u>with</u> the astonishing *line 12;* <u>more</u> fewer
line 13; nearly <u>of</u> *line 14;* <u>the</u> most famous *line 15;* <u>the</u>
Bram Stoker *line 16;* <u>being</u> fiction *line 17;* <u>is</u> called
line 18; <u>such</u> his *line 19;* have <u>been</u> *line 20;* enjoy
<u>himself</u> *line 21;* cut <u>them</u> *line 22;* <u>so</u> as *line 23;* may <u>be</u>
line 24; was <u>having</u> *line 25;* <u>to</u> how *line 26;* <u>for</u> to see

Writing: describing places p.138

1 Students work individually studying the three plans.

ANSWER
The article goes with plan C.

2 Do this exercise with the whole class.

ANSWER
The unsuitable plan would be plan B because the task asks you to write about a place you know well and it will appear in a magazine for young travellers.

3 Students work in pairs and plan what they are going to write, before writing the composition for homework. Mark the compositions using the correction code on pages 7 and 8 and paying particular attention to the use of conditionals.

FURTHER PRACTICE: **First Certificate Gold Exam Maximiser Unit 13, pp.94–95.**

Unit 13 Review

ANSWERS

1 *lion* a) tail b) mane

eagle c) beak d) wings

shark e) fin

camel f) hump

2 1 eating   2 run/sold   3 wears   4 Look   5 throw
6 stands   7 take   8 let   9 kill

3 1 would never have stayed

2 if I had taken

3 would not have been sent

4 you had tried harder

5 unless it rains

6 you speak English fluently

7 boils if you

8 if I won/were to win

9 might have lent her

10 would have got

Now your students are ready to do the test for Unit 13 on page 137.

UNIT
14 Guilty or not guilty

Reading p.140

1 Focus students' attention on the photos and get individual students to describe them. Encourage them to speculate as much as possible.

> **ANSWERS**
> The characters in the photos are: Batman (the actor, Michael Keaton), Vicki (the actress, Kim Basinger), the Joker (the actor, Jack Nicholson).

2 Set a three-minute time limit for the gist task.

> **ANSWER**
> Batman rescues Vicki from the Joker.

3 Pre-teach *henchman*, *pitcher*, *tan*, *skylight*, *nail*, *embedding*. Set a ten-minute time limit for the reading task. Students work individually and then compare answers with a partner.

> **ANSWERS**
> 1 To capture Vicki.
> 2 He was in a cheerful mood.
> 3 It made the fake tan come off. No, he just pretended it had.
> 4 Through the skylight.
> 5 The special escape wires Batman used.

EXTRA ACTIVITY: photocopy a page of a comic or a comic strip with some of the text in the speech bubbles blanked out. Students work in pairs to write their complete versions and then compare them with the rest of the class.

Writing: making your writing more interesting p.141

1 Students work in pairs before comparing answers with the whole class.

> **ANSWERS**
> 1 burst into 2 methodically 3 grab 4 drench
> 5 reveal 6 writhe 7 stagger 8 abruptly
> 9 scream 10 grin 11 shatter 12 plunge
> 13 flabbergasted

2 Students work in groups of three or four using their English – English dictionaries where necessary.

> **ANSWERS**
> **1** 1 h); 2 c); 3 g); 4 i); 5 b); 6 a); 7 d); 8 e); 9 f)
> **2** **group a):** *exclaim:* speak loudly and suddenly; *mutter:* speak in a low voice often expressing anger and dissatisfaction; *insist:* say firmly and repeatedly.
> **group b):** *giggle:* laugh in a childish silly way; *chuckle:* laugh quietly; *snigger:* laugh quietly to yourself in a disrespectful way.
> **group c):** *writhe:* twist your body because you are in great pain; *wriggle:* twist your body from side to side; *fidget:* move your body around in a restless impatient way.
> **group d):** *hurl:* throw something with force; *toss:* throw something, especially coins up to decide something; *lob:* throw or hit a ball high in the air.
> **group e):** *stagger:* move unsteadily on your feet; *wander:* walk through an area without a fixed aim; *tiptoe:* walk quietly and carefully on your toes.
> **group f):** *munch:* eat something noisily; *nibble:* eat slowly with small repeated bites; *swallow:* move something down your throat from your mouth.
> **group g):** *wonder:* express the wish to know something silently or in words; *consider:* think about something carefully; *reckon:* think or suppose.
> **group h):** *order:* give a command to someone; *inform:* tell someone something; *instruct:* give someone knowledge or information.

group i): *clutch:* hold something tightly; *grasp:* take suddenly and roughly; *hug:* hold someone tightly in your arms because you love them.

EXTRA ACTIVITY: students work in groups of three or four and mime some of the verbs while the others guess which one they are miming.

3 Students work in pairs. If possible, they should write their new versions on an overhead transparency or on separate sheets of paper to put up around the class so that they can be compared.

POSSIBLE IMPROVED VERSION

It took Vicki a few seconds to realise she had been rescued from the Joker. Batman grasped her firmly and in a flash they were in Gotham Square. He instructed her to go down a tiny side street quickly. He followed her and tossed a small object behind them. Suddenly a screen of smoke covered the entrance to the street.

He ordered her to get in the car. At first she didn't know which one, but then she saw it. It was jet black and looked incredibly weird. 'Ignition,' commanded Batman and instantly the car started.

4 Students brainstorm ideas for the continuation of the story in groups of four. The actual writing can be done in class or for homework.

Vocabulary: crime p.142

1 1 Divide the class into four groups, A, B, C and D. Encourage students to think of their own definitions for the words they know and to use you as a resource where necessary. Also encourage students to check that they know the correct pronunciation of each of the words using a dictionary if necessary.

ANSWERS

Group A: *a thief:* someone who steals, usually without violence; *a kidnapper:* someone who takes someone away in order to demand money or something else for their safe return; *a mugger:* someone who robs with violence especially in a dark street; *a shoplifter:* someone who takes things from shops without paying; *a pickpocket:* someone who steals from the pockets and bags of people in crowds; *a blackmailer:* someone who obtains money by threatening to make known something unpleasant; *a hijacker:* someone who takes control of a vehicle or aircraft illegally, often for political aims; *a forger:* a person who makes copies of things in order to deceive people; *a smuggler:* someone who takes goods or people from one country to another illegally; *an arsonist:* someone who sets fire to property in order to cause damage; *a rapist:* a man guilty of forcing a woman to have sex with him.

Group B: *a court:* a room or building in which law cases can be held and judged; *a judge:* a public official who has the power to decide cases that are brought before a court of law (in the British legal system the police investigate crimes not the judge); *a jury:* a group of twelve people chosen to hear all the details of a case in a court of law and give their decision on it (in the British, Commonwealth and American legal systems members of the general public are obliged to do jury service if they are called and cannot provide a good excuse); *a witness:* a person who sees something happen and can describe it to other people; *a defence lawyer:* the legal representative of the person accused of a crime; *a prosecution lawyer:* the lawyer who tries to prove that someone is guilty in a court of law (in the British, Commonwealth and American legal systems if there is any doubt that the accused may <u>not</u> be guilty, the jury or judge must find her/him 'not guilty'); *the accused:* a person charged with a crime (the accused is assumed innocent until proven guilty in the British, Commonwealth and American legal systems); *a verdict:* the official decision made in a court of law at the end of a trial; *a plea:* a statement by a person in a court of law saying whether or not they are guilty of a crime.

Group C: *a fine:* an amount of money paid as a punishment; *Community Service:* work done for the community instead of a fine or period of imprisonment; *capital punishment:* a legal punishment by which the person who is found guilty of a crime such as murder can be put to death; *corporal punishment:* physical punishment, usually hitting someone; *a suspended sentence:* a punishment in which, instead of going to prison immediately, the person found guilty of the crime remains free as long as s/he commits no further crimes; *a jail sentence:* a period spent in prison as a punishment for a crime.

Group D: *to arrest:* to catch someone and declare that they are believed to be guilty of a crime; *to question:* to ask someone questions about something; *to accuse:* to say that someone has done something wrong or has broken the law; *to deny:* to say that something is untrue; *to admit:* to agree, often unwillingly, that something bad or unpleasant is true; *to put on probation:* allowing someone who has broken the law to go free if they promise to behave well and report to the court; *to execute:* to kill someone as a legal punishment; *to release on bail:* to set the accused free because s/he has paid an amount of money to the court to guarantee that s/he will return to the court for her/his trial; *to acquit:* to give a decision in a court of law that someone is not guilty of a crime.

2 Regroup the students. Go round monitoring and noting mistakes to discuss with the whole class at the end of the lesson.

2 Read the example sentences aloud to the class, exaggerating the stress pattern slightly. Get students to repeat the sentences, emphasising the stress patterns chorally and individually. Point out that sentences 7 to 10 have a slightly different pattern. Students work in pairs correcting the mistakes and practising the stress pattern together before comparing answers with the whole class.

ANSWERS

1 No, a blackmailer threatens to make secrets known to the public. A mugger robs with violence especially in a dark street.

2 No, a pickpocket steals things from people's pockets, especially in a crowd. A shoplifter takes things from shops without paying.

3 No, a smuggler takes goods or people from one country to another illegally. A hijacker takes control of a vehicle or plane for political motives.

4 No, the lawyers question the witnesses. The jury listens to all the evidence and reaches a verdict

5 No, the accused pleads guilty or not guilty at the beginning of a trial. A judge decides what punishment to give the accused.

6 No, you get a fine if you are caught driving too fast on the motorway. You get a jail sentence if you commit a serious crime.

7 No, some people think Community Service is a more useful and positive way of punishing people than giving a jail sentence.

8 No, he admitted stealing the car when he saw all the evidence against him.

9 No, he was released on bail until the case could be heard.

10 No, they acquitted him when they found the police had been lying.

FURTHER PRACTICE: First Certificate Gold Exam Maximiser **Unit 14, p.98.**

Watch Out! *to steal/to rob*

1 You *steal* things.

2 You *rob* people or places.

EXTRA ACTIVITIES:

1 Play the game *Alibi*. Two students are accused of committing a crime e.g. a bank robbery, but they both provide one another with an alibi, that is they were together at the time of the crime doing something quite different. The two students leave the room to discuss the details of their alibi while the rest of the class decides on questions to ask them in a cross-examination. The class appoints a representative to conduct the cross-examination, but they can write notes suggesting further questions. Each student is cross-examined separately to try to find a 'hole' in their alibi.

2 If you have access to video recordings of a trial such as that of OJ Simpson, play an extract and ask if students can point out *the judge, witnesses, the accused* and *the lawyers*.

3 If you are in an English-speaking country, take students on a visit to the law courts.

Use of English: multiple choice cloze p.143

Read the exam information aloud to the class or get students to read it silently.

Students work individually before comparing answers with a partner and then with the whole class.

ANSWERS

1 C; 2 A; 3 B; 4 B; 5 D; 6 C; 7 A; 8 C; 9 A; 10 D; 11 B; 12 A; 13 D; 14 C; 15 B

FURTHER PRACTICE: First Certificate Gold Exam Maximiser **Unit 14, p.102.**

Grammar: *make/let/allow* p.144

1 Look at the three sentences in Column A with the whole class and discuss what the difference in meaning is.

ANSWERS

There is no difference in meaning between sentences 1 and 2. In both cases he can go home if he wants to. In the third sentence he *had to* go home.

2 Students work with a partner before checking the answers with the whole class.

> **ANSWERS**
>
> 1 b); 2 no passive form; 3 a)

Refer students to the relevant section of the *Grammar reference* on page 177.

3 Students work individually before comparing answers with a partner and then with the whole class.

> **ANSWERS**
>
> 1 allowed 2 let 3 allowed 4 make 5 let 6 made 7 let 8 allowed 9 make

4 Students discuss the questions in groups of three or four before comparing their answers with the whole class.

FURTHER PRACTICE: **First Certificate Gold Exam Maximiser Unit 14, p.100.**

Speaking: p.144

1, **2** and **3** Divide the class into groups of five and allot roles to each group member. If, because of the numbers in your class, you need to have a group of four, omit the Brian North role. If you need to have a group of three, omit the Brian North role and the Mrs North role. Allow five minutes for students to prepare what they are going to say and ten minutes for the actual roleplay. Each group reports back on what they decided to do with Brian.

ALTERNATIVE PROCEDURE: divide the class into five groups, a group for each role. The groups choose a representative to 'perform' in the actual roleplay. They work together deciding what their representative should say and how s/he should say it. After ten minutes their representatives hold their discussion with the class listening. Make a note of any errors or problems and discuss them with the whole class at the end of the activity.

Students read what actually happened to Brian. How many people came to the same decision? Do students think this was a fair decision?

4 Students discuss these items in groups before comparing their answers with the rest of the class.

Grammar: passives p.145

1 Look at the explanation of when the passive is used with the whole class or try to elicit this from them first.

Students work in pairs locating examples of the passive.

> **ANSWERS**
>
> *line 7: to be locked up*
> *line 10: (youngsters) will be held*
> *line 17: he was freed*
> *line 19: he would have been locked away*
> *line 34: a shop assistant was even handed*
> *line 43: to be taken into consideration*
> *line 46: to be remanded*
> *line 51: nowhere can be found*

2 Students work individually before comparing answers with a partner and then with the whole class.

> **ANSWERS**
>
> **Present Continuous:** *active*: The police *are questioning* the suspect; *passive*: The suspect *is being questioned* by the police.
>
> **Past Simple:** *active*: The police *questioned* the suspect; *passive*: The suspect *was questioned* by the police.
>
> **Past Continuous:** *active*: The police *were questioning* the suspect; *passive*: The suspect *was being questioned* by the police.
>
> **Future Simple:** *active*: The police *will question* the suspect; *passive*: The suspect *will be questioned* by the police.
>
> **Future Perfect:** *active*: The police *will have questioned* the suspect; *passive*: The suspect *will have been questioned* by the police.
>
> **Present Perfect Simple:** *active*: The police *have questioned* the suspect; *passive*: The suspect *has been questioned* by the police.
>
> **Past Perfect Simple:** *active*: The police *had questioned* the suspect; *passive*: The suspect *had been questioned* by the police.
>
> **Modals (Present):** *active*: The police *must question* the suspect; *passive*: The suspect *must be questioned* by the police.
>
> **Modals (Past):** *active*: The police *must have questioned* the suspect; *passive*: The suspect *must have been questioned* by the police.

3 Students work in pairs before comparing answers with the whole class.

ANSWERS

1 had been sent 2 it was/had been labelled 3 arrived
4 have had/have been having 5 have already been
shown 6 am being treated 7 have been introduced
8 are woken up 9 were even given 10 was taken
11 were welcomed 12 explained 13 went 14 were
given 15 had 16 checked 17 were leaving 18 were
handed 19 were told 20 were taken 21 are put/will be
put 22 will be told 23 will be given

Refer students to the relevant section of the *Grammar reference* on page 171.

FURTHER PRACTICE: **First Certificate Gold Exam Maximiser Unit 14, p.104.**

Exam focus: Paper 4 Listening: Part 1 (multiple choice) p.146

Read the exam information and advice aloud to the students or get them to read it silently.

Play the cassette straight through without pausing and then again so that students hear each extract twice. Check the answers through with the whole class. Play the cassette again, pausing after each relevant section to go over the answers again if necessary.

TAPESCRIPT

1 I can't believe it ... he got six months. It's just not fair. It all depends on the judge and the judge he got thought he should be made an example of. People like Reggie shouldn't be locked up. <u>I mean it was only a few packets of biscuits and some cans of beer or something.</u> And then kids who go joyriding and smash up cars and go out mugging old people get let off scot free. And anyway it won't do him any good at all – being inside.

2 A: ... and so, you see, I've been asked to go and talk to some of the people over at the other branch. I'm really sorry, but I shouldn't be too late.
   B: But it's Tania's birthday and you did promise after all.
   A: <u>I know, love,</u> but honestly I'll get back as quick as I can.

3 I've had the tests back and they're not good. It's been confirmed. I'm afraid if you're not careful, there's a definite danger of heart attacks if you don't do something about your current lifestyle. I mean, <u>you</u>

<u>really must cut down on all this smoking, drinking and these fatty foods. When did you say was the last time you did any exercise?</u>

4 A: So what did he say then?
   B: Well, he said that if that was how she felt she should go.
   A: No!
   B: Yes, that's right. He said he hated being treated like an idiot.
   A: <u>No! And they seemed such a happy couple.</u>

5 A: I'm terribly sorry, Madam, but we are fully booked this evening until 9.30 p.m.
   B: Look, I'm a regular customer. Isn't there any chance that we could be given <u>a table for two at around 7.00? We just need something very quick before the play starts.</u>

6 It was only at the beginning of this century that women were allowed to vote in this country. It was after this that women began to be taken seriously. <u>But still at the end of the century in spite of women holding important positions throughout government and industry, there are still obvious ways in which women are discriminated against and do not get the same chances as their male counterparts.</u>

7 A: What do you think we should get her?
   B: Oh, well, I thought we'd agreed ...
   A: But she's already got so many clothes. She gets them every birthday and Christmas.
   B: Okay, so let's get her something else then, something really nice. Well, what about a new stereo system? <u>I mean, it's not everyday that somebody is offered a place at the best university in the country.</u>
   A: No, you're absolutely right, but then what are we going to get her for Christmas?

8 Excuse me. I'm from Ecosafe. I wonder if you could spare a few moments of your time. As you may know the local government are planning to build a ring road around the town and we're convinced that this will do terrible environmental damage. We've already got over 1000 signatures on a petition we're going to present to the local government. <u>Would you like to add your name?</u>

ANSWERS

(see underlined sentences in tapescript)
1 A; 2 B; 3 A; 4 A; 5 B; 6 C; 7 B; 8 B

Speaking p.147

1 This information gap activity must be done in pairs. Go round monitoring and noting any errors, especially with passive forms. Discuss the errors with the whole group at the end of the activity without saying who has made the error.

ANSWERS

1 D; 2 F; 3 B; 4 H; 5 A; 6 G; 7 C; 8 E

2 Students work individually before comparing their answers with a partner and then with the whole class.

ANSWERS

line 1: delete *been*; *line 3:* delete *of*; *line 4:* delete *to*; *line 7:* delete *being*; *line 9:* delete *him*; line 10: delete *them*; *line 11:* delete *it*; *line 13:* delete *absolutely*; *line 15:* delete *having*; *line 17:* delete *at*

Listening: Guardian Angels p.148

1 Play the cassette straight through once so that students can answer the gist question.

TAPESCRIPT

H = husband   W = wife

w: Did you see this thing here in the paper about Guardian Angels?

H: No, I haven't had a chance to read it yet.

w: Well, I think it's really interesting. <u>Apparently it's been going on for a while in the States and now they're coming over here.</u>

H: Who or what exactly are you talking about?

w: The Guardian Angels! It says here that <u>they are an all-volunteer, unarmed organisation</u> dedicated to stamping out urban crime, launched in the US ten years ago by Curtis Sliwa . . .Sliva. . . or however you pronounce it.

H: So, what do they actually do?

w: Hang on, I'm coming to that ... <u>well, as far as I can make out, the idea in Britain is that they just sort of patrol the underground and try and stop crime.</u> Ah yes, now listen to this bit, one of them who was interviewed says, 'If we see a fight, we break it up and try to calm the situation down. The main thing we are taught is to separate the people and get them out of sight of each other. We don't hurt anybody. <u>We get training over three months and this covers self-defence, first aid and law.</u>'

H: That's all very well, but what if they come across someone with a gun? What happens then?

w: Well, this woman says, 'I'd make sure the public were out of the way, then I'd get the attention of the person. I'd try to distract him by saying, "Look behind you." I also think it would be a question of playing for time. I'd ask him why he was doing this, what he thought he was trying to achieve and just try to get to the root of the problem. There's a whole patrol of us, so once the message is passed down, <u>the person nearest the driver can get him to get the police.</u>'

H: Mmm. Does it say what the police think about all this?

w: Er ... yes, well, it seems that <u>a police spokesman had said they're quite suspicious about the whole thing</u> and really regard the Guardian Angels more or less as vigilantes – more trouble than they're worth. But this woman reckons that, <u>in fact the police they've actually come into contact with really appreciate them and what they're trying to do.</u> The last thing she says is, 'We're not vigilantes, we're just making sure that there aren't any violent crimes committed against people. If we can stop crime, we will. We're not making our own laws; anyone can carry out a citizen's arrest.'

H: <u>I think it's a pretty stupid idea – we've got the police already.</u>

w: <u>Yes, but there are never enough of them. Surely it can't hurt to have extra people on the look out for trouble ...?</u>

---

2 Play the cassette a second time. Students compare their answers with a partner. Play the cassette again so that they can check their answers. Go through the answers with the whole class, playing the cassette a third time and pausing after the relevant section if necessary.

ANSWERS

(see underlined sentences in tapescript)

1 True 2 False 3 False 4 True 5 True 6 True
7 True 8 False

3 Students work in groups of three or four discussing the statements. They should appoint a spokesperson to report the main points of their discussion back to the rest of the class.

ALTERNATIVE PROCEDURE: conduct a whole class discussion of the statements.

Vocabulary: phrasal verbs (*make*) p.148

Focus students' attention on the sentence from the listening, and elicit the meaning of 'to make out' *(to see, to understand)*.

1 Students work individually before comparing their answers with a partner and then with the whole class.

> **ANSWERS**
> 1 made for 2 made it up 3 made out 4 make up for
> 5 make out 6 make of 7 make up

2 Encourage students to use other phrasal verbs they have studied as well when writing their stories.

FURTHER PRACTICE: **First Certificate Gold Exam Maximiser Unit 14, p.100.**

Unit 14 Review

> **ANSWERS**
>
> **1** 2 a) staggered b) jury c) denied d) nibbles e) fidgeting f) drenched g) flabbergasted
>
> **2** 1 delete *been* 2 delete *to* 3 I haven't **been** allowed ... 4 delete *was* 5 I am **being** looked after ... 6 What do you think you will **be** doing ... 7 He could have **been** delayed ... 8 delete *be* 9 Mike really enjoys **being** asked ... 10 You know he made it all **up**. 11 delete *to* 12 delete *be*
>
> **3** 1 of 2 had 3 was 4 commit 5 be 6 of 7 were 8 to 9 been 10 the 11 was 12 of 13 was 14 for 15 were 16 to

Now your students are ready to do the test for Unit 14 on page 138.

U N I T
15 The power of words

Reading pp.150–151

1 Focus students' attention on the pictures and get individual students to describe them before discussing the questions with the whole class.

ANSWERS

a) To someone from Britain, crossing their fingers in this way indicates 'Good luck'.

b) This indicates 'Please, wait a minute.' for someone from Argentina and other Latin American countries.

c) A sharp tilt of the head backwards in Turkey and Greece indicates 'No'.

d) In many countries, for example Egypt and Italy, someone kisses their fingers in this way to indicate that they think something or someone is beautiful.

2 Set a three-minute time limit for the gist questions. Students work individually before comparing answers with the whole class.

ANSWERS

1 The aim of the experiment was to teach the apes to talk.

2 Yes. Washoe learnt 132 signs and used them even when alone.

3 Set a ten-minute time limit for the second reading task. Students work individually before comparing their answers with a partner and then with the whole class.

ANSWERS

The chimps were able to:

1 recognise the meaning of individual words.

2 ask for things.

4 use bad language.

5 talk to one another in sign language.

6 name new objects by combining words.

7 decide on correct word order.

4 Students work individually before comparing their answers with a partner and then with the whole class.

ANSWERS

2 communication 3 beliefs 4 talkative 5 indecisive
6 incorrect 7 disabled 8 application 9 invention
10 scientific 11 representative 12 doubtful

5 Students discuss the questions in groups of three or four, appointing a spokesperson to report the main points of their discussion back to the rest of the class.

ALTERNATIVE PROCEDURE: conduct a whole class discussion.

Grammar: expressing hypothetical meaning pp.151–152

1 Focus attention on the speech bubble and elicit possible ways of completing it from the whole class.

POSSIBLE ANSWERS

... would know what food they liked best.
... would be famous.
... would learn so much more about them.

2 Students work individually before comparing their answers with a partner and then with the whole class.

ANSWERS

1 False: *wish* is followed by the Past Simple when it refers to the present or future.

2 True

3 True

3 Students work in pairs before comparing their answers with the whole class.

ANSWERS

1 wasn't 2 hadn't gone 3 could 4 didn't 5 wouldn't
6 lived 7 had stayed

4 Demonstrate the task by telling students what four wishes you would make. They then write their wishes individually as you go round checking and pointing out any errors. Students read their sentences aloud to the whole class. Encourage students to listen out for anyone who made the same wishes as they did.

5 Give students time to read the sentences before eliciting the answers from the whole class.

ANSWERS

1 They haven't gone yet. 2 I'm sorry I went to the party.
3 I would like you to come early. 4 He has taken it.

6 Students work in pairs before comparing their answers with the whole class.

POSSIBLE ANSWERS

1 ... had more friends 2 ... had studied harder
3 ... stay at home 4 ... left early 5 ... would stop
fidgeting 6 ... got down to work 7 ... walk
8 ... offered to wash the car 9 ... had a car
10 ... we went home

Watch Out! *'d rather/'d better*

a) *'d rather* means 'prefer'; *'d better* means 'should'

b) *'d rather = would; 'd better = had*

7 **1** Play the song once. Have students heard it before? Do they like it?

TAPESCRIPT

Verse 1
You know I never meant to see you again,
But I only passed by as a friend, yeah.
All this time I stayed out of sight,
I started wondering why.

Chorus
Now, I ... Ooh, now, I wish it would rain down, down on me.
Ooh yes, I wish it would rain, rain down on me now.
Ooh yes, I wish it would rain down, down on me.
Ooh yes, I wish it would rain on me.

Verse 2
You said you didn't need me in your life,
Oh, I guess you were right, yeah.
Ooh, I never meant to cause you no pain,
But it looks like I did it again, yeah.

Chorus

ANSWER

He wishes it would rain. He wishes that he hadn't hurt her.

2 Students match up the two halves of the lines while they listen to the song again

ANSWERS

1 h); 2 e); 3 a); 4 c); 5 d); 6 b); 7 f); 8 g)

3 Students discuss the answers in pairs before comparing notes with the rest of the class.

POSSIBLE ANSWERS

a) Because they had split up.
b) Why he hadn't seen her again.
c) The pain caused by coming back into her life.

FURTHER PRACTICE: First Certificate Gold Exam Maximiser **Unit 15, p.105.**

Use of English: word formation p.153

1 Students work in pairs before comparing answers with the whole class.

POSSIBLE ANSWERS

1 *to translate:* when you speak two or more languages and you are with someone who does not speak one of the languages you know.

2 *to repeat:* when someone did not hear what you said.

3 *to whisper:* when you don't want someone else to hear what you want to say to a person who is sitting or standing close to you.

4 *to mutter:* when you are angry, but you don't want anyone to hear exactly what you are saying.

5 *to chat:* when you are with friends.

6 *to gossip:* when you know something about someone else which you want to tell your friends.

7 *to shout:* when the person you are talking to is too far away to hear you if you talk or because you are angry.

8 *to discuss:* when you want to express your opinions and find out what other people's opinions are about something.

9 *to row:* when you are angry about something and you talk about it with someone in an angry way.

10 *to beg:* when you want very badly to persuade someone to do/not to do something.

11 *to mention:* when you talk about something very briefly and it is not the main thing you are talking about.

12 *to inform:* when you give someone information

13 *to contradict:* when you say the opposite of something someone else has just said.

14 *to speak up:* when people didn't hear you the first time because you were speaking too softly and you repeat it in a louder voice.

2 Tell students to read the text straight through and to answer the question: What kind of event is described in the text? (A meeting of a neighbourhood association).Was it a success? (No). Students work individually before checking their answers open class.

ANSWERS
1 meeting 2 representative 3 repetitive 4 speech
5 muttering 6 argument 7 immediately 8 agreement
9 inaccuracies 10 communication

FURTHER PRACTICE: First Certificate Gold Exam Maximiser **Unit 15, p.110.**

Listening: extracts p.153

1 Students work in pairs before comparing their answers with the whole class.

ANSWERS
A a TV guide B an agenda C a diary D an instruction manual E a love letter F a telegram G a play
H a review

2 Play the cassette through once. Students compare answers with a partner. Play the cassette again before checking the answers with the whole class. Play the cassette again, pausing after the relevant section if necessary.

TAPESCRIPT

1 Hi, Mike, this is Carol and it's about 10.30. This is just to say that I phoned the sports centre and booked a court for 7.30 on Wednesday. I hope all the work you're having done on the house is going okay. Anyway, tell me all about it on Wednesday. Bye for now.

2 **A:** Oh yeah, wasn't it great, especially the ending? I really wasn't expecting it.

B: No, I wasn't either. And I thought that was so sad, I mean they were fantastic together.

A: Didn't you love that bit where they shot the petrol tank of the truck and the whole thing exploded?

B: Did you see the look on that fat guy's face? Wasn't it awful when he looked round . . .

3 And welcome to another edition of the show where we give love the chance to grow. And this week the possible destinations include ballooning over southern France, skiing in the Swiss Alps or lying amongst the palm trees on the golden sands of the Bahamas. What a wonderful opportunity for one lucky couple. But first of all let's meet our lucky contestants and our first three handsome gentlemen are Brian from ...

4 Hardly anyone would argue that he is perhaps the greatest British playwright that has ever lived and as well as that it should be remembered that between 1590 and 1610 Shakespeare wrote over 100,000 lines of drama and brought to life 1,277 characters, major and minor. His vocabulary was one of the richest of any English writer. There are over 30,000 different words used in his works, double the average vocabulary for an educated individual in the late 20th century. Of course some critics still refuse to believe that a mere actor, educated at a grammar school in the English Midlands ...

5 I don't know what to do really. I mean it was quite a relief when he had to go off on holiday with his family for six weeks. It gave me a bit of time away from it all. You know, he's a nice guy, I like him a lot, but he just gets so intense, it all gets a bit too much. And I never spend enough time with my other friends in case he gets jealous. It's ridiculous ... we end up being together all the time, just the two of us. I don't think I can go back to it being like that.

6 We are sorry to announce that all trains to Plymouth will be running late this morning due to the need to carry out essential engineering works on the line. We would like to apologise to all our customers for any inconvenience this might cause, but all normal services should be resumed by midday.

7 **A:** So, how does it actually work?

B: Well, it's terribly simple. You take any document that you want to send, up to ten pages at one time, and you place it face down just here, right?

A: Uh-huh.

B: And then you need to enter the number of the person you are sending it to.

A: Is that their telephone number?

B: Well, it could be, but sometimes people have a separate number for this.

A: I see, and then I suppose you just press 'Start'.

B: That's it and then it will feed through.

8 So, perhaps just before we actually get down to business, I could just express our congratulations to Jill for her new appointment to the position of Head of Sales. I know this has been a very popular appointment and we're all looking forward to seeing the energy and enthusiasm that Jill will be bringing to the job. Now, turning to our first item – market share in Europe. Yes, well, now I know this has been a tough year, not helped by the widespread economic recession. But, having said this ...

ANSWERS

1 *text C:* he is leaving a message on Carol's answer machine confirming a game of squash.

2 *text H:* they are discussing the film.

3 *text A:* the TV presenter is introducing 'Blind Date'.

4 *text G:* she is talking about William Shakespeare, the author of *Romeo and Juliet*.

5 *text E:* she is talking about the man who has sent her the love letter and how she feels about him.

6 *text F:* the train which the writer of the telegram was hoping to catch will be delayed.

7 *text D:* the shop assistant is explaining to a customer how to use the fax machine.

8 *text B:* this is the opening of the department meeting.

Writing: a report (2) p.154

Students work individually studying the information on p. 72 and the model report in the Writing Reference. Work with the whole class, eliciting suggestions for key words to underline (exam courses; advertising; students like yourself, potential benefits, television, radio and press advertising) and for the number of sections in the report (one section each for TV, radio and press advertising). Students work in pairs brainstorming points to include in each section. The actual writing can be done in class or at home.

FURTHER PRACTICE: First Certificate Gold Exam Maximiser Unit 15, p.111.

Grammar: *to have something done* p.154

1 Elicit an answer from the whole class.

ANSWERS

meaning: in the first sentence the person referred to as 'you' is not doing the work her/himself, whereas in the second sentence s/he is.

form: in the first sentence the form is the Present Continuous form of *have* + the past participle of *do*; in the second sentence the form is the Present Continuous form of *do*.

2 Students work in pairs before comparing their answers with the whole class.

ANSWERS

a house: to paint

a watch: to mend (*You can have your watch mended.*)

hair: to cut (*You can have your hair cut.*)

a sofa: to mend, to deliver (*You can have your sofa mended/delivered*)

eyes: to test (*You can have your eyes tested.*)

a photo: to take (*You can have your photo taken.*)

trousers: to mend, to dry-clean (*You can have your trousers mended/dry-cleaned.*)

3 Students work individually before comparing their answers with a partner and then with the whole class.

ANSWERS

Wednesday

He had his jacket dry-cleaned.

He had his eyes tested.

He had a new window in the bathroom put in.

Thursday

He is having a new sofa delivered.

He is having the bathroom painted.

He is having the oil and tyres of his car changed.

Friday

He is going to have the TV repaired.

He is going to have his photo taken.

He is going to have his hair cut.

4 Demonstrate this task yourself by telling students what you would have done. Students work individually writing at least five sentences. They read their sentences aloud to the rest of the class. Who has the most extravagant plans?

Watch Out! *to have something done*

The only verb that can replace *have* is *get*.

FURTHER PRACTICE: **First Certificate Gold Exam Maximiser Unit 15, p.107.**

Exam Focus: Paper 3 Use of English: Part 3 (key word transformation) p.155

Read the exam information and advice aloud to the class. Students work individually completing the sentences before checking their answers open-class.

> **ANSWERS**
> 1 love to be able to 2 only I had not told 3 time you children were 4 rather you didn't 5 regret not learning 6 suppose someone saw you 7 wish you wouldn't tap 8 has her hair washed 9 had their car stolen 10 must have/get our house

Listening: handwriting p.156

1 Choose a few students with very different handwriting and get them to pass their notebooks around the class for students to look at their writing. Then discuss the questions with the whole class.

2 Play the cassette once so that students can do the gist task.

> **TAPESCRIPT**
>
> **I = interviewer PM = Patricia Marne**
>
> **I:** ... and with us on today's programme we have graphologist, Patricia Marne. Patricia founded the Graphology Society and has published a number of books on the subject. Patricia, welcome.
>
> **PM:** Thank you very much.
>
> **I:** Now, it has been said that our writing gives away a great deal about our characters and <u>even just our signatures provide a large amount of information for the graphologist</u>.
>
> **PM:** That's absolutely right, and <u>graphology can be used for all sorts of things like marriage guidance</u>, career advice, staff recruitment and for solving emotional problems.
>
> **I:** Now I understand that many different features of one's writing are taken into account by the graphologist. What are these exactly?
>
> **PM:** Well, there's the slant of the writing, the pressure and spacing, the capital letters, the margins and the signature – they all play a part in handwriting analysis.
>
> **I:** Perhaps we can begin by looking at the question of slant.
>
> **PM:** Okay ... well, basically there are three kinds of slant – right, left and upright – though occasionally you may come across a mixture. If your handwriting slants to the right, it shows a friendly and sociable disposition. You enjoy human contact and like to have people around you. <u>An upright slant on the other hand reveals very good self-control and your head usually rules your heart</u>. A definite left slant shows an introspective nature, often shy and reserved – you are more interested in your own feelings than other people's.
>
> **I:** So what would you say about this first sample?
>
> **PM:** Ah yes ... this is very interesting ... you can see that there's no consistent slant here – some letters are upright, some lean to the left and some lean to the right. This shows versatility and an erratic character. The writer is impatient, intelligent and highly active. <u>She enjoys mixing and communicating with lots of people</u> as she enjoys variety and change in her life.
>
> **I:** Now, what about size of handwriting?
>
> **PM:** Yes, well, basically, very large handwriting belongs to the extroverts and socially-minded people who like attention and admiration. <u>The small writer, on the other hand, is more concerned with things than people.</u> Small writing is found in the handwriting of many scientists and intellectuals. They generally aren't particularly interested in an active social life, <u>but will often be quite careful about who they choose as close friends.</u> Medium handwriting shows a good balance between mind and emotion. Such writers are generally able to communicate and mix without being either reserved or over-familiar.
>
> **I:** So what would you say about this second sample?
>
> **PM:** <u>Well, this more rounded, medium size handwriting shows a lively personality who enjoys companionship. She is talkative – see the small open a's and o's – and has a friendly approach to people,</u> but the wide spaces between the words indicates that she can keep her personal distance when necessary.
>
> **I:** Now isn't there also something about the way we form our letters?
>
> **PM:** Yes, that's right, there are four basic types.
>
> **I:** So, what would you say about this third sample?
>
> **PM:** Oh, yes, this is a very good example of what we call 'garland' writing. This is an easy script and can be formed very quickly. It's a rather grand style and you can also see that the m's and n's tend to be

written like the letter u. Often these people are friendly, kind and affectionate, but sometimes a bit lazy. It's important for them to have an active social life and in particular they enjoy meeting glamorous people. <u>They make an excellent host or hostess, as this brings out the grand style of their nature.</u>

ANSWERS

1✔ 3✔ 4✔ 5✔ 6✔ 7✔

3 Play the cassette again. Students do this individually before comparing answers with a partner and the whole class. Play the cassette one more time if necessary, pausing after the relevant sections.

ANSWERS

(see underlined sentences in tapescript)
1 True 2 False 3 False 4 True 5 False 6 True 7 True

4 Before students analyse a partner's handwriting get them to analyse your writing from a sample on the board.

Reading pp.156–157

1 Focus students' attention on the photos and get individual students to describe them before discussing the questions with the whole class.

2 Set a three-minute time limit for the gist question.

ANSWER

His opinion is not clear.

3 Set a ten-minute time limit for the second reading task. Remind students of the suggested procedure in Unit 6, page 64 or get them to read it again.

ANSWERS

1 D; 2 B; 3 B; 4 C; 5 C

Writing: discursive (2) p.158

1 Students discuss the questions in groups of three or four appointing a spokesperson to report their conclusions back to the rest of the class.

ALTERNATIVE PROCEDURE: conduct a debate with half the class preparing arguments for the motion 'Graffiti is a crime' and the other half preparing arguments against. They

should then choose a representative to argue their case. If possible, another class can be invited in to hear the debate and to vote for or against the motion.

2 Students work individually before comparing their answers with the whole class.

ANSWERS

1 for 2 for 3 against 4 neutral 5 against 6 against
7 against 8 for 9 against

3 Read the rubric and advice aloud to the class or get students to read it silently. Students work individually writing their plans. The final version can be written for homework.

FURTHER PRACTICE: First Certificate Gold Exam Maximiser **Unit 15, p.111.**

Units 11–15 Progress check

ANSWERS

1 1 C; 2 B; 3 A; 4 D; 5 A; 6 D; 7 C; 8 C; 9 B;
10 D; 11 B; 12 C; 13 B; 14 B; 15 D

2 1 That *must be* you when you were a baby.
2 Helen *must have forgotten* that we had a meeting this morning ...
3 You *shouldn't have been* so rude to her.
4 I suppose *I could have lent* you my calculator ...
5 You *must be* freezing.
6 They *shouldn't have pulled down* that house.
7 But he *can't have done* it.
8 That *can't be* the postman.

3 1 been 2 can 3 going 4 sudden 5 must 6 them
7 going 8 had 9 make 10 trying 11 through
12 could 13 him 14 round 15 had

4 1 It took her a long time *to get over* her illness.
2 I *wish I hadn't said* that to him.
3 It *can't have been* Tony we saw. He's in London.
4 I *need to post* this letter tonight.
5 I'm sure the children *have been getting up to* something terrible while we've been out.
6 I *had the tyres checked* on my car.
7 It's *time you went* to bed.
8 I couldn't *make out* the number plate in the fog.
9 'd *rather you didn't tell* Andrew about our conversation.

10 You **could fail the exam unless** you start
studying now.

5 1 mix/get 2 hadn't told/would have been able
3 start/will have 4 will lose/play 5 will print/press
6 promise/will tell

6 1 fog 2 breeze 3 earthquake 4 charity 5 drought
6 journalist 7 headline 8 chimney 9 cellar
10 hedge 11 smuggle 12 agenda

7 *line 1:* the grammar   *line 7:* often to
line 2: makes up   *line 10:* visiting in
line 3: an English books   *line 13:* be get
line 4: like as   *line 14:* a bit of
line 5: they are   *line 15:* are being

8 1 complaints 2 delivery 3 conclusion 4 failure
5 combination 6 employees 7 representatives
8 management/managers 9 communication
10 competition

9 1 away 2 up 3 worn 4 rub 5 round 6 throw
7 out 8 make 9 stick 10 get 11 out 12 get

**Now your students are ready to do the Progress test
for Units 11–15 on pages 139–141.**

Unit 1 test

Choose the best alternative to fill the gap in each of the following sentences.

1 I find the way she keeps playing with her hair really ..... .
 A irritating **B** irritated **C** thrilling **D** thrilled

2 She was ..... to discover that she had won first prize.
 A excited **B** astonished **C** lucky **D** nervous

3 You must have felt ..... when all your exams were over.
 A relieved **B** upset **C** irritated **D** cross

4 *The Silence of the Lambs* is the most ..... film I've ever seen.
 A terrifying **B** terrified **C** scared **D** excited

5 I was ..... that Tom could come to the party after all.
 A irritating **B** nervous **C** furious **D** glad

6 Who ..... you Michael and Mandy were getting married?
 A tells **B** did tell **C** told **D** telling

7 Can you tell me where ..... a ticket for tomorrow night's concert?
 A do I buy **B** buying **C** I buy **D** get

8 ..... that we should cancel the meeting?
 A Is she agree **B** She agree **C** Agrees she
 D Does she agree

9 Do you know ..... possible to get to Lilydale by bus?
 A if is **B** is **C** if it is **D** is it

10 What time ..... tomorrow?
 A you leaving **B** you are leaving **C** you leave
 D are you leaving

11 ..... have Maria and Stelios been studying English?
 A How many time **B** How many times **C** How much
 D How long

12 They used to do extreme sports, ...?
 A didn't they **B** don't they **C** used they
 D hadn't they

13 Let's take up hang gliding, ...?
 A do we **B** let we **C** shall we **D** are we

14 I hadn't been riding before and could barely ..... the horse at first.
 A get into **B** get out of **C** get on **D** get off

15 I misread the time on the ticket and we ..... the plane.
 A caught **B** missed **C** lost **D** got on

16 If you know when you're coming back it would be better to buy a ..... ticket.
 A first-class **B** single **C** return **D** one-way

17 If they had been wearing ..... they might have survived when their plane crashed into the sea.
 A life-belts **B** seat-belts **C** cabins **D** yachts

18 How long does it usually take to ..... for a domestic flight?
 A check out **B** check in **C** check over **D** check on

19 They're starting their ..... by flying to Tokyo.
 A travel **B** voyage **C** trip **D** journey

20 The shop assistant was most ..... when I told her that there was no price on the jar of olives.
 A unhelpful **B** helpless **C** thoughtful **D** unhelpfully

21 He may not be good looking but he's one of the most ..... people I've ever met.
 A likely **B** likeable **C** unlikely **D** likeness

22 The space mission was launched ..... earlier this morning.
 A unsuccessfully **B** successfully **C** unsuccessful
 D successful

23 I don't know why exactly but I suspect him of being ..... .
 A dishonesty **B** dishonestly **C** dishonest **D** honesty

24 The organisers ..... how many people would be attending the course and there were not enough chairs.
 A estimated **B** overestimated **C** overrated
 D underestimated

25 He runs a very ..... business selling spare parts for cars on the Internet.
 A profitable **B** profiting **C** profit **D** profitably

Unit 2 test

Choose the best alternative to fill the gap in each of the following sentences.

1 The ..... in our building often falls asleep at the front desk.
A caretaker   B stockbroker   C undertaker
D bookmaker

2 There was a ..... on the door who wouldn't let us into the disco.
A referee   B lifeguard   C bouncer   D wrestler

3 The sink is completely blocked so we'll have to get a(n) ..... .
A miner   B undertaker   C surgeon   D plumber

4 He hired a ..... to try to follow her everywhere she went.
A traffic warden   B caretaker   C lifeguard
D private investigator

5 ..... a minute! I can't find my keys.
A Keep on   B Hold on   C Go on   D Carry on

6 We ..... to a concert this Friday.
A go   B have gone   C are going   D gone

7 I realise as I look at my grandmother that she ..... old.
A get   B does get   C will get   D is getting

8 As soon as he ..... into bed he falls asleep.
A will get   B gets   C is getting   D does get

9 The sun ..... at different times according to the seasons.
A rises and sets   B is rising and setting
C will rise and set   D rose and set

10 She ..... with him again unless he apologises.
A didn't work   B isn't working   C doesn't work
D won't work

11 If you ..... to Berlin, call my friend Peter and say 'hello' from me.
A will go   B go   C won't go   D going

12 She gets fifteen per cent ..... on every insurance policy she sells.
A salary   B pension   C bonus   D commission

13 My uncle is thinking of ..... next year and spending the rest of his life travelling round the world .
A retiring   B being made redundant   C being sacked
D being resigned

14 Before they opened the new factory a lot of the young people round here were ..... the dole.
A in   B on   C up   D at

15 In the interview they asked if I had much ..... with computers.
A experiences   B experiment   C experiments
D experience

16 I worked all summer but I didn't ..... enough to save any money.
A gain   B win   C pay   D earn

17 Many governments have tried to ban ..... .
A trade unions   B employers   C syndicates
D employees

18 There is a special section of the newspaper entirely devoted to job ..... .
A propaganda   B announces   C advertisements
D publicity

19 She has ..... a position as general manager.
A applied   B asked   C solicited   D applied for

20 I look forward to ..... from you and receiving your brochure.
A heard   B hearing   C hear   D hears

21 Are there any squash ..... in the area?
A greens   B pitches   C courts   D rings

22 People sometimes use baseball ..... as weapons.
A bats   B sticks   C clubs   D rackets

23 It doesn't matter which football team you support the ..... is always in the wrong.
A linesman   B umpire   C arbitrator   D referee

24 I think the ..... is a bit too high, don't you?
A pitch   B ring   C net   D set

25 ..... , I want to explain why the team has not managed to get into the first division.
A Finally   B In the end   C At the end   D Last

Unit 3 test

Choose the best alternative to fill the gap in each of the following sentences.

1 I'm not as musical ..... my sister Mary.
A than **B** as **C** that **D** like

2 Experience is often more important ..... qualifications.
A than **B** so **C** as **D** that

3 They've only got a ..... more copies of the book left.
A far **B** much **C** lot **D** few

4 They say that things often get ..... before they get better.
A more bad **B** worse **C** as bad **D** so bad

5 She seems much ..... since she broke up with Tim.
A more happy **B** happy **C** happier **D** happiest

6 She is one of ..... people I have ever met.
A most intelligent **B** a most intelligent
C the more intelligent **D** the most intelligent

7 His parents died when he was very young so he was ..... by an aunt.
A grown up **B** brought up **C** taken after
D taken care

8 I have always ..... my older brother for his courage and honesty.
A taken up **B** taken after **C** looked after
D looked up to

9 We'll have to find someone to ..... our plants while we're away on holiday.
A bring up **B** get on **C** look after **D** grow up

10 Even very active children often stop playing sport when they ..... .
A tell off **B** bring up **C** look up **D** grow up

11 I haven't been ..... Pete lately.
A getting up to **B** getting on with
C getting through to **D** getting round to

12 We used to ..... all sorts of things when our parents went out.
A get through to **B** get over **C** get up to
D get on with

13 The conductor ..... the boys off for misbehaving on the bus.
A told **B** said **C** shouted **D** cried

14 Don't be so ..... ! He was only joking.
A sensible **B** senseless **C** sensitive **D** insensitive

15 My sister has just ..... sixteen.
A turned **B** completed **C** become **D** had

16 You all ..... you're having a wonderful time.
A look as **B** look that **C** look so **D** look as if

17 My father ..... a bit bald but he's still very handsome.
A is going **B** has **C** is having **D** goes

18 How ..... is your brother?
A high **B** tall **C** long **D** height

19 She ..... long dark hair and blue eyes.
A is **B** has got **C** is getting **D** is going

20 My brother and my ..... have just had twins.
A sister-in-love **B** sister-in-low **C** sister-in-law
D political sister

21 Just think! Next month you'll be ..... and it seems like only yesterday you were a baby.
A in your teens **B** in your teenage **C** at your teens
D teenager

22 She's very ..... . She gets to work at 7.30 and almost never leaves before 6.00.
A worker **B** worked **C** working-hard
D hard-working

23 I don't think you should be so ..... with the children. Watching television for half an hour a day won't do them any harm.
A stubborn **B** strict **C** reliable **D** thoughtful

24 It was very ..... of you to lend us your car for the whole week.
A generous **B** ambitious **C** modest **D** thoughtless

25 It was very ..... of you to eat the last slice of cake without asking.
A loyal **B** sensitive **C** self-confident **D** naughty

Unit 4 test

Choose the best alternative to fill the gap in each of the following sentences.

1 The twentieth century has seen some extraordinary ..... discoveries .
   A scientific   **B** scientist   **C** science   **D** scientifically

2 There is some controversy over who is responsible for the ..... of penicillin.
   A discovery   **B** creation   **C** invention   **D** revolution

3 Nobody knows if the ..... *Mona Lisa* is in the Louvre or in a private collection.
   A really   **B** real   **C** realistic   **D** realistically

4 My uncle works as a research ..... for a big pharmaceutical company.
   A chemist   **B** chemical   **C** chemically   **D** chemistry

5 Many people are reluctant to use ..... that cause damage to the environment.
   A productions   **B** products   **C** produce
   D manufacturing

6 She's a very ..... person who enjoys fixing things.
   A practical   **B** practically   **C** practise   **D** practice

7 Would you like ..... you up from the station?
   A we picked   **B** us picking   **C** us to pick
   D us to picking

8 I look more ..... my mother than my father as I grow older.
   A than   **B** similar   **C** as   **D** like

9 What about doing something we've never done before ..... going bungee jumping?
   A such   **B** as   **C** like   **D** such like

10 ..... getting up early in the morning?
    A Do you like   **B** Are you like   **C** Like you   **D** You like

11 In the summer I like ..... at least two weeks at the seaside with friends.
    A spend   **B** to spending   **C** to spend   **D** spent

12 A: ..... ?
    B: He's a bit taller than me and he's got fair hair.
    A What is your brother like   **B** How is your brother like
    C What is your brother   **D** How is your brother

13 I've got so much spare time now I'm thinking of taking ..... a new hobby like stamp collecting.
    A in   **B** up   **C** off   **D** over

14 I wish he'd let us make some of the decisions instead of completely taking ..... all our meetings.
    A in   **B** off   **C** over   **D** up

15 I don't think they'll be taking ..... any more teachers this term because there aren't many students.
    A on   **B** in   **C** up   **D** over

16 High risk sports have really taken ..... .
    A up   **B** off   **C** in   **D** on

17 I'm going to take a couple of days ..... next month to help my sister move house.
    A off   **B** over   **C** out   **D** up

18 I had to give up going to aerobics. It was ..... up too much time.
    A giving   **B** getting   **C** putting   **D** taking

19 Everyone laughed when he took ..... the teacher so well.
    A over   **B** up   **C** out   **D** off

20 I have never met ..... person in my life.
    A such a rude   **B** so rude   **C** such rude   **D** ruder

21 I ..... a bath when the doorbell rang.
    A had   **B** have   **C** have had   **D** was having

22 She ..... the door when she realised the keys were inside the car.
    A has already locked   **B** is already locking
    C had already locked   **D** already locked.

23 First she ..... all her papers in order. Then she began to write the letter.
    A put   **B** was putting   **C** had put   **D** has put

24 It was such a shock to receive a letter like that ..... .
    A in the red   **B** in the pink   **C** out of the blue
    D over the moon

25 I knew that something ..... was going on as soon as I walked into the room.
    A huge   **B** massive   **C** vast   **D** odd

Progress test Units 1–5

1 Multiple choice cloze

Circle the alternative that best fits each of the gaps in this text. The first one (**0**) has been done for you.

My friend's wedding

My friends Laura and Ian (0) *got* married last Saturday. It was a lovely (1) ..... The music was wonderful and the (2) ..... sang beautifully. The (3) ..... looked absolutely stunning in a white silk dress with pearls around the neckline. She was carrying a (4) ..... of roses and orchids. She had asked her three sisters to be (5) ..... and they looked very pretty as well. There was one awkward moment when it seemed that the (6) ..... could not find the rings, but in the end it turned out that he was only pretending not to know where they were. The (7) ..... was held in a huge tent on the village green. All the (8) ..... enjoyed themselves thoroughly. There were some very funny (9) ..... as well. I bet Laura and Ian got a surprise when they drove off to go on their (10) ..... and heard all those tin cans that we had tied on the back of their car. Ian had to (11) ..... to stop all the noise. Laura actually looked a bit (12) ..... but we only did it for fun. No one knows exactly where they've gone but a friend is (13) ..... after Ian's flat until they get back. They're planning to live there until they (14) ..... something a bit (15) ..... .

0 **A** had   **B** are   **C** got   **D** did

1 **A** marriage   **B** engagement   **C** matrimony   **D** wedding

2 **A** choir   **B** organist   **C** singers   **D** band

3 **A** wife   **B** fiancé   **C** bride   **D** groom

4 **A** bunch   **B** branch   **C** collection   **D** bouquet

5 **A** companions   **B** bridesmaids   **C** assistants   **D** helpers

6 **A** best man   **B** best friend   **C** best boy   **D** best fellow

7 **A** party   **B** meal   **C** food   **D** reception

8 **A** guests   **B** invited   **C** hosts   **D** friends

9 **A** talks   **B** speeches   **C** discourses   **D** speaking

10 **A** holiday   **B** vacation   **C** honeymoon   **D** break

11 **A** slow out   **B** slow down   **C** slow through   **D** slow over

12 **A** annoying   **B** annoy   **C** annoys   **D** annoyed

13 **A** taking   **B** looking   **C** going   **D** watching

14 **A** will find   **B** are finding   **C** found   **D** find

15 **A** more big   **B** big   **C** bigger   **D** biggest

(15 marks)

2 Open cloze

Fill each gap with one suitable word. The first one (**0**) has been done for you.

A rewarding job

All the members (0) *of* my family have interesting and rewarding jobs. My sister works as (1) ..... social worker with the local council. She gets a (2) ..... of satisfaction from her job though the (3) ..... is not very good and she finds it difficult to save any money. She studied (4) ..... three years at university and she often goes on training (5) ..... so she has very good (6) ..... now. She has also gained a lot of experience with (7) ..... sorts of people. She is much (8) ..... patient than I am and almost (9) ..... loses her temper, even with the (10) ..... abusive or unpleasant clients.

In our area a lot of people have been (11) ..... redundant and this has caused a lot of social problems. Many families live (12) ..... the dole and this means they find it hard to get (13) ..... . They certainly do not have very (14) ..... left over to spend on entertainment. Children and young people in our neighbourhood often get really (15) ..... because they have nothing to do after school, so my sister started a club for them.

(15 marks)

3 Key word transformations

Use the word in bold and the words given to write a second sentence with a similar meaning.

1 'I will not allow you to go to the party,' she said.

refused

She .... go to the party.

2 Her spoken Italian is better than her Spanish.

speaks

She .... speaks Spanish.

3 Why don't you wear your hair in the same way as me?

like

Why don't you .... mine.

4 'I didn't eat the cake,' she said.

that

She denied .... the cake.

5 The plane took off before we got to the airport.

when

The plane .... to the airport.

6 Tony types more carefully than Peter.

as

Peter does .... Tony.

7 There is no other country in the world with a city as spectacular as Rio de Janeiro.

city

Rio de Janeiro .... in the world.

8 I don't play tennis as well as my brother.

better

My brother .... me.

9 Don't lie about the money.

lies

Don't .... about the money.

10 'Why don't you take up jogging?' said my doctor.

encouraged

My doctor .... jogging.

(20 marks)

4 Error correction

Read each line of this text carefully. In some lines there is an extra word that should not be there. Circle this word. If the line is correct put a tick at the end of the line. The first two lines (**0** and **00**) have been done for you.

Taking up tennis

0   I did not really enjoy (to) playing sports much when   *to*

00   I was at the school. I suppose this was because we did   ✔

1   not really have very good physical education teachers.

2   They were always shouting at us and telling to us to try

3   harder. If you asked them what did you had to do to improve

4   they could never give you a good advice. When I left school

5   I started playing at tennis with some friends. To my great

6   surprise, I loved to it. I became a complete tennis addict,

7   sometimes playing as many as five times a week. I played so

8   much that I eventually became quite a good player. The only

9   problem was that I wasn't very a fit and consequently I started

10   to getting all sorts of injuries. First it was my elbow and then

11   my shoulder. Once I managed to get over of those two

12   problems my knees started to give me the trouble. My only

13   consolation is that even the top players suffer from these

14   injuries too. Of course I can't compare myself to someone

15   like as Martina Hingis, but I enjoy the game and have some of the same problems.

(15 marks)

5 Word formation

Complete this text with the correct form of the words in capital letters at the end of each line. The first one (**0**) has been done for you.

A burglary

When I got home I knew (0) _immediately_ that someone	**IMMEDIATE**
had broken into the flat in my (1) ..... . The signs	**ABSENT**
that the locks had been forced were (2) ..... . Because	**MISTAKE**
I was (3) ..... that the burglars might still be there	**WORRY**
I rang the police first. Burglars can be (4) ..... when surprised	**VIOLENCE**
and it would have been very (5) ..... to put myself	**RESPONSE**
into a potentially (6) ..... situation instead of making.	**DANGER**
a phone call Two policemen arrived soon after. Their (7)	**EFFICIENT**
really impressed me. (8) ..... not a lot had been	**FORTUNE**
taken, but the flat was in a (9) ..... mess, with things	**TERROR**
all over the floor. The police were very (10)	**UNDERSTAND**
and even helped me put things away.	

(10 marks)

Unit 6 test

Choose the best alternative to fill the gap in each of the following sentences.

1 Have you checked all your ..... to make sure there are no mistakes?

   A calculates   **B** calculators   **C** calculated   **D** calculations

2 I've always been completely ..... at finding my way around new cities.

   A useless   **B** useful   **C** use   **D** usefully

3 What's the main ..... between your country and Britain?

   A different   **B** difference   **C** differ   **D** differently

4 She has a lot of really ..... habits like smoking and eating fatty foods.

   A healthy   **B** healthily   **C** unhealthy   **D** unhealthily

5 She was sent out of the examination room because the examiner caught her ..... .

   A sneaking   **B** lying   **C** cheating   **D** copying

6 He is doing a science ..... at the University of Edinburgh.

   A degree   **B** certificate   **C** title   **D** career

7 The teacher told us to learn the irregular verbs ..... heart.

   A to   **B** at   **C** in   **D** by

8 If I don't write you a note to say you have a doctor's appointment, the teacher will think you are playing ..... .

   A truant   **B** the fool   **C** for time   **D** hard to get

9 Could you speak ..... a bit? We can't hear you at the back of the room.

   A out   **B** loud   **C** over   **D** up

10 I can't remember Mary's number. I'll have to ..... in the phone book.

   A look it   **B** look it up   **C** look for   **D** look it out

11 The older children used to ..... on him in the playground at lunch time.

   A get   **B** hit   **C** beat   **D** pick

12 Slow down a bit. I can't ..... up with you when you walk so fast.

   A keep   **B** hold   **C** get   **D** work

13 Can you help me work ..... the answers to these maths problems?

   A out   **B** in   **C** up   **D** off

14 We're always playing tricks on Pete because he takes ages to ..... on.

   A get   **B** keep   **C** pick   **D** catch

15 The traffic policeman let her ..... with a warning though she was driving way over the speed limit.

   A up   **B** on   **C** off   **D** out

16 Don't forget ..... the front door when you leave.

   A locking   **B** lock   **C** locked   **D** to lock

17 Would you mind ..... the window a bit?

   A to open   **B** opened   **C** open   **D** opening

18 I can hardly remember .... this film before.

   A seeing   **B** to see   **C** see   **D** saw

19 The bouncer refused ..... us into the club.

   A let   **B** to let   **C** letting   **D** of letting

20 Do you enjoy ..... foreign languages?

   A study   **B** studying   **C** to study   **D** with studying

21 We stopped ..... some fruit at the market on the way to the picnic.

   A buy   **B** for buying   **C** buying   **D** to buy

22 They plan ..... the islands on their next trip.

   A to visit   **B** visiting   **C** to visiting   **D** visit

23 He was very thrilled when he heard he had ..... the exam.

   A failed   **B** approved   **C** passed   **D** won

24 I'm sorry but I ..... with you. I think exams are better than coursework.

   A agree   **B** am agree   **C** don't agree   **D** am not agree

25 ..... my opinion, students shouldn't have to repeat the year if they fail their exams.

   A From   **B** At   **C** On   **D** In

Unit 7 test

Choose the best alternative to fill the gap in each of the following sentences.

1 Most of the ..... were unimpressed by his latest film.

A critics   B criticising   C reviews   D comments

2 It was so embarrassing when Romeo forgot his ..... in the second act.

A paper   B part   C lines   D script

3 I hope the film has a happy ..... .

A ending   B end   C finale   D finish

4 It's surprising the performance went so well after only three ..... .

A auditions   B rehearsals   C applauses   D directions

5 The person ..... the orchestra was a young woman in her early twenties.

A composing   B directing   C conducting   D leading

6 Throughout the city there are ..... by leading local artists.

A sculpts   B sculptors   C sculptures   D sculpted

7 Their latest ..... is available on the Internet.

A disk   B recorded   C long playing   D album

8 You should ..... to get a bit more exercise.

A try   B have try   C to try   D trying

9 You ought ..... for the part of Juliet.

A auditioning   B have audition   C audition
D to audition

10 I ..... better go. It's very late.

A would   B have   C did   D had

11 If I ..... you, I'd revise the script.

A were   B would be   C have been   D am

12 I ..... a single Johnny Depp film since *Edward Scissorhands*.

A don't miss   B am not missing   C didn't miss
D haven't missed

13 ..... a famous person?

A Have you ever met   B Do you ever meet
C Did you ever meet   D Are you ever meeting

14 We have had our cat ..... just over a year.

A since   B from   C ago   D for

15 I haven't had time to go to the gym ..... classes started at the university.

A for   B from   C ago   D since

16 ..... ? Your hair is wet.

A Has it rained   B Has it been raining   C Did it rain
D Does it rain

17 ..... to get through to Carlos all afternoon but the line is still engaged.

A I have tried   B I tried   C I had tried
D I have been trying

18 ..... a lot of time with my cousin lately.

A I have been spending   B I spent   C I spend
D I was spending

19 ..... she tried not to eat any sweets, she still put on weight.

A On the one hand   B However   C Even though
D Despite

20 In spite of ..... tired, she went on working.

A She felt   B to feel   C she feels   D feeling

21 ..... another cat will be company for him, but on the other they might not get on.

A However   B Despite   C On the one hand
D Although

22 It may be the middle of July, ... that doesn't mean it won't be wet in Ireland.

A but   B despite   C in spite of   D even though

23 I was absolutely ..... in that new Stephen King film.

A terror   B terrific   C terrifying   D terrified

24 Stage fright is a very common ..... problem.

A psychological   B psychology   C psychic
D psychologist

25 Most people are frightened ..... in public at first.

A speak   B to speaking   C of speaking
D for speaking

Unit 8 test

Choose the best alternative to fill the gap in each of the following sentences.

1   The ..... felt slightly too tight around my wrist.

    A bracelet **B** vest **C** belt **D** brooch

2   She knitted him two warm ..... to wear in the winter.

    A sandals **B** slippers **C** shorts **D** scarves

3   You can't go out in the street in those ..... . Put some proper shoes on.

    A slippers **B** braces **C** leggings **D** shorts

4   In New York some women wear trainers in the street and put on ..... when they get to work.

    A flippers **B** high-heeled shoes **C** slippers
    D wellington boots

5   She doesn't usually wear much jewellery. Just an antique ..... pinned on the collar of her jacket.

    A bracelet **B** vest **C** brooch **D** braces

6   Oh no! It's pouring outside and I haven't got my ..... .

    A dungarees **B** bow-tie **C** raincoat **D** waistcoat

7   He had to give ..... tennis because of a shoulder injury.

    A off **B** up **C** away **D** back

8   Tom, could you give ..... the books? There should be enough for everyone.

    A off **B** up **C** away **D** out

9   The pile of burning rubbish gave ..... a very unpleasant smell.

    A off **B** back **C** up **D** away

10   I was furious when I discovered my mother had given all my old dolls ..... .

    A up **B** in **C** off **D** away

11   Alright. I give ..... . Tell me the answer because I'll never guess it.

    A away **B** in **C** out **D** off

12   I always try to be polite but my face sometimes gives ..... what I really think.

    A away **B** in **C** out **D** back

13   Would you mind giving me ..... that book you borrowed?

    A back **B** in **C** off **D** away

14   People say high-heels are quite comfortable once you ..... to them.

    A use **B** used **C** get used **D** be used

15   When I was a little girl, my grandmother ..... me wonderful fairy stories every night.

    A use to telling **B** would tell **C** used to telling
    D use to tell

16   My grandparents ..... playing cards before we had a TV.

    A would enjoy **B** were enjoying **C** used to enjoy
    D used to enjoying

17   He got so used ..... with his friends by e-mail that he hardly ever wrote any letters.

    A to communicate **B** communicate
    C communicating **D** to communicating

18   Don't tell me your name again. It's ..... .

    A on the tip of my tongue **B** in my mouth
    C at my fingertips **D** off my chest

19   He criticised her in the meeting and I'm afraid she's really taken it ..... .

    A to chest **B** to brain **C** to mind **D** to heart

20   She's had a ..... in her left shoulder for a week now.

    A sore **B** ache **C** hurt **D** pain

21   He was so badly injured that they had to bring on a ..... and carry him off the football pitch.

    A stretcher **B** hammock **C** bed **D** bunk

22   In some countries you don't need a doctor's ..... to buy antibiotics.

    A recipe **B** prescription **C** receipt **D** note

23   The nurse took his ..... and checked that he was comfortable.

    A temperature **B** fever **C** heat **D** thermal

24   You ..... smoke on Iberia flights anymore.

    A couldn't **B** mightn't **C** can't **D** didn't

25   You ..... be hungry again. We've just had lunch!

    A mightn't **B** mustn't **C** may not **D** can't

Unit 9 test

Choose the best alternative to fill the gap in each of the following sentences.

1 We must get ..... new furniture for the living room.

A an   **B** the   **C** a piece   **D** some

2 You don't need ..... equipment to play sports like football and tennis.

A many   **B** some   **C** much   **D** an

3 Have you had ..... news from Irene? I haven't heard from her for ages.

A any   **B** a   **C** the   **D** a piece

4 I've got so ..... to do that I don't know where to begin.

A many works   **B** work   **C** works   **D** much work

5 He's got ..... friends.

A a great deal of   **B** a great many of   **C** a great many   **D** a great deal

6 Would you like ..... cake?

A another slice of   **B** another sheet of   **C** another lump of   **D** more of

7 The vet refused to put their cat ..... .

A out   **B** down   **C** by   **D** over

8 I'm afraid it's such a small flat that we don't have any room to put our friends ..... .

A down   **B** in   **C** over   **D** up

9 We try to put some money ..... each month for a house.

A down   **B** in   **C** by   **D** up

10 They had to put the party ..... because Charles broke his leg.

A up   **B** off   **C** over   **D** through

11 Please put ..... your cigarette. You're not allowed to smoke in here.

A down   **B** over   **C** out   **D** under

12 I asked the telephonist to put me ..... to the accounts department.

A up   **B** over   **C** in   **D** through

13 He went to the doctor because he couldn't put ..... with the pain any longer.

A up to   **B** up with   **C** down with   **D** down to

14 Can you pass me a knife? I want to ..... these onions.

A fry   **B** roll   **C** chop   **D** grate

15 I don't think I could eat any ....., but I'd like a coffee.

A dessert   **B** starter   **C** main course   **D** second helping

16 Can you ..... the soup while I slice the bread?

A sprinkle   **B** whisk   **C** roll   **D** stir

17 This time next month ..... on the beach in Greece.

A I'll lie   **B** I am lying   **C** I'll be lying   **D** I lie

18 By the time you get home I ..... painting the bathroom.

A will finish   **B** will have finished   **C** am finishing   **D** finish

19 I find it really hard to walk in shoes with very high ..... .

A soles   **B** heels   **C** bottoms   **D** supports

20 Could you go down to the baker's and get me a ..... of bread and a couple of jam doughnuts.

A slice   **B** piece   **C** lump   **D** loaf

21 My sister works on the ..... in the local supermarket on Saturday mornings.

A check-out   **B** check-up   **C** check-through   **D** check-in

22 We had to wait in a ..... in the post office for over ten minutes.

A row   **B** line   **C** file   **D** queue

23 I lost the receipt and the shop assistant refused to give me a ..... .

A refund   **B** discount   **C** guarantee   **D** exchange

24 They said they could order it for me because they didn't have my size in ..... .

A shop   **B** hold   **C** stock   **D** store

25 Our local supermarket charges a lot to ..... groceries.

A deliver   **B** carry   **C** bring   **D** bear

Progress test Units 6–10

1 Multiple choice cloze

Circle the alternative that best fit each of the gaps in this text. The first one (**0**) has been done for you.

An acting career

My younger sister is a (0) *potential* star of stage and screen, or at least that's what she tells me. Last week she had an (1) ..... . It was for the (2) ..... of Juliet in Shakespeare's *Romeo and Juliet*. It went well and she starts (3) ..... next week. This is the first (4) ..... that she has been in, but she's done quite a lot of TV (5) ..... work and she's also been in a couple of films. The last film she was in was called *The Magician*. It was set in ancient Egypt and she was in a crowd (6) ..... with thousands of other people. When I went to see it I sat in the front (7) ..... so that I could see the (8) ..... really clearly, but I still couldn't pick out my sister in the crowd. She says the (9) ..... was one of the best professionals she has worked with but I must say the (10) ..... seemed a bit stupid to me. It was all (11) ..... a very clever magician who had managed to travel back through time to the court of Tutankhamen. The (12) ..... were magnificent and so were some of the sets but having an actor saying
(13) ..... in present day American English just didn't work. The (14) ..... was really ridiculous. The magician got accidentally buried with Tutankhamen. Funnily enough, the rest of the (15) ..... seemed to have rather enjoyed the film.

0 **A** potential **B** latent **C** inherent **D** likely

1 **A** trial **B** interview **C** audition **D** test

2 **A** job **B** part **C** position **D** post

3 **A** training sessions **B** practices **C** rehearsals
D exercises

4 **A** game **B** play **C** theatre **D** activity

5 **A** advertising **B** publicity **C** propaganda **D** display

6 **A** scenery **B** scene **C** view **D** spot

7 **A** line **B** queue **C** file **D** row

8 **A** board **B** screen **C** blind **D** curtain

9 **A** conductor **B** chief **C** director **D** master

10 **A** plot **B** argument **C** dialogue **D** letters

11 **A** on **B** over **C** about **D** concerning

12 **A** dressings **B** cloths **C** customs **D** costumes

13 **A** lines **B** scripts **C** plays **D** readings

14 **A** final **B** culmination **C** ending **D** end

15 **A** public **B** audience **C** spectators **D** viewers

(15 marks)

2 Open cloze

Fill each gap with one suitable word. The first one (**0**) has been done for you.

Modern banking

Modern banks make life easier and easier (0) *for* their customers all the time. Instead of (1) ..... into the bank to cash a (2) ..... you can use the cash machines. These machines (3) ..... conveniently placed outside the bank so you can use them when the banks are (4) ..... . You can withdraw (5) ....., ask the bank to send (6) ..... a statement and put money into your (7) ..... all by simply pressing a (8) ..... .

Of course if you (9) ..... overdrawn you won't be able to (10) ..... any money out until you talk (11) ..... your bank manager. If you are earning a reasonable (12) ..... the manager will generally (13) ..... you have credit. If however you are (14) ..... debt or if you (15) ..... a mortgage the manager might say no.

(15 marks)

3 Key word transformations

Use the word in bold and the words given to write a second sentence with a similar meaning.

1 'Alright. I'll let you go home early,' said the teacher.

agreed

The teacher .... us go home early.

2 Could you close the window?

mind

Would you .... the window?

3 'I won't tell anyone. I promise,' she said.

promised

She .... anyone.

4 I'm sure I put my door keys in my bag this morning.

remember

I .... my door keys in my bag this morning.

5 I want to invite some friends for dinner next week.

like

I .... some friends for dinner next week.

6 'I'll help you with your English,' she said.

offered

She .... me with my English.

7 We were late because we had a coffee on the way.

stopped

We .... and that's why we were late.

8 The emergency doors wouldn't open and the passengers were trapped inside the plane.

failed

The emergency doors .... and the passengers were trapped inside the plane.

9 I hope you took your medicine this morning.

remember

Did you .... your medicine this morning?

10 We weren't able to see Peter when we were in Berlin.

manage

We didn't .... Peter when we were in Berlin.

(20 marks)

4 Error correction

Read each line of this text carefully. In some lines there is an extra word that should not be there. Circle this word. If the line is correct put a tick at the end of the line. The first two lines (**0** and **00**) have been done for you.

A threatening phone call

0 A leading politician had been charged with corruption and ✔

00 I had been covering the trial which had finished (more) earlier   *more*

1 that day. Despite of being very tired I went on working until

2 the midnight. I had promised to finish the story and have it on

3 the editor's desk by morning. I was almost certain no other

4 journalist had to got hold of the story or not the whole

5 story anyway. Jack had told me he would wait for my version

6 because of it would be an exclusive. I was worried that

7 if I have used real names, there might be trouble later

8 but in the end I decided that to include them. After all

9 the journalism is all about giving the public information

10 and that includes the names of all those involved in the news.

11 Just as it I was reading through the final draft the telephone

12 rang. I picked up the receiver expecting it is to be Jack.

13 A woman's voice has said 'If you print this story, you know

14 what to expect,' and then the line went dead. I sat there

15 wondering what I to do and then went to bed, but not to sleep.

(15 marks)

5 Word formation

Complete this text with the correct form of the words in capital letters at the end of each line. The first one (**0**) has been done for you.

Out of work

Since my brother has been (0) _unemployed_ he has gradually	**EMPLOY**
become more and more (1) ..... . I suppose it's because he	**FORGET**
doesn't have to be so (2) ..... anymore. He doesn't have	**SYSTEM**
the same (3) ..... routine as the other members of the family.	**DAY**
We all get up quite early, (4) ..... before 7 a.m., shower	**PREFER**
have a (5) ..... breakfast and leave for work or school	**HEALTH**
before my brother gets up. We try to be (6) ..... of	**TOLERATE**
his (7) ..... but it's not always easy. Of course	**BEHAVE**
we all feel very (8) ..... towards him, because it's	**SYMPATHY**
not his fault that most of the (9) ..... at the	**TECHNOLOGY**
factory lost their jobs. (10) ..... levels were above	**PRODUCE**
average but people are not buying so many cars.	

(10 marks)

Unit 11 test

Choose the best alternative to fill the gap in each of the following sentences.

1 Don't take that road. There's always very ..... traffic along there.

   A hard   **B** strong   **C** powerful   **D** heavy

2 She's so ..... skinned that nothing offends her.

   A hard   **B** thick   **C** strong   **D** heavy

3 This tea is too ..... for me. Could you bring me some hot water?

   A hard   **B** thick   **C** strong   **D** heavy

4 He's a very ..... smoker. He gets through two and a half packets a day.

   A strong   **B** heavy   **C** thick   **D** hard

5 You shouldn't go into ..... sea if you've got a cold.

   A a   **B** the   **C** an   **D** –

6 They went canoeing on ..... Amazon when they visited Brazil.

   A a   **B** the   **C** an   **D** –

7 Hundreds of people climb ..... Mount Everest every year.

   A a   **B** the   **C** an   **D** –

8 It is one of ..... smallest populated islands in the Mediterranean.

   A a   **B** the   **C** an   **D** –

9 People say ..... love makes the world go round.

   A a   **B** the   **C** an   **D** –

10 ..... mobile phone has made communication much easier.

   A A   **B** The   **C** An   **D** –

11 I think ..... today's students should be more involved in politics.

   A a   **B** the   **C** an   **D** –

12 Pete ..... that today is our anniversary. He told me he wouldn't be home till after 10 p.m.

   A can't have forgotten   **B** must have forgotten
   C must forget   **D** can't forget

13 I suppose I ..... lent the book to Simon, but I'm almost sure I didn't.

   A might   **B** could   **C** must have   **D** might have

14 You ..... that man our phone number. I didn't trust him at all.

   A must not have given   **B** should not have given
   C might not have given   **D** could not have given

15 He ..... at school this afternoon because the headmaster phoned to ask where he was.

   A might have been   **B** must have been
   C could have been   **D** can't have been

16 You ..... the night if you had wanted to.

   A could have stayed   **B** can have stayed
   C must have stayed   **D** can't have stayed

17 The hot weather has made the ..... even worse.

   A drought   **B** famine   **C** floods   **D** hail

18 Fortunately only three passengers suffered minor ..... .

   A hurts   **B** injuries   **C** pains   **D** damages

19 The government have declared a state of ..... after yesterday's earthquake.

   A crisis   **B** urgency   **C** emergency   **D** danger

20 Scientists are working to find a cure for ..... like AIDS.

   A ills   **B** infirmities   **C** complaints   **D** diseases

21 Thousands of ..... are fleeing the war in the north.

   A refugees   **B** employees   **C** escapees   **D** emigrants

22 They have closed the centre of the city to traffic because of ..... .

   A overpopulation   **B** contamination   **C** pollution
   D famine

23 People were injured by ..... stones the size of tennis balls.

   A sleet   **B** hail   **C** gale   **D** snow

24 A ..... of wind blew my hat off.

   A gust   **B** draft   **C** puff   **D** breeze

25 Don't bring those clothes in off the line yet. They're still a bit ..... .

   A humid   **B** mild   **C** damp   **D** cool

Unit 12 test

Choose the best alternative to fill the gap in each of the following sentences.

1 I'm sorry I wasn't home when you phoned. I ..... go out.
   A have to   B must   C had to   D should

2 You ..... keep your passport in a safe place at all times.
   A must   B have to   C had to   D need

3 Teachers often ..... work in the evenings and at weekends.
   A have to   B have got to   C must   D need

4 You ..... to buy your own racket. The tennis coach can lend you one.
   A mustn't   B don't have   C needn't   D no need

5 I ..... to pay full fare. University students get discounts on public transport there.
   A needn't   B needn't have   C didn't need   D mustn't

6 You ..... so much food. There was plenty in the fridge already.
   A don't need to buy   B don't have to buy
   C mustn't buy   D needn't have bought

7 I can get ..... on a lot less now that I don't have to pay rent.
   A by   B down   C over   D through

8 We've got two cats and they get ..... very well together.
   A down   B through   C by   D on

9 I couldn't get ..... to Wendy so I left a message on her answering machine.
   A over   B by   C through   D up

10 He never really got ..... his relationship with Jenny.
   A over   B by   C through   D up

11 So what have you been getting ..... while I've been away?
   A down to   B away with   C through to   D up to

12 I am ..... furious with Charlotte. How could she forget our wedding anniversary?
   A absolutely   B extremely   C very   D terribly

13 I haven't had a chance to read anything apart from the ..... in today's paper.
   A headings   B headlines   C captions   D titles

14 How many television ..... do they have in your country?
   A canals   B numbers   C ways   D channels

15 I wish the papers weren't always so full of ..... about the royal family.
   A gossip   B rumour   C slander   D chat

16 My favourite radio ..... is Radio 3.
   A canal   B channel   C station   D way

17 Do you know what ..... Radio 3 is on?
   A frequency   B line   C dial   D position

18 *The Sun* is a newspaper with a ..... of over three million.
   A distribution   B circulation   C coverage   D sales

19 Can you pass me the ..... control? I want to see if my favourite soap has started.
   A far   B removed   C distant   D remote

20 ..... he is very generous, he can be a bit arrogant at times.
   A Despite   B Although   C In spite of   D Moreover

21 She is hard-working and efficient. ....., she has had several years' experience of this kind of work.
   A Furthermore   B Not only   C However   D As well as

22 ..... was she very rude to my mother, but she insulted my father too.
   A Furthermore   B As well as   C In addition to
   D Not only

23 Despite ..... a little arrogant, he is actually extremely shy.
   A he seems   B of seeming   C seeming   D to seem

24 ..... passing all her examinations, she won a major tennis tournament this month.
   A In addition   B Moreover   C Not only   D As well as

25 I was feeling very tired ..... I decided not to go to the party.
   A therefore   B so   C because   D as

Unit 13 test

Choose the best alternative to fill the gap in each of the following sentences.

1   Look .....! That shelf is about to fall down.

   A up   **B** down   **C** over   **D** out

2   I'm terribly sorry but we haven't got any copies of the book in stock. They sold ..... early this morning.

   A over   **B** up   **C** through   **D** out

3   A rude boy ..... his tongue out at me.

   A stuck   **B** put   **C** showed   **D** took

4   I was completely ..... out after running so far.

   A exhausted   **B** run   **C** worn   **D** rubbed

5   If you ..... a cloth over the cage, the parrot falls asleep.

   A will put   **B** put   **C** had put   **D** would put

6   I wouldn't have booked the court if ..... me you couldn't play today.

   A you tell   **B** you would tell   **C** you would have told   **D** you had told

7   If she ..... a bit more cooperative she'd be much easier to work with.

   A are   **B** were   **C** would be   **D** would have been

8   If the boat ..... at 7 p.m. you should have plenty of time to get the 7.30 bus.

   A will arrive   **B** arrives   **C** arrived   **D** would arrive

9   I won't be able to come to the party ..... someone can give me a lift.

   A if   **B** unless   **C** provided   **D** as long as

10   If I hadn't gone to bed so late I ..... so tired this morning.

   A wouldn't have felt   **B** hadn't felt   **C** wouldn't be feeling   **D** didn't feel

11   ..... some exercises every morning unless you notice that the pain is getting worse.

   A Do   **B** You would do   **C** You would have done   **D** You do

12   Our new cat is black with white ..... .

   A paws   **B** hooves   **C** wings   **D** claws

13   As the elephant walked along he swung his ..... from side to side.

   A beak   **B** trunk   **C** fin   **D** hump

14   The lion ..... when the keeper tried to make him go back into his cage.

   A barked   **B** neighed   **C** mooed   **D** roared

15   I think it's time you ..... and told him you think things should be changed.

   A took the bull by the horns   **B** put the cat among the pigeons   **C** killed two birds with one stone   **D** got out of the rat race

16   Why did you ..... and mention the party to Roger? It was supposed to be a surprise.

   A put the cat among the pigeons   **B** let the cat out of the bag   **C** have kittens   **D** kill two birds with one stone

17   It must be true. I heard it straight from the ..... mouth.

   A horse's   **B** dog's   **C** camel's   **D** cat's

18   I know you're upset about breaking up with Tony but there are plenty more ..... .

   A horses in the stable   **B** cows in the field   **C** tigers in the zoo   **D** fish in the sea

19   Half way up the mountain there was a ..... where climbers could stay over night.

   A bungalow   **B** hut   **C** cottage   **D** bedsit

20   It took them over an hour to put up their ..... .

   A hut   **B** tent   **C** caravan   **D** bungalow

21   He lives in a tiny ..... up in the mountains.

   A suburb   **B** city   **C** town   **D** village

22   He likes to spend his holidays lying on a beach and she likes to spend hers walking in ..... .

   A a country   **B** some country   **C** country   **D** the country

23   Have you seen the exhibition at that new ..... in the high street?

   A gallery   **B** theatre   **C** cathedral   **D** stadium

24   Competition from goods produced with cheaper labour has meant that many ..... have closed.

   A markets   **B** factories   **C** stadiums   **D** galleries

25   The royal wedding was celebrated in the magnificent sixteenth-century ..... .

   A cathedral   **B** theatre   **C** market   **D** gallery

Unit 14 test

Choose the best alternative to fill the gap in each of the following sentences.

1 The puppy was ..... so much I nearly dropped him.

   A sniggering **B** chuckling **C** wriggling **D** giggling

2 We were ..... that the flight would be delayed for two hours.

   A invited **B** ordered **C** instructed **D** informed

3 He managed to ..... the branch of a tree and avoid being swept away by the flood waters.

   A clutch **B** grasp **C** hug **D** munch

4 That man next to me on the bus must have been a ..... . My wallet has gone.

   A shoplifter **B** pickpocket **C** hijacker **D** kidnapper

5 The murder took place in the main street in the middle of the day, but there were no ..... .

   A witnesses **B** prosecutions **C** judges **D** juries

6 He was ..... when he was caught trying to catch a plane to France.

   A arrested **B** put on probation **C** executed
   D acquitted

7 Skilled ..... have produced perfect copies of many of the world's famous paintings.

   A muggers **B** forgers **C** rapists **D** smugglers

8 The judge released him on ..... but he'll have to appear in court again next week.

   A bail **B** sentence **C** punishment **D** fine

9 My mother used to make ..... letters to all our relatives in Canada.

   A me write **B** me writing **C** that I wrote
   D me wrote

10 The doctor told him he would be allowed ..... home the next day.

   A go **B** to go **C** going **D** to going

11 My grandfather wouldn't let my mother ..... at university.

   A studying **B** to study **C** study **D** studied

12 We were made ..... our hands over our heads.

   A putting **B** to put **C** put **D** to putting

13 Only three of the hostages ..... so far.

   A have released **B** are released **C** are being released
   D have been released

14 All mobile phones must ..... during the flight.

   A switch off **B** have switched off **C** be switched off
   D been switched off

15 Your luggage might ..... to another airport.

   A send **B** sent **C** be sending **D** have been sent

16 All the exam results ..... to candidates by the end of the month.

   A will have sent **B** will have been sent **C** will send
   D will be being sent

17 I had no idea of the time because my watch ..... .

   A was being repaired **B** was repaired
   C was repairing **D** is repairing

18 When we arrived we ..... by our tour guide who told us which bus to take to our hotel.

   A were met **B** met **C** did meet **D** meet

19 We made ..... the nearest port when we heard the storm warning.

   A out **B** for **C** up **D** of

20 What do you make ..... Wendy? I think she's a bit strange.

   A out **B** for **C** up **D** of

21 Instead of telling her where he'd really been, he made ..... a complicated story.

   A up **B** for **C** out **D** of

22 He made ..... that it was his own work, but it was easy to see that he had copied it from a book.

   A out **B** of **C** up **D** for

23 We had a terrible row a few years ago and we still haven't made it ..... .

   A out **B** for **C** up **D** of

24 I can make ..... a bed in the spare room if you'd like to stay the night.

   A out **B** up **C** for **D** of

25 We'll make ..... for lost time if we keep working for a couple more hours.

   A out **B** of **C** for **D** up

Progress test Units 11–15

1 Multiple choice cloze

Circle the alternative that best fits each of the gaps in this text. The first one (**0**) has been done for you.

The media

Lately I seem to be so tired at the (0) _end_ of the day that I can't even manage to read the (1) ..... in the newspaper before I start to fall asleep. I used to read the papers from cover to cover and discuss the stories, articles and the (2) ..... with my colleagues at work the next day. I also used to enjoy doing the crossword (3) ..... at the back of the newspaper and I used to get a laugh out of some of the (4) ..... Of course I always buy quality papers and not those dreadful things full of gossip and (5) ..... . It seems incredible to me that they have (6) ..... figures in the millions when they really are rubbish.

I don't watch much TV though there seem to be more and more (7) ..... to choose from all the time. Unfortunately, you have to pay or buy a special (8) ..... to receive most of them. They do have some good films and some really excellent (9) ..... so I am sometimes tempted to spend the extra money. On the other hand, there is so (10) ..... information available on the Internet that TV will probably disappear altogether in a few years time. I've got a computer with an Internet connection and I spend quite a lot of time looking for information about the various (11) ..... that interest me.

I also still listen to a lot of news (12) ..... on the radio and this lets me keep up with what's going on in the world. One thing that annoys me though is that the (13) ..... seem to change all the time and sometimes I have a lot of trouble finding my favourite station. Of course the problem could be that I haven't got the (14) ..... in the right position. That reminds me. I must remember to get some new (15) ..... . I could hardly hear a thing when I tried to tune in this morning so they must be running out.

0	**A** ending	**B** final	**C** end	**D** finish
1	**A** headings	**B** titles	**C** captions	**D** headlines
2	**A** opinion	**B** editorial	**C** comment	**D** criticism
3	**A** games	**B** tasks	**C** puzzles	**D** activities
4	**A** drawings	**B** cartoons	**C** comics	**D** sketches
5	**A** scandal	**B** dishonour	**C** embarrassment	**D** shame
6	**A** selling	**B** distribution	**C** issue	**D** circulation
7	**A** canals	**B** chains	**C** channels	**D** numbers
8	**A** antenna	**B** plate	**C** disk	**D** pole
9	**A** documents	**B** documentaries	**C** documentals	**D** documented
10	**A** many	**B** a lot	**C** much	**D** a deal
11	**A** matters	**B** subjects	**C** themes	**D** sections
12	**A** broadcasts	**B** publications	**C** announcements	**D** proclamations
13	**A** positions	**B** frequencies	**C** channels	**D** routes
14	**A** aerial	**B** control	**C** battery	**D** dial
15	**A** batteries	**B** charges	**C** pills	**D** electricity

(15 marks)

2 Open cloze

Fill each gap with one suitable word. The first one (**0**) has been done for you.

The joy of pets

I have three pets that (0) _give_ me great pleasure. It is often (1) ..... that people with pets live longer because (2) ..... with animals relaxes you. Just stroking the soft (3) ..... of an animal like a cat reduces your blood pressure and prevents heart attacks. Fortunately my cat loves (4) ..... stroked. When you stroke her she (5) ..... loudly to show her appreciation. She likes playing but sometimes (6) ..... gets too excited and scratches me with her sharp (7) ..... .

I have (8) ..... more active relationship with my dog, King. I often take him (9) ..... for a run in the park. My mother gets a bit fed (10) ..... with us because in winter his (11) ..... leave muddy marks all over the kitchen floor. He keeps the house safe, though, and always (12) ..... loudly whenever he hears someone coming up the drive. Once he sees that it's someone he knows he is very friendly and wags his (13) ..... to show he's pleased to see them.

My third pet is (14) ..... parrot called Robinson Crusoe. Because of the cat he has to (15) ..... kept in a cage but I spend at least an hour a day playing with him.

(15 marks)

3 Key word transformations

Use the word in bold and the words given to write a second sentence with a similar meaning.

1 You must not write anything in the middle column on the answer sheet.

   supposed

   You .... anything in the middle column on the answer sheet.

2 It was not necessary to get up so early.

   needn't

   We .... so early.

3 I don't mind if you don't wash all the clothes.

   have

   You .... all the clothes.

4 I do not want you to write to me again.

   must

   You .... to me again.

5 Doing some kind of exercise every day is essential for me.

   need

   I .... some kind of exercise every day.

6 They were forced to wash all the dishes in the hotel kitchen.

   had

   They .... all the dishes in the hotel kitchen.

7 No one said you had to pay back all the money now.

   need

   You .... pay back all the money now.

8 His mother would not allow him to go to the dance.

   let

   His mother .... to the dance.

9 She forced him to give her all his money.

   made

   She .... her all his money.

10 I regret selling my old car.

   wish

   I .... my old car.

(20 marks)

4 Error correction

Read each line of this text carefully. In some lines there is an extra word that should not be there. Circle this word. If the line is correct put a tick at the end of the line. The first two lines (**0** and **00**) have been done for you.

Studying law

0   When I first went to (a) university I studied law. Although   *a*

00 both my mother and older sister have science degrees   ✔

1   no one else in the family had ever been studied law before

2   and my parents were very proud of me. The problem was

3   that I did not really know exactly what lawyers did do.

4   I had a very romantic ideas about going to court to defend

5   people who had been falsely accused of committing the crimes.

6   I imagined myself like those lawyers on TV, arguing

7   with the judge and the prosecution lawyer and convincing to

8   the jury that my client was innocent. After only a couple of

9   weeks of very long and difficult lectures I am realised

10 that a lot of what a lawyer does is very practical and not

11 at all romantic. Nevertheless, I have began to understand

12 that to studying law was interesting and worthwhile for other

13 reasons. For example, you learn a lot of about consumers'

14 rights. With it this kind of knowledge you can really

15 help people. I am very glad about I chose to study law.

(15 marks)

5 Word formation

Complete this text with the correct form of the words in capital letters at the end of each line. The first one (**0**) has been done for you.

Earthquake damages city centre

The (0) *detection* of an earthquake measuring five	**DETECT**
on the Richter scale caused panic but no (1) ....., although	**INJURE**
there was some (2) ..... damage to many older	**STRUCTURE**
buildings. A (3) ..... issued by the Ministry of	**STATE**
the Environment said that food (4) ..... centres	**DISTRIBUTE**
have been established. Charitable (5) ..... are	**ORGANISE**
helping to provide shelter for the (6) ..... families	**FORTUNE**
affected by the earthquake. Further (7) ..... is being	**ASSIST**
provided by aid organisations but (8) ..... financial	**ADD**
(9) ..... are needed. Those wishing to make even	**DONATE**
the smallest (10) ..... should call 0171 4503456.	**CONTRIBUTE**

(10 marks)

Unit test keys

Key: Unit 1 test

1 A; 2 B; 3 A; 4 A; 5 D; 6 C; 7 C; 8 D; 9 C; 10 D; 11 D;
12 A; 13 C; 14 C; 15 B; 16 C; 17 A; 18 B; 19 C; 20 A; 21 B;
22 B; 23 C; 24 D; 25 A;

Key: Unit 2 test

1 A; 2 C; 3 D; 4 D; 5 B; 6 C; 7 D; 8 B; 9 A; 10 D; 11 B; 12 D;
13 A; 14 B; 15 D; 16 D; 17 A; 18 C; 19 D; 20 B; 21 C; 22 A;
23 D; 24 C; 25 A

Key: Unit 3 test

1 B; 2 A; 3 D; 4 B; 5 C; 6 D; 7 B; 8 D; 9 C; 10 D; 11 B; 12 C;
13 A; 14 C; 15 A; 16 D; 17 A; 18 B; 19 B; 20 C; 21 A; 22 D;
23 B; 24 A; 25 D

Key: Unit 4 test

1 A; 2 A; 3 B; 4 A; 5 B; 6 A; 7 C; 8 D; 9 C; 10 A; 11 C; 12 A;
13 B; 14 C; 15 A; 16 B; 17 A; 18 D; 19 D; 20 A; 21 D; 22 C;
23 A; 24 C; 25 D

Key: Progress test Units 1–5

1 1 D; 2 A; 3 C; 4 D; 5 B; 6 A; 7 D; 8 A; 9 B; 10 C; 11 B;
   12 D; 13 B; 14 D; 15 C

2 1 a 2 lot 3 salary/pay/money 4 for 5 courses 6
   qualifications 7 all 8 more 9 never 10 most 11 made 12
   on 13 by 14 much 15 bored

3 1 refused to let us/me   2 speaks Italian better than she
   3 wear your hair like   4 that she had eaten   5 had
   (already) taken off   6 not type as carefully as   7 is the
   most spectacular city   8 is a better tennis player/plays
   tennis better   9 tell lies   10 encouraged me to take up

4 1 ✔ 2 (telling) to 3 did 4 a 5 at 6 to 7 ✔ 8 ✔ 9 a 10 to 11
   of 12 the 13 ✔ 14 ✔ 15 as

5 1 absence 2 unmistakable 3 worried 4 violent
   5 irresponsible 6 dangerous 7 efficiency 8 fortunately
   9 terrible 10 understanding

Key: Unit 6 test

1 D; 2 A; 3 B; 4 C; 5 C; 6 A; 7 D; 8 A; 9 D; 10 B; 11 D; 12 A;
13 A; 14 D; 15 C; 16 D; 17 D; 18 A; 19 B; 20 B; 21 D; 22 A;
23 C; 24 C; 25 D

Key: Unit 7 test

1 A; 2 C; 3 A; 4 B; 5 C; 6 C; 7 D; 8 A; 9 D; 10 D; 11 A; 12 D;
13 A; 14 D; 15 C; 16 B; 17 D; 18 A; 19 C; 20 D; 21 C; 22 A;
23 D; 24 A; 25 C

Key: Unit 8 test

1 A; 2 D; 3 A; 4 B; 5 C; 6 C; 7 B; 8 D; 9 A; 10 D; 11 B; 12 A;
13 A; 14 C; 15 B; 16 C; 17 D; 18 A; 19 D; 20 D; 21 A; 22 B;
23 A; 24 C; 25 D

Key: Unit 9 test

1 D; 2 C; 3 A; 4 D; 5 C; 6 A; 7 B; 8 D; 9 C; 10 B; 11 C; 12 D;
13 B; 14 C; 15 A; 16 D; 17 C; 18 B; 19 B; 20 D; 21 A; 22 D;
23 A; 24 C; 25 A

Key: Progress test Units 6–10

1 1 C; 2 B; 3 C; 4 B; 5 A; 6 B; 7 D; 8 B; 9 C; 10 A; 11 C;
   12 D; 13 A; 14 C; 15 B

2 1 going 2 cheque 3 are 4 closed 5 money/cash 6 you
   7 account 8 button 9 are 10 take 11 to 12 salary 13 let
   14 in 15 have

3 1 agreed to let 2 mind closing 3 promised not to tell
   4 remember putting 5 would like to invite 6 offered to
   help 7 stopped to have a coffee 8 failed to open 9
   remember to take 10 manage to see

4 1 of 2 the (midnight) 3 ✔ 4 to 5 ✔ 6 of 7 have 8 that
   9 the (journalism) 10 ✔ 11 it 12 is 13 has 14 ✔ 15 I

5 1 forgetful 2 systematic 3 daily 4 preferably 5 healthy
   6 tolerant 7 behaviour 8 sympathetic 9 technicians
   10 Production

Key: Unit 11 test

1 D; 2 B; 3 C; 4 B; 5 B; 6 B; 7 D; 8 B; 9 D; 10 B; 11 D; 12 B; 13 D; 14 B; 15 D; 16 A; 17 A; 18 B; 19 C; 20 D; 21 A; 22 C; 23 B; 24 A; 25 C

Key: Unit 12 test

1 C; 2 A; 3 A; 4 B; 5 C; 6 D; 7 A; 8 D; 9 C; 10 A; 11 D; 12 A; 13 B; 14 D; 15 A; 16 C; 17 A; 18 B; 19 D; 20 B; 21 A; 22 D; 23 C; 24 D; 25 B

Key: Unit 13 test

1 D; 2 D; 3 A; 4 C; 5 B; 6 D; 7 B; 8 B; 9 B; 10 C; 11 A; 12 A; 13 B; 14 D; 15 A; 16 B; 17 A; 18 D; 19 B; 20 B; 21 D; 22 D; 23 A; 24 B; 25 A

Key: Unit 14 test

1 C; 2 D; 3 B; 4 B; 5 A; 6 A; 7 B; 8 A; 9 A; 10 B; 11 C; 12 B; 13 D; 14 C; 15 D; 16 B; 17 A; 18 A; 19 B; 20 D; 21 A; 22 A; 23 C; 24 B; 25 D

Key: Progress test units 11–15

1 1 D; 2 B; 3 C; 4 B; 5 A; 6 D; 7 C; 8 A; 9 B; 10 C; 11 B; 12 A; 13 B; 14 A; 15 A

2 1 said/thought 2 being/living 3 fur 4 being 5 purrs 6 she 7 claws 8 a 9 out 10 up 11 paws 12 barks 13 tail 14 a 15 be

3 1 are not supposed to write 2 needn't have got up 3 don't have to wash 4 must not write 5 need to get 6 had to wash 7 don't need to 8 would not let him go 9 made him give 10 wish I hadn't sold

4 1 been 2 ✔ 3 do 4 a 5 the 6 ✔ 7 to 8 ✔ 9 am 10 ✔ 11 have 12 to 13 of 14 it 15 of

5 1 injuries 2 structural 3 statement 4 distribution 5 organisations 6 unfortunate 7 assistance 8 additional 9 donation 10 contributions

UNIVERSITY *of* CAMBRIDGE
Local Examinations Syndicate

Candidate Name
If not already printed, write name in CAPITALS and complete the Candidate No. grid (in pencil).

Candidate's signature

Examination le

Centr

Supervisor

[X] e candidate is ABSENT or has THDRAWN s here □

Centre No.

Candidate No.

0	0	0	0
1	1	1	1
2	2	2	2
3	3	3	3
4	4	4	4
5	5	5	5
6	6	6	6
7	7	7	7
8	8	8	8
9	9	9	9

Examination Detail

Candidate Answer Sheet: FCE paper 1 Reading

Use a pencil

Mark ONE letter for each question.

For example, if you think **B** is the right answer to the question, mark your answer sheet like this:

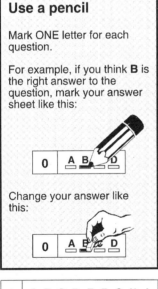

Change your answer like this:

1	A B C D E F G H I
2	A B C D E F G H I
3	A B C D E F G H I
4	A B C D E F G H I
5	A B C D E F G H I

6	A B C D E F G H I
7	A B C D E F G H I
8	A B C D E F G H I
9	A B C D E F G H I
10	A B C D E F G H I
11	A B C D E F G H I
12	A B C D E F G H I
13	A B C D E F G H I
14	A B C D E F G H I
15	A B C D E F G H I
16	A B C D E F G H I
17	A B C D E F G H I
18	A B C D E F G H I
19	A B C D E F G H I
20	A B C D E F G H I

21	A B C D E F G H I
22	A B C D E F G H I
23	A B C D E F G H I
24	A B C D E F G H I
25	A B C D E F G H I
26	A B C D E F G H I
27	A B C D E F G H I
28	A B C D E F G H I
29	A B C D E F G H I
30	A B C D E F G H I
31	A B C D E F G H I
32	A B C D E F G H I
33	A B C D E F G H I
34	A B C D E F G H I
35	A B C D E F G H I

FCE-1

DP318/92

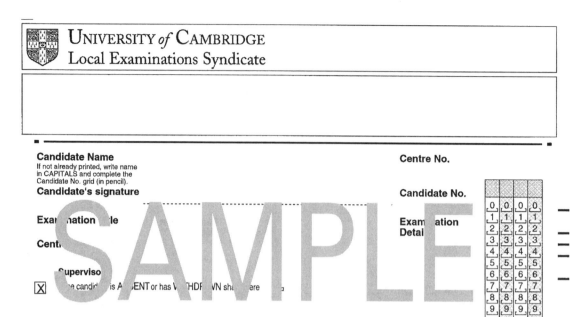

UNIVERSITY *of* CAMBRIDGE
Local Examinations Syndicate

Candidate Name
If not already printed, write name
in CAPITALS and complete the
Candidate No. grid (in pencil).

Candidate's signature

Examination Title

Centre

Supervisor

[X] the candidate is ABSENT or has WITHDRAWN shade here

SAMPLE

Centre No.

Candidate No.

Examination Details

0	0	0	0
1	1	1	1
2	2	2	2
3	3	3	3
4	4	4	4
5	5	5	5
6	6	6	6
7	7	7	7
8	8	8	8
9	9	9	9

Candidate Answer Sheet: FCE paper 3 Use of English

Use a pencil

For **Part 1**: Mark ONE letter for each question.

For example, if you think **C** is the
right answer to the question,
mark your answer sheet like this:

| 0 | A B C D |

For **Parts 2, 3, 4** and **5**: Write your
answers in the spaces next to the
numbers like this:

| 0 | |

Part 1				
1	A	B	C	D
2	A	B	C	D
3	A	B	C	D
4	A	B	C	D
5	A	B	C	D
6	A	B	C	D
7	A	B	C	D
8	A	B	C	D
9	A	B	C	D
10	A	B	C	D
11	A	B	C	D
12	A	B	C	D
13	A	B	C	D
14	A	B	C	D
15	A	B	C	D

Part 2	Do not write here
16	16
17	17
18	18
19	19
20	20
21	21
22	22
23	23
24	24
25	25
26	26
27	27
28	28
29	29
30	30

Turn over for Parts 3 - 5 →

FCE-3

DP319/93

Part 3	Do not write here
31	31 0 — 1 — 2 —
32	32 0 — 1 — 2 —
33	33 0 — 1 — 2 —
34	34 0 — 1 — 2 —
35	35 0 — 1 — 2 —
36	36 0 — 1 — 2 —
37	37 0 — 1 — 2 —
38	38 0 — 1 — 2 —
39	39 0 — 1 — 2 —
40	40 0 — 1 — 2 —

SAMPLE

Part 4	Do not write here
41	— 41 —
42	— 42 —
43	— 43 —
44	— 44 —
45	— 45 —
46	— 46 —
47	— 47 —
48	— 48 —
49	— 49 —
50	— 50 —
51	— 51 —
52	— 52 —
53	— 53 —
54	— 54 —
55	— 55 —

Part 5	Do not write here
56	— 56 —
57	— 57 —
58	— 58 —
59	— 59 —
60	— 60 —
61	— 61 —
62	— 62 —
63	— 63 —
64	— 64 —
65	— 65 —

UNIVERSITY *of* CAMBRIDGE
Local Examinations Syndicate

SAMPLE

Candidate Name
If not already printed, write name
in CAPITALS and complete the
Candidate No. grid (in pencil).
Candidate's signature

Centre No.

Candidate No.

Examiation le

Examiation Detail

Cent

Superviso

[X] e candidat AB NT or has THDF WN s ere

0	0	0	0
1	1	1	1
2	2	2	2
3	3	3	3
4	4	4	4
5	5	5	5
6	6	6	6
7	7	7	7
8	8	8	8
9	9	9	9

Candidate Answer Sheet: FCE paper 4 Listening

Mark test version below

A	B	C	D	E

Special arrangements S H

Use a pencil

For **Parts 1** and **3**:
Mark ONE letter for
each question.

For example, if you
think **B** is the right
answer to the
question, mark your
answer sheet like this:

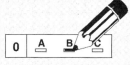

0	A	B	C

For **Parts 2** and **4**:
Write your answers in
the spaces next to the
numbers like this:

0	EXAMPLE

Part 1

1	A	B	C
2	A	B	C
3	A	B	C
4	A	B	C
5	A	B	C
6	A	B	C
7	A	B	C
8	A	B	C

Part 2

		Do not write here
9		9
10		10
11		11
12		12
13		13
14		14
15		15
16		16
17		17
18		18

Part 3

19	A	B	C	D	E	F
20	A	B	C	D	E	F
21	A	B	C	D	E	F
22	A	B	C	D	E	F
23	A	B	C	D	E	F

Part 4

		Do not write here
24		24
25		25
26		26
27		27
28		28
29		29
30		30

DP320/94